Highpoints of the United States

Highpoints
of the United States

A Guide to the Fifty State Summits

Second Edition, Revised and Updated

Don W. Holmes

The University of Utah Press
Salt Lake City

03   04   05   06

5   4   3   2

Library of Congress Cataloging-in-Publication Data

Holmes, Don W.
   Highpoints of the United States : a guide to the fifty state summits / Don W.
Holmes.—2nd ed., rev. and updated
      p.   cm.
   Includes index.
   ISBN 0-87480-645-3 (alk.paper)
      1. Mountains—United States—Recreational use—Guidebooks. 2. Hiking—
United States—Guidebooks. 3. United States—Guidebooks. I. Title

GV191.4 .H65   2000
796.52'2'0973—dc21

                                                              00-028671

To Laverne,

my life's companion,

and Mike, Mel, and David,

my mountaineering companions.

WARNING

Some of the highpoints in this guide are major mountains requiring mountaineering skill, proper equipment, and a healthy respect for weather conditions. Rely on your common sense and do not attempt an ascent that is beyond your abilities and experience.

The author and the publisher do not recommend that anyone attempt these climbs unless he or she is qualified, knowledgeable about the risks involved, and willing to assume all responsibilities associated with those risks.

Contents

Introduction

Whether your goal is to reach the highpoint of your state or the highpoint of each of the fifty states, it is a goal shared by many across the United States. You may be an experienced mountaineer accepting the challenges of Mount McKinley or Gannett Peak, a veteran hiker scaling the slopes of Guadalupe Peak or Mount Marcy, or an automobile explorer driving the roads of Mount Mitchell or Spruce Knob. Whatever your level of skill and interest, the highpoints of the United States offer a diversity of experience.

To enjoy the experience safely, *please make certain your level of expertise and preparation is equal to the route you select.* It is one thing to ride the cog railroad up Mount Washington and wish you had an extra sweater but quite another to be lost in a blinding snowstorm without proper equipment in one of the mountain's treacherous ravines. *This book is only a guide and not a substitute for your common sense.* Weather, season, road and access conditions, party numbers, and individual experience and physical condition are all variables for which only you can accept responsibility.

The highpoints of the United States range from a highway intersection, Ebright Azimuth, the highpoint of Delaware, to a world-class mountain, Mount McKinley, the highpoint of Alaska and North America. A vehicle can be driven to within a few yards of many of the highpoints. Others, such as Kings Peak and Mount Katahdin, require long and strenuous hikes. A few, including Mount Rainier, Mount Hood, Granite Peak, and Gannett Peak, require rock climbing and/or snow and glacier travel skills.

Although this guide has been assembled from firsthand observation and has been reviewed many times, errors may still be present because of new Forest Service requirements, changes in the status of private property, and new roads and access routes. Please report all errors, omissions, or recommended additions and/or corrections so that future editions of this guide can be kept as current as possible.

See you in the high country,
Don W. Holmes
P.O. Box 1675
Castle Rock, CO 80104

Introduction to the Second Edition

Although the USGS has not had to change any of the state highpoints as a result of new surveys, there have been a significant number of other events that affect the accuracy and utility of the first edition of this book. These events include changes in property ownership, modifications of Forest Service requirements, and updating and/or addition of route descriptions. In addition, errors identified in the first edition have been corrected.

This updating, of course, does not mean that this edition has no errors. Although there are only fifty state highpoints, in such a dynamic environment nothing stays the same for long. Again, please report all errors, omissions, or recommended additions and/or corrections so that future editions of this guide can be kept as current as possible.

Enjoy the pursuit of highpoints,
Don W. Holmes

Highpoints of the United States

Highpoint Guide Key

County

County or subdivision in which the highpoint is located. If the high-point is on a county boundary, both counties are listed.

Location

The general location in airline miles from a prominent point shown on most state maps.

Hiking and Gain

The round-trip distance and **gross** round-trip elevation gain in addition to the trail characteristics. These data allow an estimate of the time required and the difficulty of the route. See Appendix A, State Highpoints List, for a discussion of class and climbing difficulty.

Maps

United States Geological Survey (usgs) topographic maps that show the highpoint, as well as useful maps from other sources. If more than one topographic map is listed, the first map includes the highpoint. The others are useful for one or more of the routes described. The usgs maps are listed by exact title, including the state abbreviations. Several of the guide-books listed under "Guidebooks" also include maps. These maps are not included in this section.

Note: The maps included in this book with the route descriptions are prob-ably adequate for drive-ups and short and/or easy hikes. For all other highpoints, especially those requiring any combination of cross-country travel, difficult terrain calling for technical climbing, or areas of several trails and alternate routes, *it is strongly recommended that the appropriate topographic maps be used.* Topographic maps are invaluable in determining hiking routes, terrain characteristics, and escape routes in the event of emergency or poor weather. Knowing how to read and use a topographic map and compass is a skill all wilderness hikers should possess.

Guidebooks

Useful guidebooks and their publishers. In many cases, several guide-books are listed because of the great number of hiking opportunities in the highpoint region. Many of the guidebooks include detailed maps of the area they describe. As mentioned above, the included maps are not listed under "Maps."

Primary Route

Usually, the most commonly used route, as well as the shortest and easiest.

Approach ▲ Driving instructions to the highpoint or highpoint trailhead from a location readily found on most state maps.

Route ▲ The hiking route to the highpoint from the trailhead.

Alternate Route(s)

Alternate routes are available to many of the highpoints, certainly more than can be listed in this guide. Usually, the alternate routes listed offer special features, such as trail routes on a drive-up, approaches from other directions, trails that can be combined to form one-way or loop trips, or a route with a special means of transportation.

Special Conditions

Special conditions pertaining to the highpoint, including sources of information. Of particular concern here are those highpoints located on private property. All the current owners permit access to these highpoints. In fact, some owners encourage visits to "their" highpoint. *Please respect the rights of these private-property owners and be alert for changes in visitation policies after the publication of this guide.* Good relations with these owners will help keep the highpoints open to the public.

Historical Notes

Brief historical notes pertaining to the highpoint and the area in the immediate vicinity.

Natural History Notes

Brief natural history notes pertaining to the highpoint and the area in the vicinity.

Guides/Outfitters

A sample of guides and/or outfitters serving the area of interest. This section is usually limited to the highpoints requiring technical climbing, such as Mount McKinley, Alaska, and Mount Rainier, Washington, and/or highpoints with long approaches, such as Kings Peak, Utah. *This listing is in no way an endorsement of the guides and/or outfitters listed.*

Alabama

Cheaha Mountain

2,405 Feet

County
  Cleburne

Location
  Approximately 25 miles s of Anniston in the Cheaha State Park area of Talladega National Forest.

Hiking
  Primary Route: Drive-up.
  Alternate Route: 19.8 miles, round trip, on trail.

Gain
  Primary Route: Drive-up.
  Alternate Route: 3,300 feet, Class 1, strenuous.

Maps
  Topographic: Cheaha Mountain, Ala., and Lineville West, Ala., both 7½ minute.
  National Forest: Talladega N.F.—Talladega and Shoal Creek Ranger Districts; Cheaha Wilderness, Talladega N.F.; Pinhoti Trail, Talladega N.F.
  Other: Cheaha State Park Visitor's Guide.

Primary Route
  Approach ▲ From the junction of I-20 and U.S. Hwy 431 E of Anniston (I-20 Exit 191), proceed s on Hwy 431 for 3.5 miles to a connector road (County Road 6) to State Route 281. Turn right (sw) on the connector road and proceed 0.6 miles to State Route 281. Turn left (s) on Route 281 and continue 12.5 miles to the Cheaha State Park entrance. Enter the park and

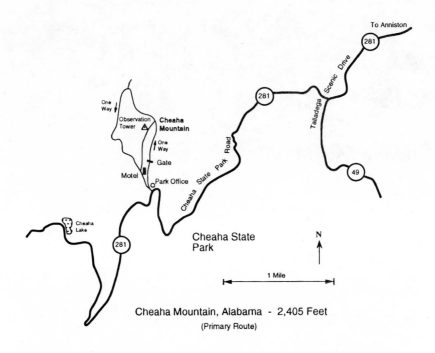

Cheaha Mountain, Alabama - 2,405 Feet
(Primary Route)

continue 0.7 miles to the parking area near the observation tower on the highpoint.

Route ▲ The usgs benchmark is in the middle of the walkway to the observation tower. The actual highpoint appears to be a boulder at the back of the building.

Alternate Route—Odum Trail/Pinhoti Trail

Approach ▲ From the junction of State Route 281 and State Route 49, 3.0 miles E of the Cheaha State Park entrance, proceed s on Route 49 for 6.0 miles to County Road 31. Turn right (sw) on County Road 31 and proceed 5.2 miles to County Road 12. Turn right (w) on County Road 12 and continue 1.5 miles to Forest Route 650 on the right. Turn right (N) on Forest Route 650 and proceed 0.4 miles to the Highfalls Trailhead parking area.

Route ▲ From the trailhead, hike generally N on the yellow-blazed Odum Trail for 4.7 miles to the point where it merges with the Pinhoti Trail, bearing left at the Nubbin Creek Trail junction at 3.9 miles. Bear right (N) on the Pinhoti Trail, identified by white, turkey-foot blazes, and continue 4.2 miles to the point where the trail crosses State Route 281. Turn left on Route 281 and continue 1.0 miles into Cheaha State Park to the observation tower on the highpoint. The usgs benchmark is in the

Stone lookout towers are on several state highpoints. This one is at the highpoint of Alabama, Cheaha Mountain.

middle of the walkway to the observation tower. The actual highpoint appears to be a boulder at the back of the building. **Note:** This can be done as a one-way hike with a car shuttle.

Special Conditions

Cheaha State Park facilities are open year-round; however, the entrance gate is locked from 9:00 P.M. until 8:00 A.M. There is a $1.00 per person day-use fee. There are cabins and a campground in the park. If a stay at the park is planned, reservations are strongly recommended. For information and cabin reservations, contact Cheaha State Park, Highway 281, 2141 Bunker Loop, Delta, AL 36258 (256/488-5115 or 800/846-2654). To make campground reservations or contact the Park Superintendent or Park Ranger, contact Cheaha State Park, 19644 Highway 281, Delta, AL 36258 (256/488-5111). A toll-free number is available for making reservations at any Alabama state park, including Cheaha State Park: 800/ALA-PARK.

The Pinhoti Trail, designated a National Recreation Trail in 1977, extends over 100 miles from Piedmont south to near Sylacauga and is the longest trail in Alabama. The name Pinhoti is derived from the Creek Indian words **pinwa** ("turkey") and **huti** ("house" or "home"). This translates literally to "turkey home"; hence the white, turkey-foot blazes. The Odum Trail, built by Boy Scouts in 1961, is the oldest trail in the state. It goes along the crests of the Cedar and Talladega Mountains on its way north. There are other trails in the Talladega National Forest that offer many interesting routes. Because there is little or no water available along the trails, be sure to carry all that you will require.

For trail information and the national forest maps, contact Talladega National Forest, Talladega Ranger District, 1001 North Street, Talladega, AL 35160 (256/362-2909).

Historical Notes

Early history of the area is one of conflicts between settlers and the Indians, escalating into the Creek Indian Wars in 1813–14. Federal troops led by Andrew Jackson fought the Creek "Red Sticks," some of the fiercest Indian warriors in the Southeast.

Cheaha State Park, established in 1933, has been in continuous operation since it opened. The derivation of the name is somewhat uncertain. It probably comes from the Choctaw Indian word *chaha*, "high," or it may derive from an Indian tribal name.

Natural History Notes

Chestnut oak and Virginia pine, with scattered longleaf pine, are found on the main ridgeline and side slopes of the higher elevations. The

Virginia pines, many of which are dwarfed, have evolved over eons of weathering from the wind, rain, snow, and sleet.

Animal life includes deer, opossum, rabbit, squirrel, fox, bobcat, weasel, and woodrat. Many species of songbirds share the area with owls, hawks, wild turkey, and dove. Several species of harmless snakes are present along with the poisonous copperhead, cottonmouth, and timber and pygmy rattlesnakes.

Alaska

Mount McKinley

20,320 Feet

Location

Approximately 140 miles NNW of Anchorage in Denali National Park.

Hiking

32 miles, round trip, on snow, ice, and glaciers.

Gain

14,450 feet, Class 4, extremely strenuous.

Maps

Topographic: Mt. McKinley (A-3), Alaska, and Talkeetna (D-3), Alaska, both 15x30 minute.

Trails Illustrated: #222, Denali National Park and Preserve, Alaska.

Other: Mount McKinley, Alaska, The Museum of Science, Boston, Massachusetts

Guidebooks

High Alaska: A Historical Guide to Denali, Mount Foraker, and Mount Hunter, by Jonathan Waterman, The American Alpine Club, Inc., New York, New York, 1988.

Hiking Alaska, by Dean Littlepage, Falcon Press Publishing Co., Inc., Helena, Montana, 1997.

Mountaineering: Denali National Park and Preserve, by the Mountaineering Rangers of Denali National Park, Alaska Natural History Association, Anchorage, Alaska, 1994.

Mt. McKinley Climber's Handbook, by Glenn Randall, Chockstone Press, Evergreen, Colorado, 1992.

The Organization of an Alaskan Expedition, by Boyd N. Everett, Jr., Gorak Books, Pasadena, California, 1984.

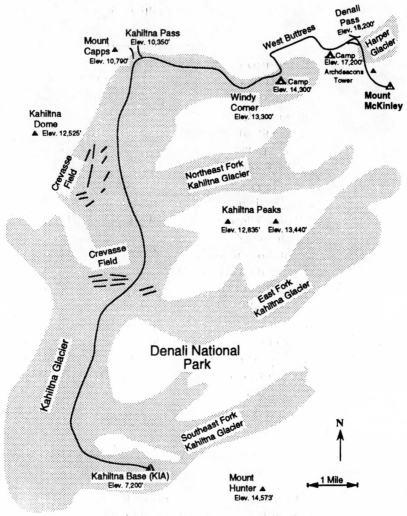

Mount McKinley, Alaska - 20,320 Feet

Surviving Denali, by Jonathan Waterman, The American Alpine Club, Inc., New York, New York, 2d revised edition, 1991.

Primary Route: West Buttress

Approach ▲ From Anchorage, proceed N on State Routes 1 and 3 approximately 115 miles to Talkeetna. From Talkeetna, fly onto the 7,200-foot level of the southeast fork of the Kahiltna Glacier to Kahiltna Base, also known as "Kahiltna International Airport," or KIA.

Mount McKinley from Kahiltna basecamp.

Route ▲ From Kahiltna Base, proceed w down the glacier to the junction with the main stream of the Kahiltna Glacier (6,900 feet). Turn right (N) and continue approximately 8 miles toward Kahiltna Pass. After gaining a small plateau E of the pass, move to the left of the prominent icefall and follow the obvious ridgeline toward the base of the West Buttress.

Continue up the snowfield, staying clear of the avalanche chutes on the buttress, and turn left (E) at Windy Corner (13,300 feet). Climb generally E up to a large basin (14,300 feet). From the basin, turn left (N) and climb the steep, icy headwall to the top of the West Buttress (16,000 feet). At the crest of the ridge, turn right (E) and climb up the ridge to the largely level area below Denali Pass (17,200 feet). Continue up the ridge and traverse left across a long snow slope to Denali Pass (18,200 feet).

From the pass, climb the ridge leading up and s for a little more than one-half mile, then turn left (E) toward Archdeacon's Tower after passing a small rocky ridge. Continue E, passing Archdeacon's Tower on the sw, and descend into and cross a broad basin. Climb up the eastern slope to the summit ridge. Turn left on the ridge and climb to the South Summit (20,320 feet).

Special Conditions

Mount McKinley, the highest mountain on the North American continent, is a world-class mountain. It is one of the coldest mountains in the world with temperatures during the spring and summer climbing season

Approach along the ridge with McKinley summit in view.

as low as -40 degrees F. and with winds of 80 to 100 mph lasting several days. Technically, the climb is not so difficult, but low temperatures and awesome winds conspire to make this mountain environment one of the harshest on earth. Although several thousand climbers of all nationalities have reached the summit, many have been killed and many have required rescue. Avalanches, crevasses, and high-altitude sickness can all prove fatal. Frostbite is the most common malady experienced.

The dangers of altitude are just as serious as storms, avalanches, and crevasses. The effects of the lower supply of oxygen can lead to life-threatening illness: acute mountain sickness (AMS), high-altitude pulmonary edema (HAPE), and/or cerebral edema (CE). There is no way of predicting who will or will not develop altitude illness. No medicine is a proven preventative. The best treatment is immediate rapid descent to a safe altitude. A relatively safe rate of ascent of 1,000 feet per day above 10,000 feet should be adequate, but even this may be too fast for some climbers. All climbers should be able to recognize the symptoms of altitude illness so descent to lower elevations can begin immediately.

Expedition-style preparation and equipment in addition to proper training and experience on glaciers and at high altitudes are necessary for a climb of Mount McKinley. Superior mountaineering skills, stamina, conditioning, equipment, and ability to survive in severe arctic conditions are essential. Experience has shown that even these qualifications do not guarantee safety or success. Climbing equipment needed for an expedition to Mount McKinley is the same as that needed for a high mountain ascent anywhere in the world, only with greater emphasis on clothing capable of keeping climbers warm and dry.

Expeditions to Mount McKinley require 15 to 30 days, depending on the weather, the strength of the party, and the rate of altitude acclimatization. The climb to the summit is done by setting up a succession of camps along the route. Usually, two days are required to move camp; the first day a carry is made to the next campsite, and then the camp is moved on the second day. Three or four rest days during the climb are often allowed for acclimatization. Severe weather conditions may require staying in camp for several days. The usual climbing season for Mount McKinley is May through mid-July in order to avoid the cold storms and high winds of winter and the increased crevasse danger of late summer. Each party should have at least four members. A large party provides greater inherent strength and self-rescue capability, as each party must depend on its own resources for the duration of the climb.

Before climbing Mount McKinley, expedition members must register with the Mountaineering Ranger in Talkeetna, Alaska, and pay the appropriate fees. Registration requirements and expedition information currently on the back of the registration form available from the Mountaineering Ranger state the following:

1. A 60-day preregistration period is required for climbing Mount McKinley and Mount Foraker. This registration form is due at the Talkeetna Ranger Station 60 days prior to your climb date. The leader of your expedition is responsible for compiling the registration forms and deposits for all expedition members and submitting them in one packet to the Talkeetna Ranger Station.

2. A Mountaineering Special Use Fee of one hundred and fifty dollars ($150.00 U.S. currency) will be charged to each expedition member attempting Mount McKinley or Mount Foraker. This fee will be paid in two installments as follows. **Deposit:** A nonrefundable, nontransferable deposit of twenty-five dollars ($25.00 U.S. currency) is due when you submit your completed registration form. Payment for this deposit may be made by money order, Visa credit card, or MasterCard credit card. Personal checks will not be accepted as payment. **Balance:** The remaining balance of one hundred and twenty-five dollars ($125.00 U.S. currency) will be due when you check in at the Talkeetna Ranger Station. Payment for the remaining balance may be made by money order, U.S. currency, Visa credit card, or MasterCard credit card. Personal checks will not be accepted as payment.

3. Registered climbers are required to check in and out at the Talkeetna Ranger Station. This includes expeditions originating on the north side of the Alaska Range. Expeditions should allow two hours for the check-in process at the Talkeetna Ranger Station. Expedition members will be required to provide a piece of picture identification. Your expedition may check in and out during regular hours of operation: 8:00 A.M. to 6:00 P.M., seven days a week. It is best to arrange for an appointment prior to your arrival.

4. Expeditions are permitted to add or substitute one new member to their expedition. This new member must pay the $25.00 deposit and be registered 30 days prior to the start date of the expedition.

5. If you plan to use a guide service, make certain that the service is authorized by Denali National Park and Preserve. Illegal guiding is prohibited, and your climb could be canceled at any time.

6. Read the National Park Service publication *Mountaineering: Denali National Park and Preserve*, which covers search and rescue requirements, clean climbing requirements, high-altitude medical problems, glacier hazards, and self-sufficiency. You should have a solid understanding of the potentially serious medical problems and the extreme mental and physical stresses associated with high-altitude mountaineering.

One of the mandatory resources for planning a Mount McKinley expedition is the booklet listed above, *Mountaineering: Denali National Park and Preserve*. This booklet and other information on climbing Mount McKinley can be obtained from the Mountaineering Ranger, Denali National Park and Preserve, Talkeetna Ranger Station, P.O. Box 588, Talkeetna, AK 99676 (907/733-2231). Current climbing information may be obtained by accessing the Denali National Park website, www.nps.gov/dena/mountaineering.

Guide services authorized for operation on Mount McKinley by the National Park Service are listed in the "Guides/Outfitters" section below. Each service meets standards established by the National Park Service and is reviewed periodically to ensure a high-quality operation. It is mandatory that climbers who do not have the skills or experience necessary to climb Mount McKinley hire a guide. Experienced climbers needing partners or who want someone to organize the equipment and pack the food may also wish to arrange for the services of a guide.

On a personal note, because of the magnitude of a climb of Mount McKinley, I believe picking a bush pilot and a guide service requires careful consideration. K2 Aviation and Alaska-Denali Guiding have always provided me with excellent service.

Several means of transportation from Anchorage to Talkeetna are available.

Air: K2 Aviation, P.O. Box 545, Talkeetna, AK 99676 (907/733-2291 or 800/764-2291)

Rust's Flying Service, Inc., P.O. Box 190325, Anchorage, AK 99519 (907/243-1595 or 800/544-2299)

Train: Alaska Railroad Corporation, Pouch 7-2111, Anchorage, AK 99510 (907/265-2685 or 800/544-0552 outside Alaska)

Limousine: Alaska Backpacker Shuttle, P.O. Box 232493, Anchorage, AK 99523-2493 (907/344-8775 or 800/266-8625 outside Alaska)

Denali Overland Transportation, P.O. Box 330, Talkeetna, AK 99676 (907/733-2384)

Talkeetna Shuttle Service, P.O. Box 468, Talkeetna, AK 99676 (907/733-1725)

For the flight from Talkeetna to the Kahiltna Glacier, there are several bush pilots who operate out of Talkeetna.

Doug Geeting Aviation, P.O. Box 42, Talkeetna, AK 99676 (907/733-2366)
Hudson Air Service, P.O. Box 648, Talkeetna, AK 99676 (907/733-2321)
K2 Aviation, P.O. Box 545, Talkeetna, AK 99676 (907/733-2291 or 800/764-2291)

McKinley Air Service, P.O. Box 544, Talkeetna, AK 99676 (907/733-1765 or 800/564-1765)

Spotted Dog Aviation, P.O. Box 786, Talkeetna, AK 99676 (907/733-SPOT)

Talkeetna Air Taxi, P.O. Box 73, Talkeetna, AK 99676 (907/733-2218 or 907/733-2681)

For information about Talkeetna, Alaska, including accommodations, contact the Talkeetna Chamber of Commerce, P.O. Box 334, Talkeetna, AK 99676.

Historical Notes

Denali National Park and Preserve was expanded to its present size in 1980. **Denali**, the "High One," is the Native American name for the mountain. Denali was renamed Mount McKinley in 1897 in honor of Senator William McKinley (1843–1901), who was the Republican candidate for president at the time. In 1980 the name Mount McKinley National Park was officially changed to Denali National Park and Preserve. The State of Alaska Board of Geographic Names has also officially changed the mountain's name back to Denali. Negotiations continue today on officially returning the original native name to this magnificent mountain.

Arguably the finest book recounting the eventful history of conquests of the mountain is *Mount McKinley: The Conquest of Denali*, by Bradford Washburn and David Roberts (Harry N. Abrams, Inc., New York, NY, 1991). The aerial photographs by Bradford Washburn are without equal. This is a "must have" book for anyone interested in Mount McKinley.

Natural History Notes

The 18,000-foot vertical relief from the 2,000-foot surroundings to the 20,320-foot summit of Mount McKinley is the largest in the world.

The only wildlife on the upper reaches of the snow- and glacier-bound Mount McKinley are ravens and an occasional rosy finch. The ravens are notorious for getting into climbers' food caches, at elevations as high as 16,000 feet.

Guides/Outfitters

Alaska-Denali Guiding, Inc., P.O. Box 566, Talkeetna, AK 99676 (907/733-2649)

Alpine Ascents International, 121 Mercer Street, Seattle, WA 98109 (206/378-1927)

American Alpine Institute, Ltd., 1515 12th Street, Bellingham, WA 98225 (360/671-1505)

Mountain Trip, P.O. Box 91161, Anchorage, AK 99509 (907/345-6499)

National Outdoor Leadership School (NOLS), P.O. Box 981, Palmer, AK 99645 (907/745-4047)

Rainier Mountaineering, Inc., 535 Dock Street, Suite 209, Tacoma, WA 98402 (206/627-6242)

Arizona

Humphreys Peak

12,633 Feet

County

Coconino

Location

Approximately 10 miles N of Flagstaff in the Kachina Peaks Wilderness Area of Coconino National Forest.

Hiking

Primary Route: 9.0 miles, round trip, on trail.
Alternate Route: 19.4 miles, round trip, on trail.

Gain

Primary Route: 3,500 feet, Class 1, strenuous.
Alternate Route: 5,100 feet, Class 1, strenuous.

Maps

Topographic: Humphreys Peak, Az., 7½ minute.
National Forest: Coconino N.F.

Guidebooks

Arizona Day Hikes: A Guide to the Best Trails from Tucson to the Grand Canyon, by Dave Ganci, Sierra Club Books, San Francisco, California, 1995.

Arizona's Mountains: A Hiking Guide to the Grand Canyon State, by Bob Martin and Dotty Martin, Cordillera Press, Inc., Evergreen, Colorado, 2d edition, 1991.

50 Hikes in Arizona, by James R. Mitchell, Gem Guides Book Co., Pico Rivera, California, 5th edition, 1985.

Hiking Arizona, by Stewart Aitchison and Bruce Grubbs, Falcon Press Publishing Co., Inc., Helena, Montana, revised edition, 1996.

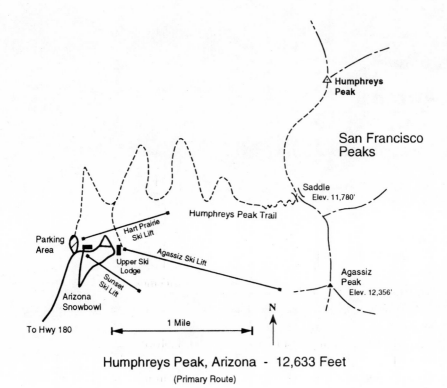

Humphreys Peak, Arizona - 12,633 Feet
(Primary Route)

Hiking Northern Arizona, by Bruce Grubbs, Falcon Press Publishing Co., Inc., Helena, Montana, 2d edition, 1996.

Hiking the Southwest: Arizona, New Mexico, and West Texas, by Dave Ganci, Sierra Club Books, San Francisco, California, 1983.

100 Hikes in Arizona: Grand Canyon, White Mountains, Valley of the Sun, Santa Catalina Mountains, San Francisco Mountains, Sedona, by Scott S. Warren, The Mountaineers, Seattle, Washington, 1994.

Primary Route: Humphreys Peak Trail

Approach ▲ From the junction of I-40 and U.S. Hwy 89A (I-40 Exit 195B) in Flagstaff, proceed N on Hwy 89A for 2.1 miles to U.S. Hwy 180. Turn left (N) on Hwy 180 and continue 7.2 miles to the Arizona Snowbowl turnoff on the right. Turn right (N) and continue 6.7 miles to the first Snowbowl parking area on the left.

Route ▲ The signed Humphreys Peak Trail begins at the north end of the parking area. Hike generally E on this trail through several switchbacks for 3.5 miles to the saddle on the ridge between Humphreys Peak

Rock shelter on Humphreys summit.

and Agassiz Peak. At the saddle, turn left (N) and hike 1.0 miles along the ridge to the summit of Humphreys Peak. There is a register, a cairn, and a USGS benchmark on the summit.

Alternate Route: Weatherford Trail/Humphreys Peak Trail

Approach ▲ From the junction of I-40 and U.S. Hwy 89A (I-40 Exit 195B) in Flagstaff, proceed N on Hwy 89A for 2.1 miles to U.S. Hwy 180. Turn left (N) on Hwy 180 and continue 2.0 miles to Forest Route 420 (Schultz Pass Road) on the right. Turn right (N) on Forest Route 420, turning right at 0.2 miles and bearing left at 0.5 miles (the intersection with westbound Forest Route 557), and continue 5.5 miles to a parking area on the S side of Forest Route 420 at Schultz Tank. Turn right (S) and park N of the pond, which is called Schultz Tank.

Route ▲ The Weatherford Trail begins at a signed trailhead on the N side of Forest Route 420, directly across from the parking area at Schultz Tank. Hike generally NNW on this trail for 8.7 miles to the saddle between Humphreys Peak and Agassiz Peak. The Weatherford Trail goes up Weatherford Canyon to Doyle Saddle (incorrectly identified as Fremont Saddle on the topographic map), skirts around the N side of Fremont Peak to Fremont Saddle (incorrectly identified as Doyle Saddle on the topographic map), and crosses the E flank of Agassiz Peak before arriving at the Humphreys Peak Trail at the Humphreys Peak–Agassiz Peak saddle.

Humphreys Peak in winter.

At the saddle, continue 1.0 miles along the ridge (N) to the summit of Humphreys Peak. There is a register, a cairn, and a USGS benchmark on the summit.

Special Conditions

Humphreys Peak is in the Kachina Peaks Wilderness, but wilderness permits are not required. The usual climbing season for Humphreys Peak is June through mid-October. Humphreys Peak Trail was built in 1984 and is not shown on the topographic map.

The San Francisco Peaks are subject to afternoon thunderstorms. In fact, it may snow during any month of the year. The thunderstorms, which may include hail and lightning, build rapidly and usually last only a short while. Be prepared to head for lower ground if a storm is threatening.

In order to protect the fragile alpine environment found in the higher elevations, hiking above 11,400 feet is restricted to designated trails. Hiking cross-country from the top of the Arizona Snowbowl Skyride to the summit of Humphreys Peak or Agassiz Peak is prohibited. In addition, hiking in the summit area of Agassiz Peak is prohibited.

Although the Skyride cannot be used to climb to the summit, it operates daily, 10:00 A.M. to 4:00 P.M., from Memorial Day through Labor Day, and on weekends through mid-October. It can be taken to the 11,500-foot elevation on Agassiz Peak and offers a spectacular view. The round-trip fare is $9.00 per adult and $5.00 per child (6–12). For information, contact the Arizona Snowbowl, P.O. Box 40, Flagstaff, AZ 86002 (520/779-1951).

Information, hiking guide sheets, and the national forest map can be obtained from Coconino National Forest, Peaks Ranger District, 5075 North Highway 89, Flagstaff, AZ 86004 (520/526-0866). Additional trail information may be obtained from the Forest Service website, www.fs.fed.us/r3/, and search for "Humphreys Peak."

The routes may be combined with a car shuttle.

Historical Notes

Humphreys Peak is one of four main peaks of the San Francisco Peaks. The peaks are remnants of an ancient volcano that reached 15,000 feet during its greatest activity a million or so years ago. Agassiz Peak at 12,356 feet is the second highest peak in Arizona.

The peaks are sacred to many northern Arizona Indians. To the Hopi, they are the home of the Kachina gods, the Source of Clouds that bring rain for their crops. To the Navajo, Humphreys Peak is the Sacred Mountain of the West, one of the cardinal mountains that border Navajo country. A major portion of the history and heritage of the San Francisco Peaks is represented by artifacts and ruins. All items of this nature are protected by federal law against damage or removal.

Humphreys Peak was named for General Andrew Atkinson Humphreys (1810–83), who served in the Union army during the Civil War. In 1866 General Humphreys was appointed chief of the United States Corps of Engineers. He served in that capacity until his retirement in 1879.

Natural History Notes

The lower slopes along Humphreys Peak Trail are covered by a forest of corkbark fir, Engelmann spruce, and quaking aspen. Near the timberline, stunted Engelmann spruce and bristlecone pine are found. At about 9,000 feet, a very noisy black, gray, and white bird, the Clark's nutcracker, makes its appearance. Black bear, wild turkey, and blue grouse are occasionally seen. Elk make their home in the Weatherford Trail region.

The higher elevations of the San Francisco Peaks are the only areas where alpine tundra is found in Arizona. A small plant, the San Francisco Peaks groundsel, is found in this region. This tundra plant, *Senecio franciscanus*, is endemic to the San Francisco Peaks and grows nowhere else in the world. It is listed as a threatened plant species.

Arkansas

Magazine Mountain

2,753 Feet

County
  Logan

Location
  Approximately 11 miles s of Paris in Ozark National Forest.

Hiking
  1.0 miles, round trip, on trail.

Gain
  225 feet, Class 1, easy.

Maps
  Topographic: Blue Mountain, Ark., and Magazine Mountain NE, Ark., both 7½ minute.
  National Forest: Ozark N.F.

Primary Route: Mount Magazine Hiking Trail
  Approach ▲ From the junction of State Routes 22 and 309 in Paris, proceed s on Route 309 for 17 miles to Forest Route 1606 on the right. (This point is 9.7 miles N of Havana via Route 309.) Turn right (W) on Forest Route 1606 and continue 1.7 miles to the Cameron Bluff Campground entrance on the right. Park along the side of the road.
  Route ▲ Hike 0.5 miles on the trail beginning on the s side of the road at the "Signal Hill Trail" sign to the summit of Signal Hill, which is the highpoint of Magazine Mountain. The USGS benchmark is on the summit.

Special Conditions
  The highpoint of Magazine Mountain is named Signal Hill. The Magazine Mountain Complex is open all year.

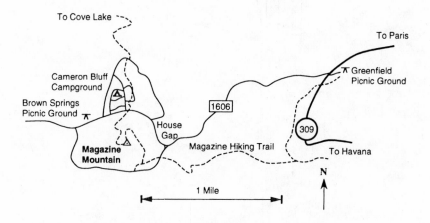

Magazine Mountain, Arkansas - 2,753 Feet

A 10.5-mile section of the Mount Magazine Trail System connects Cove Lake with the summit of Magazine Mountain after passing through Cameron Bluff Campground. It continues eastward across Mossback Ridge to the Greenfield and East End picnic areas. The trail across Mossback Ridge skirts several wildlife openings and offers vistas of the Petit Jean Valley to the south. Additional information on the Mount Magazine Trail System and an excellent map of the system may be obtained from the Ozark–St. Francis National Forest, Mount Magazine Ranger District, P.O. Box 511, Paris, AR 72855 (501/963-3076).

In 1997 the Arkansas Department of Parks and Tourism began developing the Magazine Mountain area as a state park. By the end of 2000, construction of a visitor center, camping units, a picnic pavilion, and a bath house, plus a number of other improvements, will be completed. Probably one of the most significant improvements will be the construction of a water line from the valley to the south. During 2003 and 2004 a new lodge and several cabins are expected to be built. Information on the status and availability of facilities on Magazine Mountain may be obtained from the Arkansas Department of Parks and Tourism, State Parks Division, 1 Capital Mall, Little Rock, AR 72201 (501/682-1191).

Historical Notes

The orchards found on Magazine Mountain were planted by early residents during the 1870s. At one time, there were three hotels on the mountain. They had all been destroyed by the mid-1930s. Magazine Mountain Lodge, shown on the topographic map, was completed in 1941 but burned in February 1971.

Rock cairn at the summit of Magazine Mountain.

The name, Magazine Mountain, is probably derived from the French word *magasin,* meaning "storehouse." The reason for the name is uncertain.

Natural History Notes

Because of its elevation above the Arkansas Valley, Magazine Mountain provides a home for plant species that are otherwise uncommon in this part of Arkansas. These plants include the hay-scented fern, Rocky Mountain **Woodsia**, the maple-leafed oak, and the prickly gooseberry. The diverse flora in the Ozark National Forest region includes more than five hundred species of trees and woody plants. Hardwoods occupy 65 percent of the forests; the oak-hickory types dominate.

The mammals inhabiting the Magazine Mountain area include black bear, white-tailed deer, coyote, squirrel, and rabbit. More than one hundred species of birds have been identified on the plateau, including eastern wild turkey, northern bobwhite quail, and eastern mourning dove.

California

Mount Whitney

14,494 Feet

County
Inyo-Tulare

Location
Approximately 15 miles w of Lone Pine in the John Muir Wilderness Area of Inyo National Forest.

Hiking
21.4 miles, round trip, on trail.

Gain
6,750 feet, Class 1, strenuous.

Maps
Topographic: Mount Whitney, Calif., and Mt. Langley, Calif., both 7½ minute.
Trails Illustrated: #205, Sequoia/Kings Canyon National Parks, California.
National Forest: Inyo N.F.

Guidebooks
California County Summits, by Gary Suttle, Wilderness Press, Berkeley, California, 1994.
Climbing Mt. Whitney, by Walt Wheelock and Wynne Benti, Spotted Dog Press, Bishop, California, 1998.
Guide to the John Muir Trail, by Thomas Winnett and Kathy Morey, Wilderness Press, Berkeley, California, 1998.
The High Sierra: Peaks, Passes, and Trails, by R. J. Secor, The Mountaineers, Seattle, Washington, 1992.

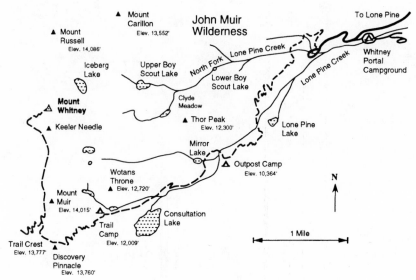

Mount Whitney, California - 14,494 Feet

High Sierra Hiking Guide to Mount Whitney, by Thomas Winnett, Wilderness Press, Berkeley, California, 2d edition, 1978.

Hiking and Climbing California's Fourteeners, by Stephen Porcella and Cameron Burns, Chockstone Press, Evergreen, Colorado, 1995.

Hiking California, by Ron Adkinson, Falcon Press Publishing Co., Inc., Helena, Montana, revised edition, 1996.

Mount Whitney Guide for Hikers and Climbers, by Paul Hellweg and Scott McDonald, Canyon Publishing Co., Canoga Park, California, 1990.

The Pacific Crest Trail, Volume 1: California, by Jeffrey P. Schaffer et al., Wilderness Press, Berkeley, California, 5th edition, 1995.

Sierra South, by Thomas Winnett et al., Wilderness Press, Berkeley, California, 6th edition, 1997.

Starr's Guide to the John Muir Trail and the High Sierra Region, by Walter A. Starr, Sierra Club Books, San Francisco, California, 12th edition, 1974.

Primary Route: Mount Whitney Trail

Approach ▲ From Lone Pine, proceed w on Whitney Portal Road for 13 miles to Whitney Portal. Park in the area designated for hikers and backpackers.

Route ▲ From Whitney Portal, hike generally wsw and then N on the well-signed Mount Whitney Trail for 10.7 miles to the summit. Elevations

Mount Whitney from the Owens Valley.

and distances from the trailhead to significant points are as follows: Whitney Portal, 8,365 feet, 0.0 miles; Outpost Camp, 10,364 feet, 3.5 miles; Trail Camp, 12,009 feet, 6.0 miles; Trail Crest, 13,777 feet, 8.2 miles; John Muir Trail junction, 13,480 feet, 8.6 miles; Mount Whitney summit, 14,494 feet, 10.7 miles. On the summit there is a plaque and the USGS benchmark.

Special Conditions

Mount Whitney is in the John Muir Wilderness, and wilderness permits are required. The Mount Whitney trailhead quota for dayhikes (150/day) and overnight trips (50/day) in the John Muir Wilderness is in effect from May 22 through October 15. In addition to a wilderness permit, Mount Whitney hikers are required to have a special stamp on their permits to enter the Mount Whitney Zone. Hikers are reminded that wilderness permits are required year-round for the John Muir Wilderness; however, there are no quotas in the off-season. Permits may be reserved from six months to two days in advance of the planned entry date. Permits must be obtained through the Inyo National Forest Wilderness Reservation Service. The entire daily quota is available for advance reservations. The overnight trip permit is $15.00 per person. The dayhiker permit is $15.00 per person. These fees are for the reservation service. There is no charge for wilderness permits that are issued at the ranger stations on a first-come, first-served

The Smithsonian hut near the summit of Mount Whitney.

basis. There are generally some unreserved and/or unclaimed permits available on a first-come, first-served basis on the day of entry.

Application forms for permit reservations are available at the Inyo National Forest website, www.r5.fs.fed.us/inyo/, beginning in December. Permit reservations will be accepted beginning February 1 by mail or fax. The mailing address is Inyo National Forest Wilderness Reservation Office, 837 N. Main Street, Bishop, CA 93514 (fax 760/873-2484). Be sure to determine where and how the permit will be obtained, by mail or picked up at an Inyo National Forest ranger station.

As of July 25, 1997, the Inyo National Forest has a new forest order that is effective in the John Muir Wilderness. It prohibits possessing or storing any food or refuse unless in a bear-proof container or in another manner designed to keep bears from gaining access to the food or refuse. Both websites given in this chapter have detailed information regarding this issue.

Information and hiking guide sheets can be obtained from Inyo National Forest, Mount Whitney Ranger District, P.O. Box 8, Lone Pine, CA 93545 (760/876-6200). Two websites offer a wealth of information about hiking Mount Whitney. The Inyo National Forest site is mentioned above. The Sequoia and Kings Canyon National Park's website address is www.nps.gov/seki/.

Maps, trail guides, and other books and items of interest can be obtained from the Eastern Sierra Inter-agency Visitor Center, P.O. Drawer R, U.S. Hwy 395 at State Route 136, Lone Pine, CA 93545 (760/876-6222).

Mount Whitney has been climbed as a very long and strenuous day-hike. It is usually done as a two-to-three-day backpacking trip. There are several campsites available along the trail, most notably at Outpost Camp and Trail Camp. Camping is prohibited at Mirror Lake and Trailside Meadow.

Because of the altitude, hikers without sufficient acclimatization may experience symptoms of altitude sickness. Immediately return to a lower altitude if the symptoms become severe.

Water is available near the trail as far as Trail Camp. There is no dependable water source above Trail Camp.

Thunderstorms, and even an occasional snowstorm, are common in the summer and early fall. Take care not to get caught on the peaks or exposed ridges during one of these storms.

Normally, the trail is free of snow from mid-July to early October. Ice patches frequently remain on the switchbacks above Trail Camp all summer long. The road from Lone Pine to Whitney Portal is usually open from May to early November. In the winter, the last 6 miles of the road are not plowed.

Two major trails that are in the Mount Whitney vicinity are the John Muir Trail and the Pacific Crest National Scenic Trail. The John Muir Trail, whose southern terminus is at the summit of Mount Whitney, extends north some 210 miles to Happy Isles in Yosemite National Park. On the west side of the mountain, the John Muir and Pacific Crest Trails follow the same track for approximately 177 miles. The Pacific Crest National Scenic Trail extends some 2,640 miles from Mexico to Canada along the Pacific Crest through California, Oregon, and Washington. Approximately 1,679 miles of the trail are in California. In 1968 Congress passed the National Trails System Act, which made the Pacific Crest and the Appalachian Trails the first two National Scenic Trails.

Historical Notes

Mount Whitney was named in 1864 by Clarence King, a member of the Whitney survey team, in honor of Josiah Dwight Whitney (1819–96), chief of the California State Geological Survey from its creation in 1860 to 1874. A geological expedition under Whitney's direction first measured the height of Mount Whitney in 1864. King, for whom Kings Peak, the highest point in Utah, is named, made two attempts to be the first to climb Mount Whitney. Both times he climbed the wrong mountain. The summit was first reached on August 18, 1873, by three fishermen.

The small stone hut near the summit was built in 1909 by the Smithsonian Institution. It was used from 1909 to 1913 to shelter scientists making observations on the summit.

Natural History Notes

Although several biological life zones are encountered during the ascent of Mount Whitney, they are not easily distinguished because of the steepness of the eastern slope. What is found is a general intermingling, cosmopolitan arrangement of both plant and animal life except at the extreme altitudes.

Glaciers, which carved much of the High Sierra during the last glacial advance, did not cover the top of Mount Whitney, leaving a relatively flat area at the summit. The summit area is littered with huge granite boulders and slabs that are largely the result of frost wedging—the action of water freezing in small cracks, thereby breaking the granite.

Guides/Outfitters

Jackson Hole Mountain Guides and Climbing School, P.O. Box 7477, 165 North Glenwood Street, Jackson, WY 83002 (800/239-7642).

Mammoth Mountaineering School, P.O. Box 7299 (located at Sandy's Ski and Sports on Main Street), Mammoth Lakes, CA 93546 (760/924-9100).

Colorado

Mount Elbert

14,433 Feet

County
   Lake

Location
   Approximately 12 miles sw of Leadville in the San Isabel National Forest.

Hiking
   Primary Route: 11.0 miles, round trip, on trail.
   Alternate Route 1: 9.0 miles, round trip, on trail.
   Alternate Route 2: 12.4 miles, round trip, on trail.

Gain
   Primary Route: 5,300 feet, Class 1, strenuous.
   Alternate Route 1: 5,000 feet, Class 1, strenuous.
   Alternate Route 2: 4,850 feet, Class 1, strenuous.

Maps
   Topographic: Mount Elbert, Colo.; Mount Massive, Colo.; and Granite, Colo., all 7½ minute.
   National Forest: San Isabel N.F.
   Trails Illustrated: #127, Aspen/Independence Pass, Colorado; #110, Leadville, Fairplay, Colorado.

Guidebooks
   A Climbing Guide to Colorado's Fourteeners, by Walter R. Borneman and Lyndon J. Lampert, Pruett Publishing Company, Boulder, Colorado, 3d edition, 1997.

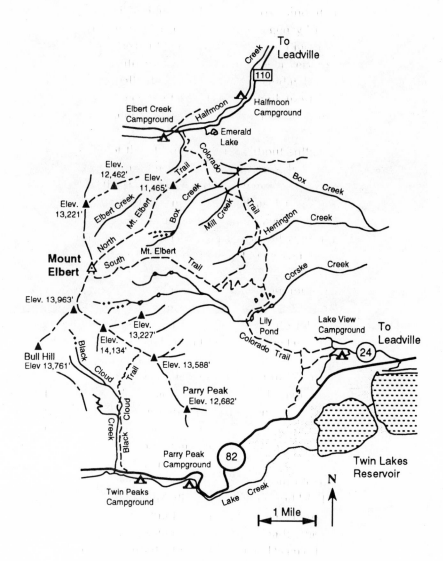

Mount Elbert, Colorado - 14,433 Feet

Colorado's Fourteeners: From Hikes to Climbs, by Gerry Roach, Fulcrum Publishing, Golden, Colorado, 2d edition, 1999.

The Colorado Trail: The Official Guidebook, by Randy Jacobs, Westcliff Publishers, Inc., Englewood, Colorado, 4th edition, 1994.

Dawson's Guide to Colorado's Fourteeners, Volume 1: The Northern Peaks, by Louis W. Dawson II, Blue Clover Press, Monument, Colorado, 1994.

Mount Elbert in the distance.

Guide to the Colorado Mountains, by Robert M. Ormes, The Colorado Mountain Club, Denver, Colorado, 9th revised edition, 1997.

Hiking Colorado, by Caryn Boddie and Peter Boddie, Falcon Press Publishing Co., Inc., Helena, Montana, 2d edition, 1996.

Hiking Colorado's Summits, by John Drew Mitchler and Dave Covill, Falcon Press Publishing Co., Inc., Helena, Montana, 1999.

100 Hikes in Colorado, by Scott S. Warren, The Mountaineers, Seattle, Washington, 1995.

Primary Route: Black Cloud Trail

Approach ▲ From the junction of U.S. Hwy 24 and 6th Street in Leadville, proceed s on U.S. Hwy 24 approximately 15 miles to State Route 82 on the right. Turn right (w) on Route 82 and continue 10.4 miles to the obscure trailhead on the right with a small sign reading "Black Cloud Trail." The trailhead is 4.1 miles w of the village of Twin Lakes. There is a small parking area approximately 50 yards N of Route 82.

Route ▲ Hike N up the Black Cloud Trail for 5.5 miles to the summit. The trail follows Black Cloud Creek to near the 11,600-foot level, where it turns NE just beyond an old cabin and climbs up to the ridge. Turn left (NW) on the ridge and continue approximately 1.3 miles, climbing over 14,134-foot South Mount Elbert, to where the ridge turns N. Continue 0.6 miles N to the summit. There is a USGS benchmark and a register on the summit.

Mount Elbert summit.

Alternate Route 1: Colorado Trail/North Mount Elbert Trail

Approach ▲ From the junction of U.S. Hwy 24 and 6th Street in Leadville, proceed s on U.S. Hwy 24 for 4.0 miles to State Route 300 on the right. Turn right (w) on Route 300 and continue 0.8 miles to County Road 11 on the left. Turn left (s) on County Road 11 and continue 1.2 miles to Halfmoon Road on the right. Turn right (w) on Halfmoon Road and proceed 5.2 miles, passing Halfmoon Campground at 3.9 miles, to the trailhead on the left. The trailhead is approximately 0.2 miles w of Elbert Creek Campground.

Route ▲ Hike s along the Colorado Trail for 1.0 miles to the junction with the North Mount Elbert Trail. Turn right onto the North Mount Elbert Trail and continue 3.5 miles to the summit. There is a USGS benchmark and a register on the summit.

Alternate Route 2: Colorado Trail/South Mount Elbert Trail

Approach ▲ From the junction of U.S. Hwy 24 and 6th Street in Leadville, proceed s on U.S. Hwy 24 approximately 15 miles to State Route 82 on the right. Turn right (w) on Route 82 and continue 4.0 miles to the Lake View Campground turnoff on the right, County Road 24. Turn right onto County Road 24 and continue 1.0 miles to the Lake View Campground. Turn into the campground and park in the area designated for hikers.

Route ▲ Hike w then N on the Colorado Trail, which passes through the w end of the campground, for 2.0 miles to the junction with the South Mount Elbert Trail. Turn left (w) on the South Mount Elbert Trail and continue 4.2 miles to the summit. There is a USGS benchmark and a register on the summit.

Special Conditions

Because of the heavy use of the North Mount Elbert Trail and the South Mount Elbert Trail, the Black Cloud Trail has been chosen as the Primary Route.

Technical ability or special mountain climbing experience is not necessary to climb Mount Elbert. The usual climbing season is June through September. The ascent and return requires a good full day of strenuous hiking. Altitude can affect even the fittest climbers; be sure to be aware of the signs of altitude sickness: headaches, dizziness, and nausea. If you feel these symptoms, get down to lower elevation immediately. Start for the summit of Mount Elbert early since showers and/or thunderstorms often occur in the afternoons. These storms build quickly and may bring freezing rain, sleet, or snow. Take care not to get caught on the peaks or exposed ridges during one of these storms. Temperatures at the summit are rarely above 50 degrees and may drop to below freezing. Check local weather forecasts before climbing. There is no safe, reliable water source on Mount Elbert. Carry all the water required.

Halfmoon Road in Alternate Route 1 is a narrow, rough road, but it is usually suitable for passenger cars. The road is closed by snow during the winter months. The hiking routes can be combined with a car shuttle to create one-way routes over Mount Elbert.

Information, maps, and hiking guide sheets can be obtained from San Isabel National Forest, Leadville Ranger District, 2015 N. Poplar Street, Leadville, CO 80461 (719/486-0749).

The two Alternate Routes offer an opportunity to hike a small distance on the Colorado Trail. The Colorado Trail concept, which linked several existing trails with new trail segments, was developed in 1973. Completed in 1987, the trail is now a continuous recreational trail that extends some 471 miles between Denver and Durango, passing through seven national forests and six wilderness areas along the way. For more information on the Colorado Trail, contact the Colorado Trail Foundation office in the American Mountaineering Center, 710 10th Street, #210, Golden, Colorado 80401-1022 (303/384-3729, ext. 113), or the Colorado Trail Foundation website, www.coloradotrail.org.

Historical Notes

Mount Elbert was named in honor of Samuel Hitt Elbert (1833–99), who, after statehood was granted in 1876, served as chief justice of the Colorado State Supreme Court for eight years, 1876–82 and 1886–88. Before Colorado became a state, President Lincoln appointed Elbert territorial secretary under territorial governor Evans, and Elbert served in that capacity from 1862 to 1866. In 1873 he was appointed the sixth territorial governor by President Grant and served from 1873 to 1874.

Nearby Leadville has a rich mining history. Gold was first discovered in 1860. After the easily obtained gold petered out, the heavy black sand that clogged sluice boxes and made gold difficult to mine was found to contain a large percentage of silver. Since the beginning of the silver boom, more than $2 billion in gold, silver, lead, zinc, copper, iron, bismuth, manganese, and molybdenum has been produced by Leadville district mines.

Natural History Notes

The lower portions of the trails pass through spruce, fir, aspen, and lodgepole pine forests. Above the treeline, alpine tundra with its many different flowers is found.

Animals that live on Mount Elbert include marmot, pika, pocket gopher, mule deer, and many species of birds. The high mountains around Mount Elbert also afford summer range for bear, elk, mountain sheep, grouse, and turkey.

Connecticut

Mount Frissell
(South Slope)
2,380 Feet

County
Litchfield

Location
Approximately 6 miles NE of Salisbury.

Hiking
Primary Route: 2.6 miles, round trip, on trail.
Alternate Route: 3.6 miles, round trip, on trail.

Gain
Primary Route: 1,000 feet, Class 1, moderate.
Alternate Route: 450 feet, Class 1, easy.

Maps
Topographic: Bashbish Falls, Mass.-Conn.-N.Y., and Sharon, Conn.-N.Y., both 7½ minute.

Guidebooks
Appalachian Trail Guide to Massachusetts-Connecticut, edited by Norman Sills and Robert Hatton, Appalachian Trail Conference, Harpers Ferry, West Virginia, 10th edition, 1996.

Connecticut Walk Book, edited by John S. Burlew, Connecticut Forest and Park Association, Rockfall, Connecticut, 17th edition, 1993.

50 Hikes in Connecticut: From the Berkshires to the Coast, by David Hardy et al., Backcountry Publications/The Countryman Press, Woodstock, Vermont, 4th edition, 1996.

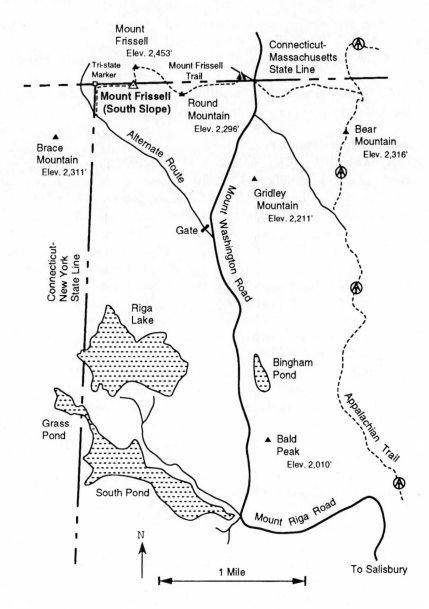

Mount Frissell (South Slope), Connecticut - 2,380 Feet

Hiking Southern New England, by George Ostertag et al., Falcon Press Publishing Co., Inc., Helena, Montana, 1997.

Hiking Trails and Short Walks around Salisbury, Connecticut, Salisbury Association, Salisbury, Connecticut, 1995.

Short Nature Walks in Connecticut, by Eugene Keyarts, The Globe Pequot Press, Old Saybrook, Connecticut, 1999.

Primary Route: Mount Frissell Trail

Approach ▲ From the junction of U.S. Hwy 44/State Route 41 and Washinee Street (identified as Library Street on the E side of Hwy 44), immediately s of the courthouse in Salisbury, proceed NW on Washinee Street for 0.7 miles to the signed Mount Riga Road on the left. Turn left and follow Mount Riga Road 2.9 miles to its junction with Mount Washington Road at the SE end of South Pond. Turn right and proceed N on Mount Washington Road 3.3 miles to the Connecticut-Massachusetts state line, where there are signs and a concrete marker. (See Special Conditions for an alternate approach.) Park in the small parking area approximately 100 feet s of the state line. Do not block the woods road at the state line.

Route ▲ From the parking area, hike N on Mount Washington Road to the woods road at the state line on the left. Hike NW up the road approximately 200 yards to a trail on the left. This is the Mount Frissell Trail, marked with red blazes. Hike w on the Mount Frissell Trail for 1.3 miles to the highpoint via the summit of Round Mountain at 0.7 miles and the summit of Mount Frissell at 1.2 miles. From the summit of Mount Frissell, the highpoint is approximately 0.1 miles almost due s via the trail. There is a pile of rocks on the N side of the trail at the highpoint. There is no USGS benchmark, but there is a brass rod set into the ground next to the highpoint.

Alternate Route

Approach ▲ From the junction of U.S. Hwy 44/State Route 41 and Washinee Street (identified as Library Street on the E side of Hwy 44), immediately s of the courthouse in Salisbury, proceed NW on Washinee Street for 0.7 miles to the signed Mount Riga Road on the left. Turn left and follow Mount Riga Road 2.9 miles to its junction with Mount Washington Road at the SE end of South Pond. Turn right and proceed N on Mount Washington Road 2.1 miles to a metal gate across a Jeep trail on the left. (See Special Conditions for an alternate route.) Park off the road.

Route ▲ Hike NW on the Jeep road 1.2 miles to a trail on the right marked by a 1-foot-high cairn. This point is beyond the first small bridge and approximately 30 yards before a second small bridge. Bear right on this trail approximately 100 yards to a 3-foot stone Connecticut–New York state line marker. Proceed 0.3 miles N on the trail to the Connecticut–Massachusetts–New York tri-state marker, then E on the trail 0.3 miles to the highpoint. There is a pile of rocks on the N side of the trail at the highpoint. There is no USGS benchmark, but there is a brass rod set into the ground next to the highpoint.

Special Conditions

Although Mount Riga Road and Mount Washington Road are gravel roads, they are well maintained and suitable for any type of vehicle. They are, however, subject to winter closure. An alternate approach to the trailheads is as follows: From Salisbury, proceed N on State Route 41 approximately 13 miles to State Route 23 at Mill Pond. On the E side of Mill Pond, 0.1 miles S of Route 23, turn W on Mount Washington Road. Continue W then S on Mount Washington Road 4.4 miles to East Street, bearing to the left. Proceed S on East Street 4.4 miles to a scissors crossing of West Street near Hunts Pond. Continue S on East Street for 4.1 miles to the Connecticut-Massachusetts state line and the Primary Route trailhead. East Street becomes Mount Washington Road at the state line. Continue S for 1.1 miles to reach the trailhead for the alternate route. The topographic map showing this route is Egremont, Mass.-N.Y., 7½ minute.

This alternate approach to Mount Frissell is convenient if one is coming S from Mount Greylock, Massachusets, via U.S. Hwy 7. Continue S on U.S. Hwy 7 to Great Barrington, Mass. Turn right (W) on State Route 23 to its intersection with State Route 41. Follow the alternate approach from there.

On the Primary Route, there is a "Private Property—No Trespassing" sign at the entrance to the woods road. Hikers are allowed access to the Mount Frissell Trail. The routes may be combined with or without a car shuttle to create a loop trip or a one-way trip.

The Appalachian Trail passes near the Connecticut highpoint. It goes over Bear Mountain, which is approximately 1½ miles ESE of Mount Frissell. The Appalachian Trail can be reached by hiking E 0.7 miles on an old woods road (Northwest Road) that begins on the E side of Mount Washington Road just S of the Connecticut-Massachusetts state line. The summit of Bald Mountain is 0.6 miles S of where the woods road meets the Appalachian Trail. The entire Appalachian Trail is marked for travel in both directions with white paint blazes on trees or poles and rocks, about 2 inches wide and 6 inches high. Two blazes, one above the other, are a signal of an important trail feature such as an obscure turn or a change in route. Side trails from the Appalachian Trail are usually blazed in blue. Information on hiking the Appalachian Trail can be obtained from the Appalachian Trail Conference, P.O. Box 807, 799 Washington Street, Harpers Ferry, WV 25425-0807 (304/535-6331).

In addition to the Appalachian Trail, which traverses 51 miles north-south across Connecticut, there is an extensive trail system in Connecticut. The trails in this system are usually referred to as the "Connecticut Blue Trails" because of the blue blazes marking almost all the trails. There are over 500 miles of blue-blazed trails sponsored by the Connecticut Forest and Park Association. Information and the *Connecticut Walk Book*, which is a complete guide to the "Blue Trails," with descriptions and maps, can be obtained from the Connecticut Forest and Park Association, 16 Meriden Road, Rockfall, CT 06481-2961 (860/346-2372).

Historical Notes

Nearby 2,316-foot-high Bear Mountain is the highest mountaintop within Connecticut. However, the **highpoint** in Connecticut is on the s slope of Massachusetts's Mount Frissell.

The Appalachian Trail, completed in 1937, extends over 2,150 miles from Mount Katahdin, the highpoint of Maine, to Springer Mountain in northern Georgia.

Natural History Notes

Mountain laurel grows in profusion here, along with hemlock and beech trees. Blueberries can be found in season.

Delaware

Ebright Azimuth

448 Feet

County

New Castle

Location

Approximately 5 miles N of Wilmington.

Hiking

Drive-up.

Gain

Drive-up.

Maps

Topographic: Wilmington North, Del.-Pa., 7½ minute.

Primary Route

Approach ▲ From the junction of I-95 and U.S. Hwy 202 (I-95 Exit 8) in Wilmington, proceed N on Hwy 202 for 4.3 miles to State Route 92 (Naamans Road). Proceed E on Route 92 for 1.1 miles to Ebright Road on the left. (This point may also be reached by proceeding W on Route 92 for 4.5 miles from its junction with I-95, Exit 11.) Proceed N on Ebright Road 0.6 miles to Ramblewood Drive (a little N of the radio tower) on the right. Turn right (E) on Ramblewood Drive and park along the side of the road.

Route ▲ Walk to the large sign at the highpoint on the SE corner of Ebright Road and Ramblewood Drive. There is no USGS benchmark at the highpoint.

Special Conditions

There is a USGS benchmark, identified as Ebright Azimuth, on the NW corner of the Ebright Road/Turf Road intersection. There is a boulder

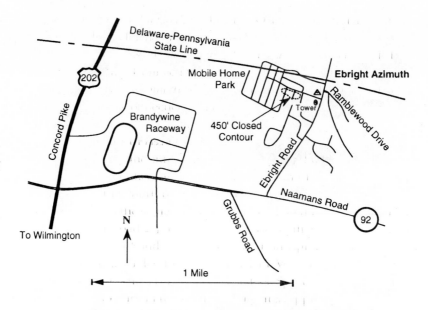

Delaware-Pennsylvania State Line

202

Concord Pike

Mobile Home Park

Ebright Azimuth

Ramblewood Drive

Brandywine Raceway

450' Closed Contour

Tower

Ebright Road

To Wilmington

N

Grubbs Road

Naamans Road

92

1 Mile

Ebright Azimuth, Delaware - 448 Feet

Delaware highpoint, Ebright Azimuth. Be sure to look both ways when crossing the street.

immediately N of Turf Road approximately 150 yards w of Ebright Road next to a mobile home, which is, in fact, higher than the base of the Ebright Azimuth sign. A survey of the elevation of these points is as follows: base of the Ebright Azimuth sign, 448.25 feet; the Ebright Azimuth benchmark, 447.85 feet; the boulder in the trailer park, 450.85 feet. Although higher than the base of the Ebright Azimuth sign, the boulder is probably the result of grading and landscaping for the mobile home park and is, therefore, manmade and not recognized as the highpoint.

Another issue yet to be resolved is that, on the 1993 edition of the Wilmington North, Del.-Pa., topographic map, there is a closed contour with an elevation of 450 feet. This area is in the trailer park approximately 230 yards w of the tower on the w side of Ebright Road. It is unknown whether this is a natural or manmade feature. The 450-foot contour is shown on the map included herein.

Historical Notes

In 1933, when the USGS originally surveyed and monumented the station in the highpoint area, the primary benchmark was located on property owned by James and Grant Ebright. Accordingly, the benchmark was named Ebright after the owners of the land. The primary benchmark was placed near the Ebrights' stone house, which survives today and is located on the south side of Winterset Road 0.2 miles west of Ebright Road near the Delaware-Pennsylvania boundary monument number 17. The azimuth reference mark, named Ebright Azimuth, provides an azimuth reference for the primary benchmark. The benchmark, the road, and the highpoint have inherited the name.

Florida

Lakewood Park

345 Feet

County
Walton

Location
Approximately 2 miles ENE of Paxton.

Hiking
Drive-up.

Gain
Drive-up.

Maps
Topographic: Paxton, Fla.-Ala., 7½ minute.

Guidebooks
Hiking Florida, by M. Timothy O'Keefe, Falcon Press Publishing Co., Inc., Helena, Montana, 2d edition, 1997.

Primary Route
Approach ▲ From the junction of U.S. Hwy 331 and Alabama State Route 54 E of Florala, Ala., proceed E on Route 54 for 1.1 miles to a junction with a paved road on the right. This road becomes Walton County Road 285 on the Florida side of the Alabama-Florida state line. Proceed s on County Road 285 for 0.8 miles to Lakewood Park on the right. Park in the parking area.

Route ▲ Walk to the gray granite monument that "marks" the highpoint. There is no USGS benchmark. The actual highpoint appears to be approximately 30 yards WSW of the monument.

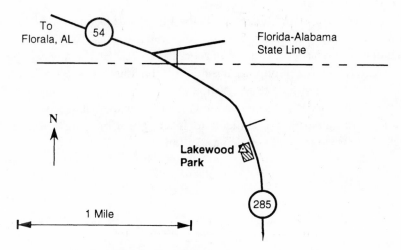

To Florala, AL — 54

Florida-Alabama State Line

N

Lakewood Park

285

1 Mile

Lakewood Park, Florida - 345 Feet

Lakewood, Florida

Florida's Highest Point
345 FT.

Florida Department of Natural Resources,
National Park Service
and
Land and Water Conservation Fund as Cooperators
with
Walton County Board of Commissioners

Florida's highpoint would be difficult to find if not marked.

Special Conditions

Lakewood Park, which surrounds the highpoint, has been developed by Walton County and is in the unincorporated hamlet of Lakewood. It includes nature trails and a large gazebo. Lakewood Park is always open. Although the Florida highpoint has no official name that is recognized by the USGS, the signs put up by Walton County identify the plateau surrounding the highpoint as Lakewood Park. The relatively flat 400-foot-by-900-foot plateau makes it difficult to locate the actual highpoint. The highpoint region is locally known as Britton Hill.

Georgia

Brasstown Bald

4,784 Feet

County
Towns-Union

Location
Approximately 12 miles E of Blairsville in Chattahoochee National Forest.

Hiking
Primary Route: 1.0 miles, round trip, on paved trail.
Alternate Route 1: 12.2 miles, round trip, on trail.
Alternate Route 2: 5.6 miles, round trip, on trail.
Alternate Route 3: 14.4 miles, round trip, on trail.

Gain
Primary Route: 400 feet, Class 1, easy.
Alternate Route 1: 4,330 feet, Class 1, strenuous.
Alternate Route 2: 2,350 feet, Class 1, moderate.
Alternate Route 3: 3,300 feet, Class 1, strenuous.

Maps
Topographic: Jacks Gap, Ga.; Hiawassee, Ga.-N.C.; and Blairsville, Ga.-N.C., all 7½ minute.
National Forest: Chattahoochee N.F.

Guidebooks
Appalachian Trail Guide to North Carolina–Georgia, edited by Jack Coriell, Appalachian Trail Conference, Harpers Ferry, West Virginia, 11th edition, 1998.
The Georgia Conservancy's Guide to the North Georgia Mountains, edited by Fred Brown, Longstreet Press, Atlanta, Georgia, 2d edition, 1991.

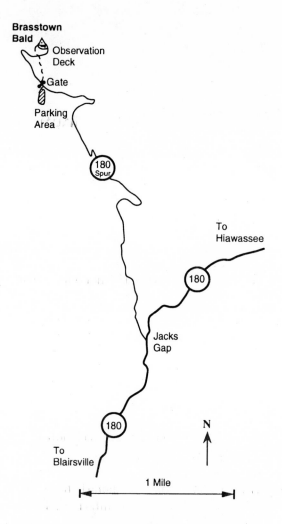

Brasstown
Bald

Observation
Deck

Gate

Parking
Area

180
Spur

To
Hiawassee

180

Jacks
Gap

180

To
Blairsville

N

1 Mile

Brasstown Bald, Georgia - 4,784 Feet
(Primary Route)

The visitor center atop Georgia's Brasstown Bald.

Hiking Georgia, by Donald W. Pfitzer, Falcon Press Publishing Co., Inc., Helena, Montana, 2d edition, 1996.

The Hiking Trails of North Georgia, by Tim Homan, Peachtree Publishers, Ltd., Atlanta, Georgia, 3d edition, 1997.

Summits of the South: A Visitor's Guide to Twenty-Five Southern Appalachian Peaks, by Brian A. Boyd, Fern Creek Press, Clayton, Georgia, 1990.

Primary Route

Approach ▲ From Blairsville, proceed s on U.S. Hwy 19/129 for 7.5 miles to State Route 180. Turn left (E) on Route 180 and proceed 7.3 miles to State Route 180 Spur. (This point may also be reached by proceeding w on Route 180 for 5.2 miles from its junction with U.S. Hwy 76/State Routes 17/75 approximately 12 miles s of Hiawassee.) Turn left on Route 180 Spur and continue 2.5 miles to the parking area at the end of the road.

Route ▲ From the N end of the parking area, hike 0.5 miles N on the signed paved trail to the summit. There is a Visitor Center on the summit. There is a USGS benchmark just inside the locked gate next to the wooden stairway leading up to the observation platform. The rangers there will open the gate on request.

Alternate Route I: Arkaquah Trail

Approach ▲ From Blairsville, proceed s on U.S. Hwy 19/129 for 2.8 miles to Town Creek School Road on the left. Turn left (E) and continue

1.0 miles to Trackrock Gap Road on the left. Turn left (NE) and proceed 3.9 miles to the signed trailhead and a small parking area on the right. A larger parking area is on the left about 50 yards before the trailhead. This point is just s of the crest at Trackrock Gap.

Route ▲ Hike generally w 5.6 miles along the blue-blazed trail to the NW corner of the Brasstown Bald parking area. Continue N 0.5 miles on the signed paved trail to the summit. There is a Visitor Center on the summit. There is a USGS benchmark just inside the locked gate next to the wooden stairway leading up to the observation platform. The rangers there will open the gate on request.

Alternate Route 2: Jacks Knob Trail

Approach ▲ From Blairsville, proceed s on U.S. Hwy 19/129 for 7.6 miles to State Route 180. Turn left (E) on Route 180 and proceed 7.2 miles to State Route 180 Spur. (This point may also be reached by proceeding w on Route 180 for 5.2 miles from its junction with U.S. Hwy 76/State Routes 17/75 approximately 9 miles s of Hiawassee.) Turn left on Route 180 Spur and continue approximately 100 yards to the point where Jacks Knob Trail crosses the road at Jacks Gap. Park on the side of the road.

Route ▲ Hike N on the blue-blazed trail for 2.3 miles to the s end of the Brasstown Bald parking area. Cross the parking area and continue N 0.5 miles on the signed paved trail to the summit. There is a Visitor Center on the summit. There is a USGS benchmark just inside the locked gate next to the wooden stairway leading up to the observation platform. The rangers there will open the gate on request.

Alternate Route 3: Wagon Train Trail

Approach ▲ From the junction of U.S. Hwy 76 and State Route 66 in the town of Young Harris, proceed s on U.S. Hwy 76 for 0.2 miles to Bald Mountain Road on the left. Turn left (E) on Bald Mountain Road and park in the Sharp Memorial United Methodist Church parking lot on the NE corner of U.S. Hwy 76 and Bald Mountain Road on the Young Harris College campus.

Route ▲ Hike E on Bald Mountain Road approximately 0.2 miles to the trail, which at this point is a gated dirt road. Hike generally SE for 6.6 miles up the road, which becomes more of a trail in approximately 1.0 miles at the wilderness boundary, to the paved trail to the summit. Turn right (N) on the paved trail and continue 0.4 miles to the summit. There is a Visitor Center on the summit. There is a USGS benchmark just inside the locked gate next to the wooden stairway leading up to the observation platform. The rangers there will open the gate on request.

Special Conditions

Brasstown Bald Visitor Center is open daily from Memorial Day through October and on weekends in the early spring, depending on the weather. When the Visitor Center is open, a shuttle bus operates from the parking area to the summit for a fee. For information, contact the Brasstown Bald Visitor Center (706/896-2556). For information during the off-season and the national forest map, contact the Chattahoochee National Forest, Brasstown Ranger District, P.O. Box 9, 1881 Hwy 515, Blairsville, GA 30514 (706/745-6928).

There is no water available along any of the trails. Carry all that you will require. The Arkaquah Trail and the Jacks Knob Trail have been designated National Hiking Trails. The Jacks Knob Trail continues s 2.2 miles beyond Jacks Gap, where it meets the Appalachian Trail. All three trail routes can be done as one-way hikes with a car shuttle. They may also be combined with a car shuttle to provide one-way routes across Brasstown Bald.

Portions of the Arkaquah Trail are shown on all three topographic maps listed. The Jacks Knob Trail requires only the Jacks Gap, Ga., topographic map; the Wagon Train Trail appears on the Hiawassee, Ga.-N.C., and Jacks Gap, Ga., topographic maps.

As noted above, the Appalachian Trail passes near Brasstown Bald. The trail can be reached by hiking s from Brasstown Bald on the Jacks Knob Trail for 5.0 miles, meeting the Appalachian Trail at Chattahoochee Gap. Approximately 75 miles of the Appalachian Trail are in Georgia, and the summit of Springer Mountain, Georgia, is the southern terminus of the trail. The entire Appalachian Trail is marked for travel in both directions with white paint blazes on trees or poles and rocks, about 2 inches wide and 6 inches high. Two blazes, one above the other, are a signal of an important trail feature such as an obscure turn or a change in route. Information on hiking the Appalachian Trail can be obtained from the Appalachian Trail Conference, P.O. Box 807, 799 Washington Street, Harpers Ferry, WV 25425-0807 (304/535-6331).

Historical Notes

An observation tower has existed on Brasstown Bald since the 1920s. The present tower portion of the Brasstown Bald complex was completed in 1965, the exhibit building in 1967, and the parking area in 1968.

The Cherokee Indians called the summit area *Itse'yi*, "place of fresh green." Early settlers confused *Itse'yi* with *Untsaiyi*, the Cherokee word for "brass"; hence the name Brasstown.

The Appalachian Trail, completed in 1937, extends over 2,150 miles from Mount Katahdin, the highpoint of Maine, to Springer Mountain.

Hawaii

Mauna Kea

13,796 Feet

County
Hawaii

Location
Approximately 27 miles WNW of Hilo in the Mauna Kea Forest Reserve on the Big Island of Hawaii.

Hiking
0.4 miles, round trip, cross-country.

Gain
230 feet, Class 1, easy.

Maps
Topographic: Mauna Kea, Hawaii, and Puu Oo, Hawaii, both 7½ minute.

Guidebooks
Hawaii Trails: Walks, Strolls, and Treks on the Big Island, by Kathy Morey, Wilderness Press, Berkeley, California, 1992.

Primary Route
Approach ▲ From the junction of State Route 19 and State Route 200 (Waianuenue Avenue), in Hilo, proceed "Mauka" (toward the mountain) on Route 200. After a short distance Route 200 becomes Kaumana Drive and, later, the Saddle Road. Continue on Route 200 for 27.5 miles to the summit road on the right at Humuula Saddle. (This point is 58 miles NE of Kailua-Kona via State Routes 190 and 200.) Turn right (N) and proceed 6.3 miles on the paved road to the Onizuka Center for International

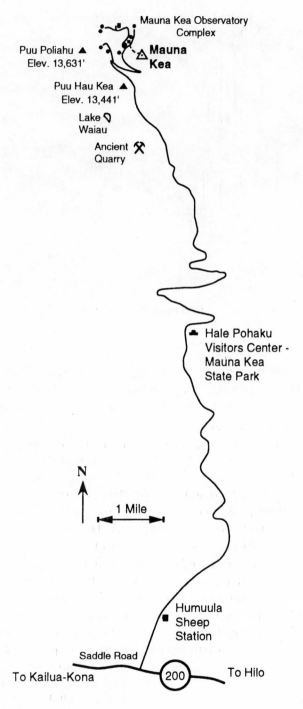

Mauna Kea Observatory
Complex

Puu Poliahu ▲
Elev. 13,631'

△ **Mauna
Kea**

Puu Hau Kea ▲
Elev. 13,441'

Lake ᕼ
Waiau

Ancient ✕
Quarry

Hale Pohaku
Visitors Center -
Mauna Kea
State Park

N
↑

|← 1 Mile →|

Humuula
Sheep
Station

Saddle Road

To Kailua-Kona   (200)   To Hilo

Mauna Kea, Hawaii - 13,796 Feet

54

Mauna Kea from the air with Mauna Loa behind it.

Astronomy Visitors Center (also known as Hale Pohaku, "Stone House" in Hawaiian). Continue on the gravel road 8.4 miles to the Mauna Kea observatory complex near the summit. Park near the University of Hawaii 2.2-meter telescope.

Route ▲ The trail to the summit is opposite the University of Hawaii observatory. Hike 0.2 miles SE up to the obvious highpoint. There is a USGS benchmark and a rock cairn on the summit.

Special Conditions

The summit road beyond the Visitors Center at the 9,240-foot level is a steep, mostly unpaved gravel road and requires a 4WD vehicle. 4WD vehicles can be rented in Hilo or Kailua-Kona.

Snow is common at the higher elevations even in the summer and often prevents driving to the summit. Be prepared with proper clothing and equipment in case it is necessary to hike to the summit from a lower elevation. Summit conditions can be checked by calling the Visitors Center, which is open Thursday (5:30–10:00 P.M.), Friday (9:00 A.M.–12 noon, 1:00–4:30 P.M., 6:00–10:00 P.M.), and Saturday and Sunday (9:00 A.M.–10:00 P.M.).

Visitors should be aware of the sudden change in altitude: from sea level to nearly 14,000 feet. Symptoms of altitude sickness may be experienced. If so, head back down the mountain. Be alert to park in the area closest to the summit.

Observatory complex near the summit of Mauna Kea.

Information on the Mauna Kea observatories, the evening programs, and the weekend tours can be obtained from the Visitors Center at 808/961-2180. Additional information is available on the Web at www.ifa.hawaii.edu/info/bif.

Harper's Car and Truck Rental rents 4WD vehicles that can be driven to the summit. Its Hilo office is at 456 Kalanianaole Avenue, Hilo, HI 96720 (808/969-1478). Its Kona office is at the Ke-ahole Airport, Kailua-Kona, HI 96740 (808/329-6688).

A tour company that allows one to hike to the highpoint from the observatory complex is Paradise Safaris, P.O. Box 9027, Kailua-Kona, HI 96745 (808/322-2366).

Historical Notes

Mauna Kea means "white mountain" in the Hawaiian language. Mauna Loa, the second highest mountain in Hawaii, is the Hawaiian phrase for "long mountain."

Approximately 0.4 miles w of the road at the 12,400-foot level, there is a cave where ancient Hawaiians mined stones for their adzes. It is the world's most extensive adze quarry and is listed as a National Historic Landmark.

In 1988 the Mauna Kea observatory complex was named the Onizuka Center for International Astronomy in honor of Air Force Lt. Col. Ellison

S, Onizuka, a native of the Kona Coast region of Hawaii, who lost his life January 28, 1986, on the ill-fated space shuttle *Challenger* flight.

Natural History Notes

The dry, clear atmosphere on Mauna Kea makes it a premier astronomical site.

Birds found in the area include ring-necked pheasant, chukar, and California quail.

Lake Waiau, at an elevation of 13,020 feet, is the highest lake in the United States.

Idaho

Borah Peak

12,662 Feet

County
Custer

Location
Approximately 18 miles NNW of Mackay in the Challis National Forest.

Hiking
6.8 miles, round trip, on trail and cross-country.

Gain
5,550 feet, Class 3, strenuous.

Maps
Topographic: Borah Peak, Idaho, 7½ minute.
National Forest: Challis N.F.

Guidebooks
Exploring Idaho's Mountains: A Guide for Climbers, Scramblers, and Hikers, by Tom Lopez, The Mountaineers, Seattle, Washington, 1990.
Hiking Idaho, by Ralph Maughan and Jackie Johnson Maughan, Falcon Press Publishing Co., Inc., Helena, Montana, 2d edition, 1997.
Trails of Eastern Idaho, by Margaret Fuller and Jerry Painter, Trail Guide Books, Weiser, Idaho, 1998.

Primary Route
Approach ▲ From the junction of U.S. Hwy 93 and Trail Creek Road approximately 16 miles N of Mackay, proceed N on Hwy 93 for 4.7 miles to a dirt road on the right, between mileposts 129 and 130, with signs indicating "Mt. Borah Trailhead." Turn right (E) and continue 3.1 miles on

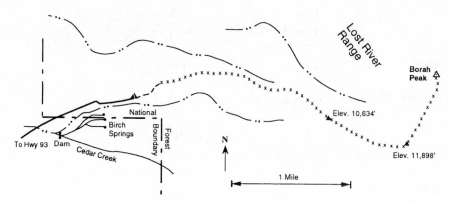

Borah Peak, Idaho - 12,662 Feet

Birch Springs Road, passing a large flat area for trailers and motorhomes on the right at 2.0 miles, to the trailhead and a parking area for dayhikers and picnickers.

Route ▲ From the E end of the trailhead turn-around, follow the trail generally ENE 0.6 miles to the top of the ridge. Hike ESE along the ridge 2.1 miles to the 11,700-foot level and the s arête of Borah Peak. Continue N up the arête 0.7 miles to the summit. There is a register and USGS benchmark on the summit.

Special Conditions

The route up the ridge from the 11,300-foot level and the s arête has some exposed Class 3 sections and requires some rock and boulder climbing. A knife-edged ridge, known as Chicken Out Ridge, extends from approximately 11,300 feet to approximately 11,700 feet. This knife-edged ridge has a more dangerous slope on the N side than on the s side and involves Class 3 climbing. Where the knife-edged ridge meets the s arête of Borah Peak, there is a notch on the ridge that has steep slopes on both sides and is frequently filled with steep, hard snow. In moderate to heavy snow years, snow remains in the notch until late summer. This section can sometimes be passed by dipping below the snow on the w side of the ridge. There is a small cliff along the ridge that requires a short pitch of rock climbing. The character of this area changes with the amount of snow present. Depending on winter snowfall and the time of year, the short rock pitch may be completely covered with snow. The usual climbing season for Borah Peak is June through mid-September. This is a steep climb. The net gain is in excess of 5,000 feet in a little less than 3.5 miles. Except for melting snow, there is no water source on Borah Peak. Carry all the water required.

Thunderstorms are common in the summer and early fall. The first buildup of clouds should be the signal for getting off the mountain. Take care not to get caught on the peaks or exposed ridges during one of these storms.

This climb can be done as a backpack. There are suitable campsites at the timberline and near the 11,600-foot level. At the trailhead there is a small campground with three campsites. There is no water available at the campground.

Information, hiking guide sheets, and the national forest map can be obtained from Salmon and Challis National Forest, Lost River Ranger District, P.O. Box 507, 716 W. Custer Street, Mackay, ID 83251 (208/588-2224).

Historical Notes

Borah Peak was named in honor of William Edgar Borah (1865–1940), who served in the U.S. Senate from 1907 to 1940. A man of imposing presence, Senator Borah had a leonine head with a majestic mane and rugged features that conveyed the sense of an elder statesman, and he was known as the "Lion of Idaho."

Natural History Notes

The Lost River Range, which includes Borah Peak, is a long, narrow fault block of sedimentary rock pushed up between two downdropped blocks forming valleys. Most of the rocks that outcrop in the range are lithified ocean sediments. Fossils of bivalve shells and corals can be found high on the mountain. Leatherman Peak, also in the Lost River Range, is approximately 7 miles SE of Borah Peak. At an elevation of 12,228 feet, it is the second highest peak in Idaho. In fact, Idaho's 24 highest mountains are in or border the Lost River Ranger District.

On October 28, 1983, a magnitude 7.3 earthquake shook the Borah Peak area. It left a fault scarp 21 miles long and up to 14 feet high near the western base of Borah Peak. The fault scarp is clearly evident as one drives to the trailhead. There is an earthquake interpretive center NE on Doublesprings Road, which intersects U.S. Hwy 93 about 2 miles N of the Borah Peak turnoff.

Wildlife in the area include antelope, deer, elk, bighorn sheep, mountain lion, and bobcat.

Guides/Outfitters

Jackson Hole Mountain Guides and Climbing School, P.O. Box 7477, 165 North Glenwood Street, Jackson, WY 83001 (800/239-7642).

Sawtooth Mountain Guides, P.O. Box 18, Stanley, ID 83278 (208/774-3324).

Illinois

Charles Mound

1,235 Feet

County

Jo Daviess

Location

Approximately 12 miles NE of Galena.

Hiking

0.4 miles, round trip, cross-country.

Gain

75 feet, Class 1, easy.

Maps

Topographic: Shullsburg, Wis.-Ill.; Scales Mound East, Ill.; and Scales Mound West, Ill., all 7½ minute.

Primary Route

Approach ▲ From Galena, proceed ENE on the Stagecoach Trail (Jo Daviess County Road 3) for approximately 11 miles to Elizabeth–Scales Mound Road (Jo Daviess County Road 4). (This point can also be reached by proceeding NW then W approximately 29½ miles on the Stagecoach Trail from its junction with U.S. Hwy 20 approximately 2¾ miles NW of Eleroy. From here, the Stagecoach Trail follows Stephenson County Road 6, which becomes Jo Daviess County Road 13 and continues W from Warren on Jo Daviess County Road 3.) Turn left (N) on Elizabeth–Scales Mound Road and continue 1.0 miles to Charles Mound Road, which is 0.4 miles N of the railroad tracks in the village of Scales Mound. Elizabeth–Scales Mound Road is called Franklin Street in Scales Mound. At the railroad tracks, bear right, cross the tracks, then bear left back to Franklin Street, which

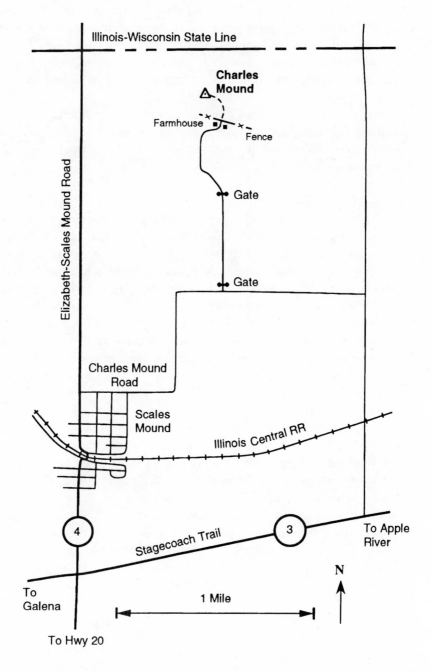

Charles Mound, Illinois - 1,235 Feet

becomes Elizabeth–Scales Mound Road at Charles Mound Road. Turn right (E) on Charles Mound Road and continue 0.5 miles, where the road turns N. Continue N for 0.5 miles to where the road turns E again. Proceed 0.3 miles to a gravel road on the left with a gate. Proceed N on the gravel road, through the gate. Continue 1.1 miles through a second gate to a signed parking area near the old farmhouse.

Route ▲ From the signed parking area at the farmhouse, follow the road up the slope to the ridge. Continue NW along the ridge approximately 200 yards to the highpoint. There is a USGS benchmark and a guest register at the highpoint.

Special Conditions

Charles Mound and the property surrounding it are private property. Please respect the rights of the property owner. The land surrounding the highpoint is owned by Wayne and Jean Wuebbels, who welcome Highpointers. The Wuebbels would prefer that permission be obtained to cross their property; however, in the event that they cannot be reached, it is not mandatory. They can be reached in the daytime at 815/845-2625 and in the evening or on weekends at 815/845-2552. If no one is available, please leave a message on the answering machine. The Wuebbels would prefer no visits after dark and, if you bring pets, for you to please leave them in your vehicle.

Historical Notes

Old records indicate that White Oak Fort was once located on Charles Mound to protect the Kellogg Trail, an old stagecoach and wagon road. The Wuebbels are only the third family to own this property. Elijah Charles, for whom Charles Mound is named, settled in a log house at the base of the mound in 1827. He was not allowed to purchase the property because it was part of a land grant given to Richard Magoon by President Polk in 1848. There is no record that Richard Magoon ever lived at Charles Mound. The land was sold to Seth Glanville in 1868 and remained in the Glanville family until the Wuebbels purchased it in 1994. The view from the summit encompasses three states: Illinois, Iowa, and Wisconsin.

Indiana

Hoosier High Point

1,257 Feet

County
Wayne

Location
Approximately 12 miles N of Richmond.

Hiking
0.1 miles, round trip, cross-country.

Gain
20 feet, Class 1, trivial.

Maps
Topographic: Spartanburg, Ind.-Ohio, and Whitewater, Ind.-Ohio, both 7½ minute.

Primary Route
Approach ▲ From the junction of I-70 and State Route 227 (Exit 153) N of Richmond, proceed N on Route 227 for 10.1 miles through Middleboro, Whitewater, and Bethel to County Line Road (this road is on the Wayne-Randolph county line). Turn left (w) on County Line Road and continue 1.0 miles to Elliott Road. Turn left (s) on Elliott Road and continue 0.3 miles to the s end of a wooded area on the right (w). Park along the side of the road.

Route ▲ Hike w along the s end of the wooded area approximately 50 yards until you come to a stile crossing the fence on the right (N). The highpoint, marked with a small rock cairn and a steel pole with a sign reading "Indiana High Point, Elev. 1,257 Feet," should be visible immediately N of the stile.

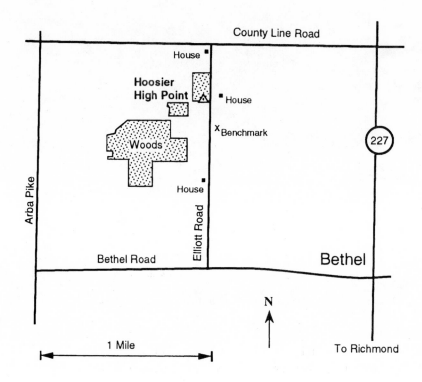

Hoosier High Point, Indiana - 1,257 Feet

Special Conditions

There is a USGS benchmark approximately 0.4 miles S of County Line Road on the E side of the road in a shallow hole approximately 6 feet off the pavement. As is obvious, the USGS benchmark is not the highpoint.

The stile over the fence was installed by members of the Highpointers Club. Exercise caution when using the stile to avoid both injury and damage to the fence.

The Indiana highpoint is on private property. Please respect the rights of the property owner. The land surrounding the highpoint is owned by Kim Goble. Ms. Goble would prefer that permission be obtained to cross her property. She can be reached by telephone at 765/966-5674. However, in the event that she cannot be reached, permission is not mandatory.

Historical Notes

On July 1, 1993, the General Assembly of the State of Indiana officially adopted "Hoosier High Point" as the name of the Indiana highpoint. The

Stone cairn at the highpoint of Indiana.

name is derived from "Hoosiers," the nickname for Indiana natives or inhabitants. Although the people of Indiana have been called the "Hoosiers" for more than a century and a half, the origin of the nickname is unknown. The earliest written references to "Hoosier" date from the early 1830s. How long the name had been used orally before that time is unknown. There are several popular theories as to the origin of the nickname, but probably the most plausible one was championed by Jacob Piatt Dunn, an Indiana historian. Dunn noted that "Hoosier" was frequently used in many parts of the South in the nineteenth century for woodsmen or rough hill people. He traced the word back to "hoozer," in the Cumberland dialect of England, which meant anything unusually large, presumably such as a hill. It is easy to see how this word was attached to a hill dweller or highlander. Immigrants from Cumberland, England, settled in the southern mountains (Cumberland Mountains, Cumberland River, Cumberland Gap, etc.). Their descendants brought the name with them when they settled in the hills of southern Indiana.

Iowa

Hawkeye Point

1,670 Feet

County
Osceola

Location
Approximately 5 miles NNE of Sibley.

Hiking
0.1 miles, round trip, cross-country.

Gain
10 feet, Class 1, trivial.

Maps
Topographic: Sibley East, Iowa, 7½ minute.

Primary Route
Approach ▲ From the junction of State Routes 60 and 9 N of Sibley, proceed N on Route 60 for 2.3 miles to a gravel road (130th Street). (This point is 2.9 miles s of the Iowa-Minnesota state line via Route 60.) Turn E on the gravel road and proceed 0.2 miles to the first farm on the right. Turn into the second of two driveways and park. This is the farm of Merrill and Donna Sterler, who own the property surrounding the Iowa highpoint. Ask permission of the Sterlers to go to the highpoint.

Route ▲ From the farmhouse, walk SE up a slight slope between farm buildings approximately 100 yards to the s end of a cattle feed trough. This is the location of the highpoint as indicated on the Sibley East topographic map. There is a silo at the immediate N end of the feed trough. There is no USGS benchmark at the highpoint, but Mr. Sterler has

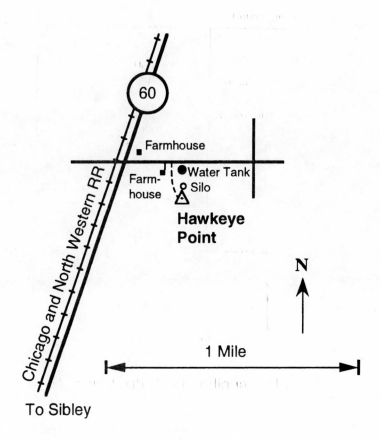

Hawkeye Point, Iowa - 1,670 Feet

placed his expired Iowa license plate, "HIGH PT," on the s end of the trough roof.

Special Conditions

The Sterlers would prefer that permission be obtained to cross their property. In the event no one is home to grant permission, however, it is not mandatory. Remember, the Iowa highpoint is on private property. Please respect the rights of the property owner. The Sterlers' telephone number is 712/754-2045.

Iowa's highpoint is at the near end of the cattle trough.

A convenient landmark is a large water tower labeled "Osceola Rural Water" on the Sterlers' farm just beyond the second driveway. The highpoint is approximately 150 yards almost due s of the water tower.

Historical Notes

Before the 1972 Geological Survey, Ocheyedan Mound, approximately 10 miles to the ESE, was considered the highpoint of Iowa. On March 23, 1998, Iowa governor Terry Branstad signed Iowa State Legislature Joint Resolution 2004, officially naming the Iowa highpoint Hawkeye Point. Iowa has been traditionally referred to as the Hawkeye State, and the highpoint was named in honor of all Iowa "Hawkeyes."

License plate shows exact location.

Kansas

Mount Sunflower

4,039 Feet

County
    Wallace

Location
    Approximately 19 miles NW of Sharon Springs.

Hiking
    Primary Route: Drive-up.
    Alternate Route: Drive-up.

Gain
    Primary Route: Drive-up.
    Alternate Route: Drive-up.

Maps
    Topographic: Mount Sunflower, Colo.-Kans., 7½ minute.

Primary Route
    Approach ▲ From the rest area in Weskan, proceed w on U.S. Hwy 40 for 2.7 miles to a gravel road. (This point is 1.5 miles E of the Colorado-Kansas state line via U.S. Hwy 40.) Turn right (N) on the gravel road and proceed 10.7 miles to a gravel road on the left with a sign reading "Mt. Sunflower." Turn left (w) on the gravel road and continue 1.1 miles to a dirt road on the right (N) with a cattle guard. Mount Sunflower is in sight to the N. Turn right and continue across the cattle guard and N through the pasture for 0.4 miles to the highpoint.
    Route ▲ In a fenced area on the highpoint will be found a 6-foot-high sunflower made of railroad spikes and a large boulder. There is no USGS benchmark.

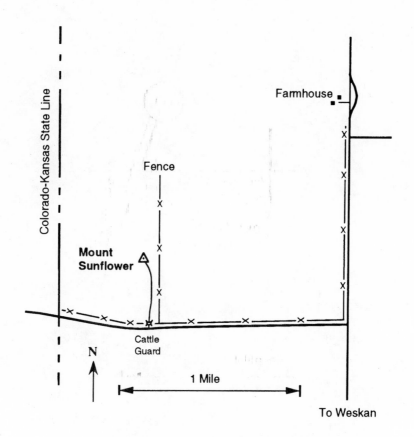

Mount Sunflower, Kansas - 4,039 Feet

Alternate Route

Approach ▲ From the Kanorado interchange on I-70 (Exit 1), 1.4 miles
E of the Colorado-Kansas state line, proceed s on the paved road 13.5 miles
(pavement ends at 6.5 miles) to a gravel road on the left. Turn left (E) on the
gravel road and proceed 0.4 miles to a gravel road on the right. Turn right
(s) and continue 8.1 miles to a gravel road on the right with a sign reading
"Mt. Sunflower." Turn right (w) on the gravel road and continue 1.1 miles
to a dirt road on the right (N) with a cattle guard. Mount Sunflower is in
sight to the N. Turn right and continue across the cattle guard and N
through the pasture for 0.4 miles to the highpoint.

Route ▲ In a fenced area on the highpoint will be found a 6-foot-high
sunflower made of railroad spikes and a large boulder. There is no USGS
benchmark.

Mount Sunflower in Kansas.

Special Conditions

Mount Sunflower is on private property, but it is open to the public. Please respect the rights of the property owner. There is a register at the highpoint for visitors to sign.

Although most of the Primary Route and a portion of the Alternate Route are on gravel roads, the roads are very well maintained and suitable for any type of vehicle in good weather.

Historical Notes

Mount Sunflower is named for the sunflower, *Helianthus annuus*, the state flower of Kansas. The property surrounding Mount Sunflower is managed by Ed and Cindy Harold. The property was purchased by Ed's grandfather in 1940. The old Harold homestead is 1.2 miles north of the westward turnoff to the highpoint. The ranch is on the w side of the road. The Harolds welcome highpoint visitors.

About 6 miles s of Mount Sunflower, just N of Smoky Hill River, was the Smoky Hill Trail. This trail was the quickest route to the Denver goldfields in 1859. The Butterfield Overland Despatch stage line traveled the trail from 1865 to 1870.

Natural History Notes

The abundant wildlife in the area includes antelope, deer, prairie dog, coyote, jackrabbit, fox, and many species of birds.

The productivity of the high plain around the highpoint depends on water that falls in the Colorado Rockies and percolates eastward underground via the Ogallala Aquifer. As development continues along the Front Range in Colorado and demand there for water increases, the available water and, hence, the productivity of this area will likely decrease significantly.

Kentucky

Black Mountain

4,139 Feet

County

Harlan

Location

Approximately 4 miles sse of Lynch and 6 miles e of Appalachia, Virginia.

Hiking

Drive-up.

Gain

Drive-up.

Maps

Topographic: Benham, Ky.-Va., and Appalachia, Va.-Ky., both 7½ minute.

Primary Route

Approach ▲ From the point where U.S. Hwy 119 crosses over State Route 160 in Cumberland, proceed e on Route 160 for 10.9 miles to the Kentucky-Virginia state line, where Route 160 turns abruptly e at the crest of the ridge and starts downhill. (See Special Conditions for an alternate approach to this point.) Two other roads are evident at this junction. One is a paved road that turns w downhill and has a locked gate across the entrance. The other is a narrow paved road that continues s through the woods with a sign indicating the way to a Federal Aviation Administration facility. Proceed on this latter road 1.7 miles to a spur road on the left, passing an FAA Long Range Radar Facility on the right at 1.5 miles. At 1.6 miles the paved road becomes a dirt road. Turn left onto

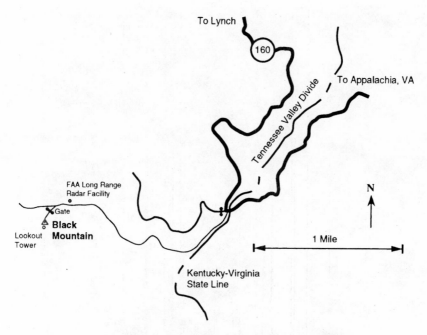

Black Mountain, Kentucky - 4,139 Feet

the spur road and continue 0.1 miles to an abandoned lookout tower on the summit.

Route ▲ The USGS benchmark is under the tower.

Special Conditions

The highpoint area is owned by the Penn Virginia Coal Company, and it has been posted with "No Trespassing" signs. An agreement has been reached with the coal company to provide Highpointers access to the summit. This special agreement is necessary because the coal company is concerned about being held liable if one of the coal mine tunnels under Black Mountain should collapse. This is still an active coal mining area. You must not leave the road to the summit.

In order to access the Black Mountain summit, you must sign the waiver printed at the end of this chapter and mail it to Penn Virginia Coal Company, Attn: Steve Looney, P.O. Box 386, Duffield, VA 24244. The waiver can be copied for use. Exhibit A, as referred to in the waiver, is the map in this chapter. Include a copy with the waiver. Once you have mailed the waiver, you are free to visit the highpoint.

Lookout tower atop Black Mountain.

The Primary Route describes an approach from the w side of Black Mountain. An alternate approach from the E is as follows: From the junction of U.S. Hwy 23-Business and Virginia State Route 68 in Appalachia, Virginia, proceed NW on Route 68 for 0.2 miles to Virginia State Route 160 on the right. Turn right (N) onto Route 160 and continue 7.8 miles to the Kentucky-Virginia state line. Virginia State Route 160 becomes, not surprisingly, Kentucky State Route 160 at the Kentucky-Virginia state line, and vice versa.

There is a gate just after the turn onto the spur road leading up to the summit. It is occasionally locked. If so, park so that none of the roads are blocked and hike up the spur road to the tower on the summit.

Historical Notes

This is a major coal mining region of Kentucky and Virginia. Numerous mining operations can be observed in the area.

The lookout tower on the summit was built by the Aermotor Company, Chicago. The Aermotor Company began manufacturing windmills and towers in 1888 and continues to do so today. As a logical extension, it manufactured steel towers for high-tension lines, triangulation towers, coast surveillance towers during World War II, and forest fire lookout towers. Several thousand fire lookout towers were placed throughout the United States. With the advent of forest fire detection by satellites, the fire lookout towers are being removed from the landscape. Few remain as testimony to the men and women who spent many lonely hours in the towers keeping our forests safe from fire.

In addition to the lookout tower, there are six other communications towers in the summit area.

WAIVER AGREEMENT FOR ACCESS TO THE SUMMIT OF BLACK MOUNTAIN, KENTUCKY

The undersigned ("Visitor"), for and in consideration of the access to private property granted to the undersigned by Penn Virginia Coal Company, Inc. hereby agrees as follows:

1. Visitor agrees to stay on the roadway marked on the map attached hereto as Exhibit A and understands and agrees that the access granted to Visitor is limited to such roadway. Visitor understands and agrees that entry into any areas outside those marked on the map attached as Exhibit A will be a trespass, and Visitor will be prosecuted for any such trespass.

2. Visitor, for him or herself, his or her heirs, successors, personal representatives, and assigns, hereby waives, holds harmless, and releases the owners of each and every interest, including coal lessees and coal operators and their contractors ("Owners") in the property to be visited ("Property") from and against all and any damage or injury to Visitor's person or property, including Visitor's death, regardless of the cause of such damage or injury, including any injury or damage which may result from negligence, gross negligence, criminal negligence, or criminal act of any Owner or any employee, agent or representative thereof, or of any other person or entity.

3. Visitor recognizes that there may be hidden, latent, or undisclosed dangers on the Property and assumes all risks therefrom and ENTERS THE PROPERTY AT VISITOR'S OWN RISK. Visitor further recognizes that the roadway marked on Exhibit A is not maintained for public travel and may not be passable by passenger car or four-wheel drive vehicle. Visitor assumes all risk to any damage (regardless of cause) to Visitor's vehicle or other personal property.

4. Visitor agrees to abide by all safety rules and regulations imposed by any Owner of the Property, and further agrees to obey and abide by any statutory or regulatory requirements imposed upon any Owner of any interest in the Property by any state, federal or local governmental or regulatory agency.

5. Visitor agrees to conduct any and all of Visitor's activities on the Property in such a way as to not interfere with any business activities being conducted on the Property.

6. Visitor agrees that Visitor will not, under any circumstances, nor at any time, assert that the Property, or any part thereof is, has become or should be deemed a "public park" as that term is defined at KRS Chapter 350 and the regulations promulgated pursuant thereto.

7. Visitor states he or she is over eighteen years of age, understands the terms and conditions of this Waiver Agreement and executes it willingly, voluntarily, knowingly, and intending to be bound thereby in all respects.

OR

Visitor is a minor under the age of eighteen (18), and this Waiver Agreement is executed by such minor Visitor's parent or guardian on behalf of such minor Visitor willingly, voluntarily, knowingly and with the intention that both the minor Visitor and the parent or guardian will be bound thereby in all respects.

Witness	"Visitor"	Date

	Name of Minor Visitor

Witness	Parent or Guardian	Date

Please sign and return to:
Penn Virginia Coal Company
Attn: Steve Looney
P.O. Box 386
Duffield, VA 24244

Louisiana

Driskill Mountain

535 Feet

County
Bienville Parish

Location
Approximately 10 miles s of Arcadia.

Hiking
1.8 miles, round trip, on dirt road and cross-country.

Gain
150 feet, Class 1, easy.

Maps
Topographic: Bryceland, Louisiana, 7½ minute.

Primary Route

Approach ▲ From Arcadia, proceed s on State Route 147. At 7.3 miles from Arcadia, bear right on State Route 797 and continue s on Route 797 for 3.8 miles to a T-intersection with State Route 507. Turn right (sw) on Route 507 and proceed 0.8 miles to Mount Zion Presbyterian Church and Driskill Memorial Cemetery on the right. Park in the church parking lot.

Route ▲ Hike N on the dirt road that begins on the w side of the church parking lot. Bear left around the hill with the radio tower. Continue approximately 0.3 miles to a fork at a small saddle, passing two spur roads and an old rusted gate along the way. At the fork, one road heads downhill to the left and the other continues up the ridge to a false summit. Go left downhill, staying right at a second fork about 100 yards from the first fork, and contour around the false summit to the right 0.4 miles to a saddle between the false summit and the true highpoint. Hike N along the road

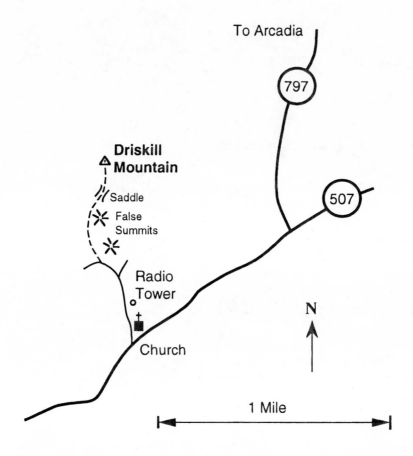

To Arcadia

797

Driskill Mountain

Saddle

False Summits

507

Radio Tower

Church

N

1 Mile

Driskill Mountain, Louisiana - 535 Feet

0.2 miles up the ridge to the cairn at the highpoint. There is a register but no USGS benchmark at the summit. (There is a USGS marker approximately 25 yards N of the summit.)

Special Conditions

There is a considerable amount of slash from logging operations in the area. The correct "road" can be difficult to follow. This is a popular deer hunting area. Use caution during hunting season, which is usually in November and December.

Part of the route crosses private property marked "No Trespassing," but Highpointers are welcome. Some of the land is owned by Margie

Don Holmes at the summit of Driskill Mountain.

Bowman. Mrs. Bowman does not require that permission be obtained to cross her property; however, she may be contacted for information at 318/263-9668. Please respect the rights of the property owners.

Historical Notes

Driskill Mountain was named for James Christopher "Grancer" Driskill (1817–1901), who settled in the farm and timber land surrounding the mountain in the late 1830s after moving from Macon, Georgia. Eventually, Mr. Driskill owned 960 acres in the area. In 1874 he donated two acres of land for what has become the Mount Zion Presbyterian Church and the Driskill Memorial Cemetery. Many of Grancer Driskill's descendants still live near Driskill Mountain.

Maine

Mount Katahdin

5,267 Feet

County

Piscataquis

Location

Approximately 20 miles NNW of Millinocket in Baxter State Park.

Hiking

Primary Route: 10.4 miles, round trip, on trail.
Alternate Route 1: 7.6 miles, round trip, on trail.
Alternate Route 2: 8.6 miles, round trip, on trail.
Alternate Route 3: 11.0 miles, round trip, on trail.

Gain

Primary Route: 4,200 feet, Class 1, strenuous.
Alternate Route 1: 4,000 feet, Class 2, strenuous.
Alternate Route 2: 4,300 feet, Class 2, strenuous.
Alternate Route 3: 3,900 feet, Class 1, strenuous.

Maps

Topographic: Mount Katahdin, Maine; Abol Pond, Maine; and Katahdin Lake, Maine, all 7½ minute.

Other: DeLorme's Map and Guide of Baxter State Park and Katahdin, DeLorme Publishing Co., Freeport, Maine.

Guidebooks

AMC *Maine Mountain Guide*, by Elliot Bates et al., Appalachian Mountain Club Books, Boston, Massachusetts, 1999.

Appalachian Trail Guide to Maine, edited by Dean Cilley and Susan Cilley, Maine Appalachian Trail Club, Inc., Augusta, Maine, 1998.

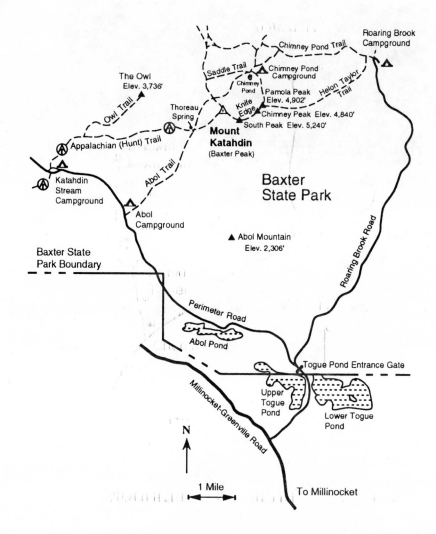

Mount Katahdin, Maine - 5,267 Feet

50 Hikes in the Maine Mountains, by Cloe Chunn, Backcountry Publications/The Countryman Press, Woodstock, Vermont, 1997.

High Peaks of the Northeast, by Bruce Scofield, New England Cartographics, Inc., North Amherst, Massachusetts, 1994.

Hiking Maine, by Tom Seymour, Falcon Press Publishing Co., Inc., Helena, Montana, 1996.

Katahdin: A Guide to Baxter State Park and Katahdin, by Stephen Clark, North Country Press, Unity, Maine, 1985.

Heading toward the summit of Mount Katahdin via the Knife Edge.

Primary Route: Appalachian (Hunt) Trail

Approach ▲ From Millinocket Center, proceed NW on the Millinocket-Greenville Road for 15.6 miles to the Togue Pond entrance to Baxter State Park. Turn right (NE) and continue 1.8 miles to the Togue Pond entrance gate. Bear left on Perimeter Road at the junction 0.1 miles beyond the gate. Continue on Perimeter Road 7.6 miles to Katahdin Stream Campground. Park in the Appalachian Trail parking area.

Route ▲ From Katahdin Stream Campground, hike NE via the white-blazed Appalachian Trail for 5.2 miles to Baxter Peak, the highpoint of Mount Katahdin. A USGS benchmark is on the summit.

Alternate Route 1: Abol Trail

Approach ▲ From Millinocket Center, proceed NW on the Millinocket-Greenville Road for 15.6 miles to the Togue Pond entrance to Baxter State Park. Turn right (NE) and continue 1.8 miles to the Togue Pond entrance gate. Bear left on Perimeter Road at the junction 0.1 miles beyond the gate. Continue on Perimeter Road 5.6 miles to Abol Campground. Park in the entrance parking area.

Route ▲ From Abol Campground, hike NE along the blue-blazed Abol Trail for 2.8 miles to the junction with the Appalachian Trail at Thoreau Spring. Turn right on the white-blazed Appalachian Trail and continue

1.0 miles to Baxter Peak, the highpoint of Mount Katahdin. A USGS benchmark is on the summit.

Alternate Route 2: Chimney Pond Trail/Helon Taylor Trail/Knife Edge Trail

Approach ▲ From Millinocket Center, proceed NW on the Millinocket-Greenville Road for 15.6 miles to the Togue Pond entrance to Baxter State Park. Turn right (NE) and continue 1.8 miles to the Togue Pond entrance gate. Stay right on Roaring Brook Road at the junction 0.1 miles beyond the gate. Continue on Roaring Brook Road 8.0 miles to Roaring Brook Campground. Park in the entrance parking area.

Route ▲ From the parking area, hike W along the blue-blazed Chimney Pond Trail for 0.2 miles to the Helon Taylor Trail. Turn left (SW) onto the blue-blazed Helon Taylor Trail and continue 3.0 miles to Pamola Peak and the junction with the Knife Edge Trail. Turn left on the unblazed Knife Edge Trail and continue 1.1 miles to Baxter Peak, the highpoint of Mount Katahdin. A USGS benchmark is on the summit.

Alternate Route 3: Chimney Pond Trail/Saddle Trail

Approach ▲ From Millinocket Center, proceed NW on the Millinocket-Greenville Road for 15.6 miles to the Togue Pond entrance to Baxter State Park. Turn right (NE) and continue 1.8 miles to the Togue Pond entrance gate. Stay right on Roaring Brook Road at the junction 0.1 miles beyond the gate. Continue on Roaring Brook Road 8.0 miles to Roaring Brook Campground. Park in the entrance parking area.

Route ▲ From the parking area, hike W along the blue-blazed Chimney Pond Trail for 3.3 miles to the Saddle Trail at Chimney Pond. Continue W on the blue-blazed Saddle Trail for 1.2 miles to the rim of the tableland. Bear left (S) at a signed trail junction and proceed uphill 1.0 miles, passing two trail junctions along the route, to Baxter Peak, the highpoint of Mount Katahdin. A USGS benchmark is on the summit.

Special Conditions

Baxter State Park is open for hiking nominally from May 15 through October 15. It is a wilderness park, and the Baxter State Park Authority vigorously controls the number of persons in the park. All persons entering the park must register at one of the three entry gates. The Togue Pond gate is open from 6:00 A.M. to 10:00 P.M. When the park campground limits are reached, the gates are closed. Camping is permitted only by reservation in authorized campgrounds and campsites. Nonresident motor vehicles entering the park are required to pay a daily fee. There are several other rules and regulations that must be followed. It is advisable to obtain the rules and regulations before planning a trip to the park. For hiking routes, probably the best guidebook for Mount Katahdin is *Katahdin: A Guide to Baxter State Park and Katahdin*, by Stephen Clark. Maps, books, rules and regulations, and information on facilities and fees can be obtained from Baxter State Park, Reservation Clerk, 64 Balsam Drive, Millinocket, ME 04462 (207/723-5140).

The most spectacular trail to Mount Katahdin is the Knife Edge Trail, Alternate Route 2. It is a ridge, sometimes less than five feet wide, which drops off precipitously on both sides. Ascending via Alternate Route 2 and descending via Alternate Route 3 makes a very nice loop hike. Also, the various routes can be combined with a car shuttle to create several one-way routes over Mount Katahdin. The Saddle Trail, Alternate Route 3, is usually considered the easiest way to climb Mount Katahdin. Hikers should register at the Ranger Station or at the trailhead before starting a hike. Be sure to sign in on your return.

Approximately 281 miles of the Appalachian Trail traverse Maine, from Mount Katahdin to the Maine–New Hampshire state line. The entire Appalachian Trail is marked for travel in both directions with white paint blazes on trees or poles and rocks, about 2 inches wide and 6 inches high. Two blazes, one above the other, are a signal of an important trail feature such as an obscure turn or a change in route. Side trails from the Appalachian Trail are usually blazed in blue. This includes most of the other trails listed in this chapter. Information on hiking in the Mount Katahdin area and the Appalachian Trail can be obtained from the Appalachian Mountain Club, 5 Joy Street, Boston, MA 02108 (617/523-0636), and the Maine Appalachian Trail Club, Inc., P.O. Box 283, Augusta, ME 04330.

Historical Notes

The highpoint of Maine is on Mount Katahdin, whose name is an Abenaki Indian word meaning "greatest mountain." The actual highpoint is named Baxter Peak. Both Baxter Peak and Baxter State Park are named in honor of Percival Proctor Baxter (1876–1969), who served as governor of Maine from 1920 to 1925. From 1930 to 1962, former governor Baxter purchased the land that constitutes Baxter State Park, an area exceeding 200,000 acres, and gave it to the state of Maine to be maintained as a wilderness park.

Baxter Peak on Mount Katahdin is the northern terminus of the Appalachian Trail. The Primary Route affords the opportunity to hike along a portion of the Appalachian Trail. This trail, completed in 1937, extends over 2,150 miles from Mount Katahdin to Springer Mountain in northern Georgia.

Natural History Notes

Mount Katahdin is an isolated, massive, gray granite monolith. Continental glaciers have planed off the top of the mountain, leaving the flat tableland rising toward the south. The last local glacier disappeared between ten and fifteen thousand years ago.

Because of the wilderness nature of Baxter State Park, wildlife abounds. The predominant large animals are moose, black bear, white-tailed deer, and eastern coyote. Smaller animals include beaver, muskrat, mink, otter, raccoon, and woodchuck. Bobcat, lynx, red fox, fisher, marten, snowshoe hare, porcupine, red squirrel, and eastern chipmunk are common in all wooded areas. More than 100 species of birds have been identified in the park. The eastern brook trout is the fish most commonly found in the lakes and streams.

Maryland

Backbone Mountain

3,360 Feet

County
Garrett

Location
Approximately 5 miles ssw of Redhouse.

Hiking
Primary Route: 2.2 miles, round trip, on dirt road and cross-country.
Alternate Route: 2.8 miles, round trip, cross-country.

Gain
Primary Route: 750 feet, Class 1, moderate.
Alternate Route: 950 feet, Class 2, moderate.

Maps
Topographic: Davis, W.Va.-Md., 7½ minute.

Primary Route
Approach ▲ From the junction of U.S. Hwy 219 and West Virginia
State Route 24 just N of Silver Lake, W.Va., proceed s on Hwy 219 for 1.1
miles to an old logging road on the uphill (E) side of the highway. Park off
the highway at this point.

Route ▲ Hike SE 0.5 miles up the logging road to a Y-intersection. Bear
right (s) and continue 0.4 miles on the road, which now parallels the
Maryland–West Virginia state line, to the top of the ridge. Be alert because
the ridge is poorly defined at this point and it is easy to go too far. Turn
hard left (NE) and hike along the ridge 0.2 miles to the highpoint, passing
the Maryland–West Virginia state line marker number 3 at 0.1 miles. There
is a cast aluminum sign identifying the highpoint.

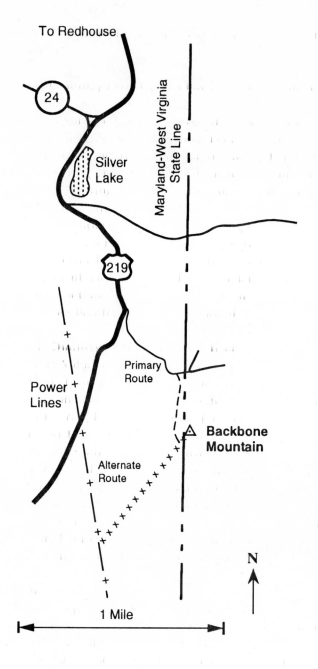

To Redhouse

24

Silver
Lake

Maryland-West Virginia
State Line

219

Power
Lines

Primary
Route

Backbone
Mountain

Alternate
Route

N

1 Mile

Backbone Mountain, Maryland - 3,360 Feet

Alternate Route

Approach ▲ From the junction of U.S. Hwy 219 and West Virginia State Route 24 just N of Silver Lake, W.Va., proceed S on Hwy 219 for 1.7 miles to the point where power lines cross the road. Park along the side of the road.

Route ▲ From U.S. Hwy 219, hike generally S under the power lines 0.6 miles to the top of Backbone Mountain ridge. Turn hard left (NE) and hike along the ridge 0.8 miles to the highpoint. The Maryland–West Virginia state line marker number 3 is approximately 0.7 miles from the power lines. There is a cast aluminum sign identifying the highpoint.

Special Conditions

Backbone Mountain is in an area of some of the wildest country on the East Coast. The undergrowth and brush can be very heavy. In the spring and summer, when the leaves are on the trees, it may be difficult to locate the sign on the highpoint. This is especially true because the width of the sign is parallel to the ridgeline and all that is seen from along the ridge is the edge of the sign.

Although most of both routes are on national forest land, the highpoint of Backbone Mountain is on private property; however, permission is not required to go to the highpoint. A private vacation home community, Backbone Ridge, which adjoins the summit of Backbone Mountain, is being developed. Please respect the rights of the property owner.

Historical Notes

The name Backbone Mountain is likely derived from the rough and rocky ridge that resembles a backbone. The fact that the ridge is part of the "Eastern" Continental Divide separating the Atlantic Ocean and Gulf of Mexico drainages may have contributed to the choice of name.

The sign on the highpoint, placed there in 1960, names the highpoint Hoye Crest in memory of Captain Charles Edward Hoye (1876–1951). He was the great-great-grandson of one of the first permanent settlers in what is now Garrett County. Captain Hoye served in the Spanish-American War and World War I. After the Spanish-American War, he worked as an educator for 25 years in the Philippines. When he retired, he returned to Garrett County and eventually founded the Garrett County Historical Society. On Labor Day 1952, because of his Maryland family heritage, his knowledge of local history, and his career in education, the Garrett County Historical Society and the state of Maryland through Governor Theodore McKeldin dedicated the highpoint of Maryland to Captain Charles Edward Hoye.

Massachusetts

Mount Greylock

3,487 Feet

County
Berkshire

Location
Approximately 6 miles SSE of Williamstown in Mount Greylock State Reservation.

Hiking
Primary Route: Drive-up.
Alternate Route 1: Drive-up.
Alternate Route 2: 6.4 miles, round trip, on trail.
Alternate Route 3: 8.4 miles, round trip, on trail.

Gain
Primary Route: Drive-up.
Alternate Route 1: Drive-up.
Alternate Route 2: 2,000 feet, Class 1, moderate.
Alternate Route 3: 2,300 feet, Class 1, moderate.

Maps
Topographic: Williamstown, Mass.-Vt., and Cheshire, Mass., both 7½ minute.
State Reservation: Mt. Greylock State Reservation Trail Map, Mt. Greylock State Reservation.
Other: Mt. Greylock Map, New England Cartographics, North Amherst, Massachusetts.

Guidebooks
AMC *Massachusetts and Rhode Island Trail Guide*, edited by Jeff Wulfson, Appalachian Mountain Club, Boston, Massachusetts, 7th edition, 1995.

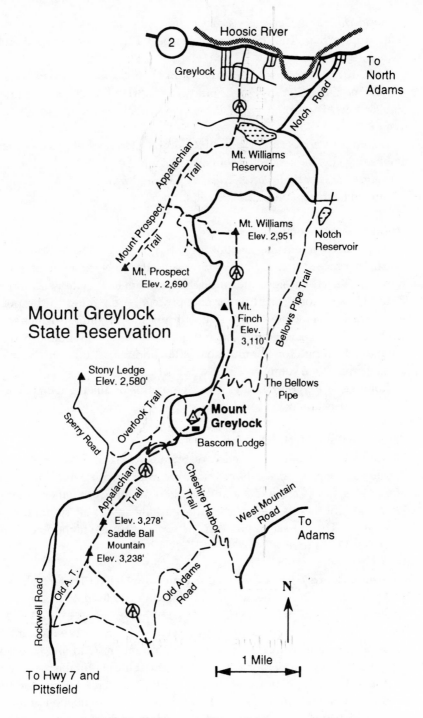

Mount Greylock, Massachusetts - 3,487 Feet

Appalachian Trail Guide to Massachusetts-Connecticut, edited by Norman Sills, Appalachian Trail Conference, Harpers Ferry, West Virginia, 10th edition, 1997.

50 Hikes in Massachusetts: Hikes and Walks from the Top of the Berkshires to the Tip of Cape Cod, by John Brady and Brian White, Backcountry Publications/The Countryman Press, Woodstock, Vermont, 3d edition, 1999.

Hiking Southern New England, by George Ostertag et al., Falcon Press Publishing Co., Inc., Helena, Montana, 1997.

Nature Walks in the Berkshire Hills, by Charles W. G. Smith, Appalachian Mountain Club, Boston, Massachusetts, 1997.

Primary Route: Rockwell Road

Approach ▲ From the junction of U.S. Hwy 7 and State Route 9 in Pittsfield, proceed N on U.S. Hwy 7 for 5.9 miles to North Main Street on the right. Watch for signs indicating Mount Greylock State Reservation. Bear right on North Main Street and proceed N 0.7 miles to the point where the main road goes to the right. Turn right and continue E then N on Rockwell Road, bearing left at 0.4 miles, for 8.0 miles to Summit Road on the right. Turn right on Summit Road and continue 0.3 miles to the large parking area at the summit.

Route ▲ The Massachusetts War Memorial is on the highpoint. There is no USGS benchmark.

Alternate Route 1: Notch Road

Approach ▲ From the junction of State Route 2 and Notch Road in North Adams, proceed s on Notch Road, bearing left at 1.2 miles and right at 2.4 miles, for 8.5 miles to Summit Road on the left. Turn left on Summit Road and continue 0.3 miles to the large parking area at the summit.

Route ▲ The Massachusetts War Memorial is on the highpoint. There is no USGS benchmark.

Alternate Route 2: Cheshire Harbor Trail/Appalachian Trail

Approach ▲ From the President McKinley Monument on State Route 8 in Adams, proceed NW on Maple Street 0.4 miles to West Road. Turn left (SW) onto West Road and proceed 0.6 miles to West Mountain Road on the right. Turn right (W) on West Mountain Road and continue 1.5 miles to Cheshire Harbor Trail on the right at the end of the road.

Route ▲ Hike NW on the white-over-orange-blazed Cheshire Harbor Trail for 2.6 miles, through several switchbacks, to the junction with the Appalachian Trail at Rockwell Road. Keep alert for the main trail, as there are several other trails in the area. Turn right on the Appalachian Trail and continue 0.6 miles to the summit. The Massachusetts War Memorial is on the highpoint. There is no USGS benchmark.

Alternate Route 3: Bellows Pipe Trail/Appalachian Trail

Approach ▲ From the junction of State Route 2 and Notch Road in North Adams, proceed s on Notch Road, bearing left at 1.2 miles, for 2.4 miles to the point where Notch Road makes a sharp right heading w and is joined by Reservoir Road coming from the E. Park at the trailhead on the s side of Notch Road.

Route ▲ From the parking area, hike s on the Bellows Pipe Trail, initially a dirt access road for Notch Reservoir, for 3.7 miles to the junction with the Appalachian Trail. At 2.2 miles the trail reaches the saddle between Mount Greylock and Ragged Mountain. A few hundred yards beyond the saddle, the trail makes a sharp right turn and heads NW. At 2.7 miles, a shelter is passed on the right. At 3.2 miles, the trail ascends a ridge in a series of switchbacks, arriving at the Appalachian Trail at the 3.7 milepoint. Turn left on the Appalachian Trail and continue 0.5 miles to the summit. The Massachusetts War Memorial is on the highpoint. There is no USGS benchmark.

Special Conditions

The roads to the summit of Mount Greylock are usually open from mid-May through early December. In addition to the trails included above, several other trails approach Mount Greylock, including the Appalachian Trail. By combining the trails, with or without a car shuttle, several one-way trips or loop trips can be created. The summit of Mount Greylock can also be reached via the Appalachian Trail from the north or the south. The Appalachian Trail traverses Massachusetts for approximately 90 miles in a north-south direction and passes over the summit of Mount Greylock. The entire Appalachian Trail is marked for travel in both directions with white paint blazes on trees or poles and rocks, about 2 inches wide and 6 inches high. Two blazes, one above the other, are a signal of an important trail feature such as an obscure turn or a change in route. Side trails from the Appalachian Trail are usually blazed in blue.

Information on hiking in the Mount Greylock area and the Appalachian Trail can be obtained from the Mount Greylock State Reservation, P.O. Box 138, Lanesboro, MA 01237 (413/499-4263); the Appalachian Mountain Club, P.O. Box 1800, Lanesboro, MA 01237 (413/443-0011); and the Appalachian Trail Conference, P.O. Box 807, 799 Washington Street, Harpers Ferry, WV 25425-0807 (304/535-6331).

Bascom Lodge is at the highpoint and is operated by the Appalachian Mountain Club. It is usually open from mid-May through mid-October.

Lodging and meals are available, and reservations are required for both. Reservations may be made by calling the Appalachian Mountain Club (413/443-0011). Additional information can be obtained from AMC Bascom Lodge, P.O. Box 1800, Lanesboro, MA 01237 (413/743-1591).

Historical Notes

Just how Mount Greylock got its name is uncertain. Of the several theories about the derivation of the name, two seem to be the most popular. The first is that the name originated from Mount Greylock's position at the head of the mountain range, its frosty winter appearance, and the fact that it is often "locked" in "grey" clouds. Perhaps the most interesting suggestion is that Mount Greylock was named in honor of Chief Greylock, believed to be a leader of the Mohawk Indians who inhabited northwestern Massachusetts.

During the late 1800s loggers had stripped the timber from the entire east face of Mount Greylock, resulting in serious erosion and landslides. In 1885, in order to preserve the area, the Greylock Park Association purchased 400 acres around the summit. In 1898 the property was given to the state for the establishment of the Mount Greylock State Reservation. Today the reservation comprises nearly 12,600 acres. Since 1966 Mount Greylock State Reservation has been a part of the state park system.

Sometime before 1833 the first wooden tower was built on the summit. In 1841 a second wooden tower was built to be used as a weather observatory. This tower eventually reached a height of 60 feet. It was destroyed by fire in 1878. In 1889 an iron tower was constructed on the summit. This tower was 40 feet tall and had four observation levels. The 90-foot granite Massachusetts War Memorial now on the highpoint was built in 1933. In 1963, because of the toll taken by the weather over the years, the granite tower was declared unsafe and was closed to the public. In 1973 the tower was torn down block by block and rebuilt to better withstand the harsh environment. In June 1975 the Massachusetts War Memorial was rededicated.

Bascom Lodge, built by the Civilian Conservation Corps, was completed in 1936. Stone fireplaces, high ceilings with hand-hewn oak beams, and a porch with large windows are a tribute to the CCC's fine work. During the 1930s the CCC also built Notch Road and the Thunderbolt Ski Trail.

The Appalachian Trail, completed in 1937, extends over 2,150 miles from Mount Katahdin, the highpoint of Maine, to Springer Mountain in northern Georgia.

Natural History Notes

Northern hardwoods, including birch, beech, and ash, are found on the lower slopes of Mount Greylock. In the glacial cirque known as "The

Hopper," there are huge conifers over 100 years old. On the summit of Mount Greylock are red spruce and balsam fir dwarfed and gnarled by the wind.

Many species of birds and mammals inhabit Mount Greylock and environs. The birds include grouse, owls, and hawks. Large mammals—deer, bear, and bobcat—are found in the forest. Other common mammals are porcupine, raccoon, snowshoe hare, woodchuck, and red and gray squirrel.

Michigan

Mount Arvon

1,979 Feet

County
Baraga

Location
Approximately 12 miles E of L'Anse.

Hiking
2.0 miles, round trip, on old logging road and cross-country.

Gain
300 feet, Class 1, easy.

Maps
Topographic: Skanee South, Mich., 7½ minute.

Guidebooks
Hiking Michigan, by Mike Modrzynski, Falcon Press Publishing Co., Inc., Helena, Montana, 1996.

Primary Route
   Approach ▲ From the intersection of U.S. Hwy 41 and Broad Street immediately s of L'Anse, proceed NW into L'Anse on Broad Street for 0.7 miles to Main Street. Turn right (NE) on Main Street, which becomes Skanee Road, and continue 16.1 miles to Church Road on the right, where the Zion Lutheran Church is on the SE corner. Church Road becomes Roland Lake Road in approximately a mile. Turn right (s) on Church Road/Roland Lake Road and proceed 2.9 miles to Ravine River Road at Roland Lake (see below for detailed description of the approach from this point). Turn right on Ravine River Road and continue 6.1 miles to a T-intersection. Turn right (s) at the T-intersection and continue 1.1 miles

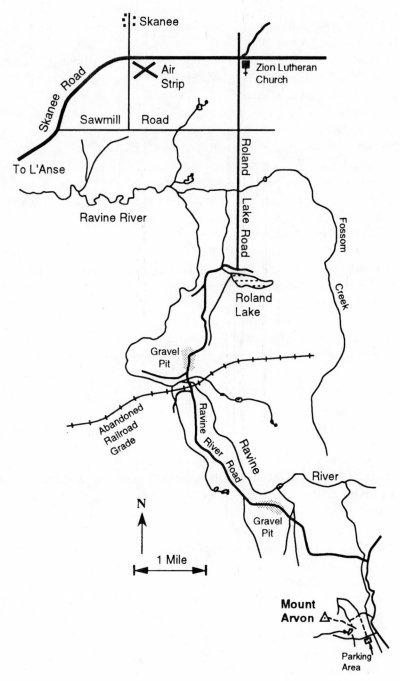

:¦: Skanee

Skanee Road

✕ Air Strip

🔲 Zion Lutheran Church

Sawmill Road

To L'Anse

Roland Lake Road

Ravine River

Fossom Creek

Roland Lake

Gravel Pit

Abandoned Railroad Grade

Ravine River Road

Ravine River

N

1 Mile

Gravel Pit

Mount Arvon △

Parking Area

Mount Arvon, Michigan - 1,979 Feet

to a road on the right. Turn right (w) and proceed 0.1 miles to a road on the right with a blue and white diamond-shaped sign indicating the route to Mount Arvon. Park here.

There are many less well developed roads in the Ravine River Road area. Unless indicated below, stay on the obvious "main track" as you proceed along Ravine River Road. The route on Ravine River Road is as follows: At 0.7 miles, fork, go straight; 1.8 miles, pass through gravel pit; 2.0 miles, leave gravel pit at a fork, go straight; 2.1 miles, cross creek on bridge; 2.2 miles, fork, go straight; 3.0 miles, fork, bear left; 3.4 miles, fork, bear right; 4.0 miles, 4.5 miles, and 4.7 miles, forks, go straight; 6.1 miles, T-intersection, main road goes left, turn right (s) (depending on road conditions and vehicle, parking at this point may be advisable); 6.3 miles, fork, go left; 6.4 miles, fork, go right; 6.8 miles, fork, go right; 7.2 miles, road on the right, turn right; 7.3 miles, trailhead.

Route ▲ Hike generally N slightly downhill, crossing two streams, then uphill on an old logging road/trail approximately 0.3 miles to another logging road/trail (all streams referred to may be dry, depending on weather and time of year). Turn left, generally wsw, and continue another 0.2 miles of relatively level hiking to a Y-intersection. Bear left, downhill, immediately crossing a stream, and continue approximately 170 yards to another Y-intersection just NE of a pond. Bear right and continue approximately 0.4 miles uphill to the point where the logging road/trail comes to an end in a large open area. On the left there is a faint path to the obvious highpoint 75 yards up the hill. A USGS benchmark and a mailbox containing a register will be found on the summit.

Special Conditions

The approach and route description for Mount Arvon differ in format from those of the other chapters because route finding in this area can be difficult. Special attention must be paid in order to reach the summit. A current topographic map is essential in locating Mount Arvon. A number of the "trails" indicated on the topographic map are, in fact, old logging roads and not narrow hiking trails. Blue and white diamond-shaped signs indicating the route to Mount Arvon have been placed along Ravine River Road at critical points and along the hiking route. These signs are very helpful if they are still in place.

Because of logging operations, the roads in the Mount Arvon area are frequently changed. The roads s of Skanee Road become impassable in winter owing to snow. During the rainy season the roads are muddy and often unfit for passenger cars.

For information about Baraga County, L'Anse, and Mount Arvon, contact the Baraga County Tourist and Recreation Association, 755 E. Broad

Street, L'Anse, MI 49946 (906/524-7444). Information on the route to Mount Arvon can also be obtained from Steve Koski at Indian Country Sports, Inc., 17 S. Front Street, L'Anse, MI 49946 (906/524-6518).

Historical Notes

Before 1963 Government Peak in the Porcupine Mountains, which are located in the Upper Peninsula along the NW shore of Lake Superior, was believed to be the highpoint. In 1963 the USGS identified Mount Curwood, which is approximately 5.5 miles SW of Mount Arvon, as the highpoint. During the USGS survey conducted in 1982, Mount Curwood was measured at a height of 1,978.24 feet above sea level and Mount Arvon was measured at 1,979.238 feet above sea level. Thus, Mount Arvon beat out Mount Curwood for the distinction of being Michigan's highpoint by a mere foot.

In 1871 substantial deposits of good quality slate were discovered in the Arvon area. A majority of the quarry workers came from Vermont and were of Welsh and Irish descent. The location was named after the capital of North Wales, Cairnarvon, but the name was soon shortened to Arvon. The name was given to the slate quarry village, Arvon Township, and Mount Arvon. Mount Curwood was named in memory of James Oliver Curwood (1879–1927), a noted American author. Mr. Curwood did much of his writing in his cabin in Baraga County's Huron Mountains during the 1920s.

The Upper Peninsula, on which Mount Arvon is located, became a part of Michigan as a result of an unpopular compromise that won Michigan statehood. The issue was a strip of land along the Michigan-Ohio border that included Toledo. A bitter fight in Congress resulted in Michigan's ceding that land to Ohio in exchange for statehood. Michigan grudgingly accepted the Upper Peninsula as a sort of consolation prize for losing Toledo. In terms of natural resources alone, the raw deal turned out to be a steal.

The area near Mount Arvon has yielded a vast amount of native copper. Indians mined the copper for thousands of years before Michigan became a state. When the copper deposits played out, several ghost towns were left. The Mount Arvon area now produces timber.

Natural History Notes

The forest consists of maple, birch, aspen, spruce, and fir trees, which shelter such animals as white-tailed deer, black bear, elk, moose, and eastern timber wolf. Numerous species of birds and reptiles can also be found.

The "hazards" around Mount Arvon are mosquitoes, deer flies, and ticks.

Guides/Outfitters

Brian Jentoft, Route 1, Box 27, Bay Shore Dr., L'Anse, MI 49946 (906/524-6267), e-mail: bjentoft@up.net.

Minnesota

Eagle Mountain

2,301 Feet

County
   Cook

Location
   Approximately 17 miles NW of Grand Marais in the Boundary Waters
Canoe Area Wilderness of Superior National Forest.

Hiking
   7.0 miles, round trip, on trail.

Gain
   600 feet, Class 1, moderate.

Maps
   Topographic: Eagle Mountain, Minn., and Mark Lake, Minn., both 7½
minute.
   National Forest: Superior N.F.

Guidebooks
   Hiking Minnesota, by John Pukite, Falcon Press Publishing Co., Inc.,
Helena, Montana, 1998.

Primary Route: Eagle Mountain Trail
   Approach ▲ From the junction of U.S. Hwy 61 and County Road 12
(Gunflint Trail) in Grand Marais, proceed N on County Road 12 for
3.7 miles to County Road 8. Turn left (w) onto County Road 8 and proceed
5.7 miles to a junction with County Roads 27 and 57. Turn right (N) onto
County Road 27 and continue 5.1 miles to Forest Route 170. Turn left (w)
onto Forest Route 170 and proceed 5.0 miles to the trailhead parking area

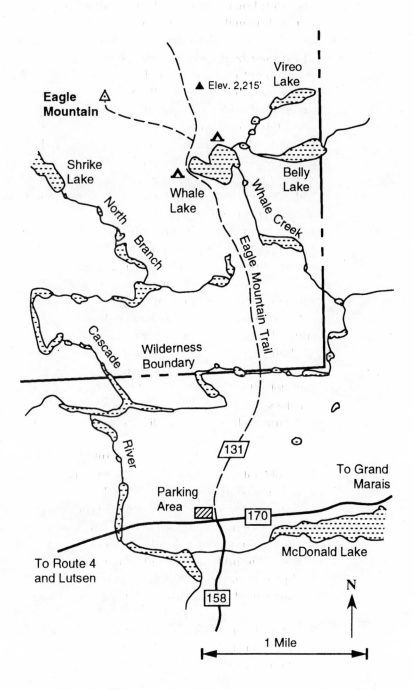

Eagle Mountain, Minnesota - 2,301 Feet

The summit of Minnesota's Eagle Mountain.

on the right (N). The parking area is directly N of the point where Forest Route 158 ends at Forest Route 170. (For an alternate approach to the trailhead, see Special Conditions.)

Route ▲ From the parking area, hike N on the well-marked Eagle Mountain Trail 3.5 miles to the summit. Be alert for the summit trail turnoff to the left just beyond the NW corner of Whale Lake. This point is approximately 2.6 miles from the trailhead. There is a sign indicating Eagle Mountain just beyond this junction. A large metal plaque on a boulder marks the summit. There is no USGS benchmark.

Special Conditions

Most of the Eagle Mountain Trail, which is not shown on the topographic map, is in the Boundary Waters Canoe Area Wilderness. Permits are required year-round. Self-issue permits are available for day use year-round and for overnight visitors between October 1 and April 30. Self-issue permits can be obtained at the main Boundary Waters Canoe Area Wilderness entry points, including the trailhead for Eagle Mountain.

For overnight stays from May 1 through September 30, a summer quota permit is required. The number of permits available is limited, and reservations are recommended. There is a $12.00 nonrefundable fee for each reservation. Permits can be obtained on a walk-in basis on the day of or the day before a trip if the permit quota is not filled for the entry point of interest. These permits can be obtained from the Forest Service office nearest the entry point.

For permits, reservations, and detailed information on the permit requirements, contact BWCAW Reservations Center, P.O. Box 462, Ballston Spa, NY 12020 (800/745-3399). The center can also be contacted via its website, www.bwcaw.org.

For information, hiking guides, and the national forest map, contact Superior National Forest, Gunflint Ranger District, 2020 W. Hwy 61, P.O. Box 790, Grand Marais, MN 55604 (218/387-1750), or Superior National Forest, Tofte Ranger District, North Hwy 61, P.O. Box 2159, Tofte, MN 55615 (218/663-7280).

An alternate approach to the trailhead is as follows: From Lutsen, proceed NE on U.S. Hwy 61 approximately 1 mile to County Road 4. Turn left (N) onto County Road 4 (Caribou Trail) and continue 17.7 miles, staying on the main track and continuing N at several side road junctions, to Forest Route 170. Turn right (E) onto Forest Route 170 and continue 3.8 miles to the trailhead parking area on the left (N). The parking area is directly N of the point where Forest Route 158 ends at Forest Route 170.

Historical Notes

Eagle Mountain was probably named for the bald eagles or the eagle nests frequently found in the area.

The remains of an old logging camp are near the sw corner of Whale Lake. White pine, Norway pine, spruce, balsam, jackpine, aspen, and fir were harvested in the area.

The first white explorer to travel by canoe along the north shore of Lake Superior was probably Etienne Brule in 1623 or 1624. This exploration was directed toward finding a water passage to the West. The Eagle Mountain Trail continues 7 miles beyond Whale Lake to its northwestern terminus at Brule Lake.

Natural History Notes

The view from Eagle Mountain provides outstanding vistas of the Superior National Forest and the Boundary Waters Canoe Area Wilderness. It is especially good in the fall. On a clear day, Lake Superior can be seen to the south.

Many species of large and small mammals inhabit the area, including moose, bear, timber wolf, and fox, as well as eagles and a variety of songbirds. Fish in the lakes and streams include lake trout, brook trout, brown trout, rainbow trout, walleye, and northern pike. Northern Minnesota is the last stronghold of the timber wolf in the contiguous United States. Between 300 and 400 of the large carnivores still roam the forest.

One-third of the 3-million-acre Superior National Forest is the Boundary Waters Canoe Area Wilderness. Over 445,000 acres of the forest is surface water. More than 1,300 miles of cold-water streams and 950 miles of warm-water streams flow within the national forest boundaries. The Boundary Waters Canoe Area Wilderness, protected as a true American wilderness, has over 1,500 miles of canoe routes, nearly 2,200 designated campsites, and more than 2,000 lakes and streams.

Mississippi

Woodall Mountain

806 Feet

County
Tishomingo

Location
Approximately 3 miles sw of Iuka.

Hiking
Drive-up.

Gain
Drive-up.

Maps
Topographic: Iuka, Miss., 7½ minute.

Primary Route

Approach ▲ Immediately s (0.1 miles) of the junction of U.S. Hwy 72 and State Route 25 s of Iuka, turn right (w) on Fairground Road. Proceed 1.2 miles on Fairground Road, which becomes County Road 187 as it soon turns s to County Road 176 on the right. Turn right (w) onto County Road 176 and continue 0.7 miles to a gravel road on the right. Turn right (n) on the gravel road and proceed 1.0 miles to the tower on the summit.

Route ▲ The USGS benchmark is 25 yards E of the tower on a small concrete pillar in the middle of the parking area.

Special Conditions

There is a gate across the gravel road to the highpoint that is almost always open. The road is well maintained and is suitable for all vehicles. In the event the gate is closed, hike up the gravel road to the summit. Permission is not required to use the gravel road for driving or hiking.

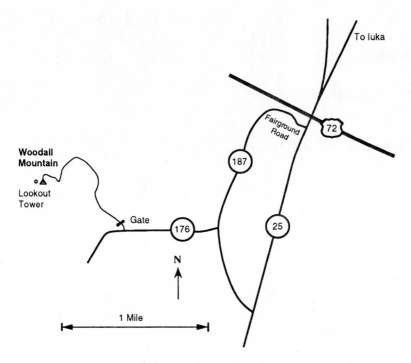

Woodall Mountain, Mississippi - 806 Feet

The tower on the summit used to be a Forest Service lookout tower. With the advent of satellite surveillance of potential forest fires, most of the Forest Service towers are being dismantled. During 1997 the lookout tower was converted to a communications repeater station.

Historical Notes

According to tradition, Woodall Mountain was called Yow Hill or Yow Mountain before 1878. It was renamed for Zephaniah H. Woodall, who was the sheriff of Tishomingo County when, in 1887, the first Tishomingo County Courthouse at Iuka, along with the county records, burned down. It is suspected that the fire was started to destroy evidence in a murder case.

On September 19, 1862, the Union Army of the Mississippi, commanded by Major General William S. Rosecrans, and the Confederate Army of the West, commanded by Major General Sterling Price, fought a fierce and bloody battle approximately 1½ miles sw of Iuka. During the battle nearly one-third of those engaged fell. The Battle of Iuka took place in the immediate vicinity of the U.S. Hwy 72/State Route 25 interchange. Because of the wide views afforded at the summit, it is likely that Woodall Mountain was used as an observation post by both armies during their campaigns in this region. The armies met again on October 3–4, 1862, during the battle for control of the railroad junction at Corinth, approximately 22 miles wNw of Iuka. Some Civil War historians believe that the defeats suffered by the Confederate Army at Iuka and Corinth forever turned the tide of war against the Confederacy.

Missouri

Taum Sauk Mountain

1,772 Feet

County
Iron

Location
Approximately 6 miles wsw of Ironton.

Hiking
Primary Route: 0.4 miles, round trip, on paved trail.
Alternate Route: 11.8 miles, round trip, on trail.

Gain
Primary Route: 30 feet, Class 1, easy.
Alternate Route: 2,000 feet, Class 1, moderate.

Maps
Topographic: Ironton, Mo., 7½ minute.

Primary Route
    Approach ▲ From the junction of State Route 21 and State Route 72 SE of Ironton, proceed s on Route 21/72 for 4.5 miles to County Road CC on the right. Turn right and continue 3.7 miles on County Road CC, bearing right at 2.9 miles, to Taum Sauk Mountain State Park and the Taum Sauk Mountain trailhead at the end of the road.
    Route ▲ From the parking area, hike generally sw for 0.2 miles on the paved trail to the highpoint. There is no USGS benchmark.

Alternate Route: Ozark Trail
    Approach ▲ From the junction of State Route 21 and State Route 72 SE of Ironton, proceed s on Route 21/72 for 5.6 miles to a parking area

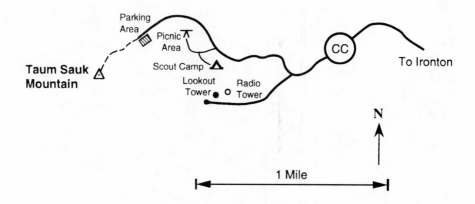

Taum Sauk Mountain, Missouri - 1,772 Feet

(Primary Route)

and the Ozark Trail trailhead on the right. Park in the designated parking area.

Route ▲ From the parking area, hike E, then N, and then E again on the Ozark Trail for 5.5 miles to a spur trail on the right. Keep left at a trail junction at approximately 2.8 miles. Turn right (NW) and continue on the spur trail 0.4 miles, bearing right at 0.3 miles, to the highpoint of Taum Sauk Mountain. There is no USGS benchmark.

Special Conditions

Taum Sauk Mountain State Park, dedicated May 1, 1993, is one of the newest additions to the Missouri State Park System. The park is located in the St. Francois Mountains and covers over 6,500 acres. Information on Taum Sauk State Park and other parks in the Missouri State Park System can be obtained from the Missouri Department of Natural Resources, Division of State Parks, P.O. Box 176, Jefferson City, MO 65102-0176 (800/334-6946).

The Alternate Route affords the opportunity to hike on a portion of the 33-mile-long Taum Sauk Section of the Ozark Trail. Currently, more than 230 miles of the Ozark Trail are open for public use. When complete, the trail will cover almost 500 miles across Missouri from St. Louis to Arkansas. The Ozark Trail is usually blazed with a green **O** superimposed on a green **T** on a white rectangular marker. Occasionally, white diamond-shaped blazes are found. Only the eastern access to the Taum Sauk Section of the Ozark Trail is described above. This section of the trail may also be

Taum Sauk summit on a winter day.

accessed on the west at either a location on the east side of County Road A approximately 3 miles north of the Hwy 49 intersection at Edgehill or in Johnson's Shut-Ins State Park. The one-way distances to the highpoint are 13 miles and 28 miles, respectively. With a car shuttle, the Alternate Route can be done as a one-way hike. For information and maps of the Ozark Trail, contact the Missouri Department of Natural Resources, Ozark Trail Coordinator, P.O. Box 176, Jefferson City, MO 65102-0176 (800/334-6946).

Historical Notes

The exact derivation of the name Taum Sauk remains a mystery. One story is that the name was derived from a legendary Piankishaw Indian Chief, Sauk-ton-qua. Another theory suggests that Sauk comes from the name of an Algonquin Indian tribe affiliated with the Sauk-Fox tribes and that Taum was derived from the Indian word *Tongo,* abbreviated *Ton,* meaning "big"; the conclusion being that Ton Sauk was the original name given to the mountain and that it signifies Big Sauk. Ton Sauk was later corrupted to Taum Sauk when whites came into the region. It is said that the men of the Sauk tribe were tall and well formed, perhaps leading to the naming of the tallest mountain Taum Sauk.

Natural History Notes

Within Taum Sauk State Park are several interesting natural features: Mina Sauk Falls, at 132 feet the highest waterfall in the state; Taum Sauk Valley, the deepest valley in the state; and the clear Taum Sauk Creek. Another interesting geologic feature is Devil's Toll Gate, which is an 8-foot-wide gap in a 30-foot-high igneous rock formation.

The mountainous domes in the Taum Sauk Mountain region contain open woodlands of white oak, post oak, and shortleaf pine. Interspersed throughout these woodlands are rocky openings called glades. These glades are home to many unusual desert-adapted plants and animals, such as the sundrop flower and eastern collared lizard. Prairie plants, including Indian grass, little bluestem, prairie blazing star, rattlesnake master, and white wild indigo, flourish in the adjacent woodlands. The Taum Sauk Mountain area is the only location in Missouri where azaleas grow wild.

Numerous birds and mammals can be found in the area, including wild turkey, bobcat, and white-tailed deer.

Montana

Granite Peak

12,799 Feet

County
Park

Location
Approximately 28 miles w of Red Lodge in the Absaroka-Beartooth Wilderness Area of Custer and Gallatin National Forests.

Hiking
Primary Route: 22.2 miles, round trip, on trail and cross-country.
Alternate Route 1: 23.2 miles, round trip, on trail and cross-country.
Alternate Route 2: 25.6 miles, round trip, on trail and cross-country.

Gain
Primary Route: 7,700 feet, Class 4, strenuous.
Alternate Route 1: 8,200 feet, Class 4, strenuous.
Alternate Route 2: 8,600 feet, Class 4, strenuous.

Maps
Topographic: Granite Peak, Montana, and Alpine, Montana, both 7½ minute.
National Forest: Absaroka-Beartooth Wilderness, Custer N.F.

Guidebooks
Climbing Granite Peak: A Beartooth Challenge, by Donald B. Jacobs, Jacobs Enterprises, Vashon, Washington, 1992.
Hiking Montana, by Bill Schneider, Falcon Press Publishing Co., Inc., Helena, Montana, 5th edition, 1995.
Hiking the Beartooths, by Bill Schneider, Falcon Press Publishing Co., Inc., Helena, Montana, 2d edition, 1996.

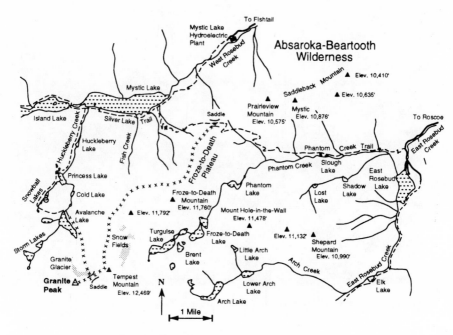

Granite Peak, Montana - 12,799 Feet

Rock Climbing Montana, edited by Randall Green, Falcon Press Publishing Co., Inc., Helena, Montana, 1997.

Primary Route: Silver Lake Trail/Huckleberry Creek

Approach ▲ From the junction of State Routes 78 and 420 in Absarokee, proceed s on Route 78 for 2.9 miles to State Route 419. (This point is approximately 32½ miles N of Red Lodge via Route 78.) Turn right (sw) on Route 419 and continue approximately 4.5 miles, turning right (w) at 3.4 miles, passing through Fishtail, and turning left (s) at 3.9 miles, to a junction with State Route 425 (West Rosebud Road), where Route 419 turns w. Turn left (E) on Route 425, which turns s in 0.3 miles, and proceed 6.3 miles to Forest Route 72. Bear left onto Forest Route 72 and continue approximately 14.2 miles to the Mystic Lake Hydroelectric Plant. There are several junctions along West Rosebud Road, and the correct road follows the West Rosebud Creek drainage all the way to the hydroelectric plant. Park in the parking area provided for hikers.

Route ▲ Hike sw from the hydroelectric plant on the Silver Lake Trail for 4.6 miles to a trail leading s up the slope on the w side of Huckleberry Creek near the w end of Mystic Lake. This point is just w of the bridge

The impressive south face of Montana's Granite Peak.

crossing Huckleberry Creek as it flows into Mystic Lake. Turn left (s) and continue up the steep slope 2.1 miles to Princess Lake. When passing Huckleberry Lake, stay on the minor ridge immediately w of the lake. The ridge consists of large boulders that are tedious to pass through, but the area closer to the lake is virtually impassable. At the s end of the boulder field, a use trail leads up a second steep slope to Princess Lake. Traverse around the w side of Princess Lake and continue 1.3 miles up to the Snowball Lakes. There is a use trail on the w side of the stream flowing down from the Snowball Lakes into Princess Lake. From the southernmost lake of the four Snowball Lakes, hike E to the N end of Avalanche Lake. Continue around the E side of Avalanche Lake through the boulder field and s up to the saddle between Granite Peak and Tempest Mountain. The distance from the Snowball Lakes to the saddle is 2.6 miles. From the saddle, follow a use trail along the s side of the ridge to a snowbridge. Ropes and, depending on the amount of snow present, an ice ax are strongly recommended for crossing the snowbridge. Cross the snowbridge and continue on the s face of Granite Peak, up a chimney, and to a prominent V-notch on the ridge. From the V-notch, the route passes through a jumble of ledges, cracks, gullies, cliffs, and chimneys. Good route-finding skills are required to navigate successfully through this area. The objective is a "keyhole" on the ridge above. From about 15 feet below the keyhole, climb up the chute to the left of the keyhole to the top of the ridge. From the top of the ridge, it is an easy scramble on the w side of the ridge to the summit. It is 0.5 miles from the saddle to the summit. There is a USGS benchmark and a register on the summit.

Alternate Route 1: Silver Lake Trail/Phantom Creek Trail/Froze-to-Death Plateau

Approach ▲ From the junction of State Routes 78 and 420 in Absarokee, proceed s on Route 78 for 2.9 miles to State Route 419. (This point is approximately 32½ miles N of Red Lodge via Route 78.) Turn right (sw) on Route 419 and continue approximately 4.5 miles, turning right (w) at 3.4 miles, passing through Fishtail, and turning left (s) at 3.9 miles, to a junction with State Route 425 (West Rosebud Road), where Route 419 turns w. Turn left (E) on Route 425, which turns s in 0.3 miles, and proceed 6.3 miles to Forest Route 72. Bear left onto Forest Route 72 and continue approximately 14.2 miles to the Mystic Lake Hydroelectric Plant. There are several junctions along West Rosebud Road, and the correct road follows the West Rosebud Creek drainage all the way to the hydroelectric plant. Park in the parking area provided for hikers.

Route ▲ Hike sw from the hydroelectric plant on the Silver Lake Trail for 2.6 miles to the Phantom Creek Trail junction near the SE end of Mystic Lake. Turn left (SE) onto the Phantom Creek Trail and continue 3.1 miles to the saddle on Froze-to-Death Plateau. From the saddle continue sw cross-country up the plateau, contouring to the w around the N side of Froze-to-Death Mountain above the 11,000-foot level. Turn s about a mile w of Froze-to-Death Mountain and hike to the w edge of Tempest Mountain near its summit. Past climbers have marked the route with a series of cairns. The distance from Phantom Creek Trail to Tempest Mountain is approximately 5.0 miles, depending on the route chosen. It is 0.9 miles from Tempest Mountain to the Granite Peak summit along the ridge between Tempest Mountain and Granite Peak. From Tempest Mountain, hike down to the saddle between Tempest Mountain and Granite Peak. From the saddle, follow a use trail along the s side of the ridge to a snow-bridge. Ropes and, depending on the amount of snow present, an ice ax are strongly recommended for crossing the snowbridge. Cross the snow-bridge and continue on the s face of Granite Peak, up a chimney, and to a prominent V-notch on the ridge. From the V-notch, the route passes through a jumble of ledges, cracks, gullies, cliffs, and chimneys. Good route-finding skills are required to navigate successfully through this area. The objective is a "keyhole" on the ridge above. From about 15 feet below the keyhole, climb up the chute to the left of the keyhole to the top of the ridge. From the top of the ridge, it is an easy scramble on the w side of the

Granite Peak from just above the saddle.

ridge to the summit. It is 0.5 miles from the saddle to the summit. There is a USGS benchmark and a register on the summit.

Alternate Route 2: Phantom Creek Trail/Froze-to-Death Plateau

Approach ▲ From the junction of State Routes 78 and 420 in Absarokee, proceed s on Route 78 for 13.0 miles to Forest Route 177 in the village of Roscoe. (This point is approximately 20½ miles N of Red Lodge via Route 78.) From Roscoe, continue s on Forest Route 177 approximately 13.6 miles to East Rosebud Lake. The trailhead for the Phantom Creek Trail is 0.3 miles N of East Rosebud Lake.

Route ▲ Hike w on the Phantom Creek Trail for 6.9 miles to the saddle on Froze-to-Death Plateau. From the saddle continue sw cross-country up the plateau, contouring to the w around the N side of Froze-to-Death Mountain above the 11,000-foot level. Turn s about a mile w of Froze-to-Death Mountain and hike to the w edge of Tempest Mountain near its summit. Past climbers have marked the route with a series of cairns. The distance from Phantom Creek Trail to Tempest Mountain is approximately 5.0 miles, depending on the route chosen. It is 0.9 miles from Tempest Mountain to the Granite Peak summit along the ridge between Tempest Mountain and Granite Peak. From Tempest Mountain, hike down to the saddle between Tempest Mountain and Granite Peak. From the saddle, follow a use trail along the s side of the ridge to a snowbridge. Ropes and, depending on the amount of snow present, an ice ax are strongly recommended for crossing the snowbridge. Cross the snowbridge and continue on the s face of Granite Peak, up a chimney, and to a prominent V-notch on the ridge. From the V-notch, the route passes through a jumble of ledges, cracks, gullies, cliffs, and chimneys. Good route-finding skills are required to navigate successfully through this area. The objective is a "keyhole" on the ridge above. From about 15 feet below the keyhole, climb up the chute to the left of the keyhole to the top of the ridge. From the top of the ridge, it is an easy scramble on the w side of the ridge to the summit. It is 0.5 miles from the saddle to the summit. There is a USGS benchmark and a register on the summit.

Special Conditions

Granite Peak is in the Absaroka-Beartooth Wilderness, but wilderness permits are not required. It is climbed during a multiday backpack trip. Usually, one or two days are spent getting to basecamp near the 11,600-foot level of Tempest Mountain or near Avalanche Lake, depending on the route chosen. The next day, weather permitting, the summit is climbed. An additional one or two days are necessary for the return to the trailhead. On the routes over Froze-to-Death Plateau, basecamp is usually set up in a group of rock shelters near the 11,600-foot level of the Tempest Mountain plateau. The rock shelters are on the w edge 1.6 miles NE of Granite Peak. The shelters are low rock walls built over the years to protect climbers from the frequent strong winds. On the Huckleberry Creek route, basecamp is usually set up at the N end of Avalanche Lake, although sometimes it is set up near the Snowball Lakes. The usual climbing season for Granite Peak is mid-July through mid-September.

Sudden storms with strong winds and subzero wind chill are common. Thunderstorms around Granite Peak are legendary. Snowstorms can occur any month of the year. Take care not to get caught on the peaks or exposed ridges during one of these storms. Be prepared with warm and wind-proof clothing and a tent sufficient to withstand high winds. Before starting the climb, be aware of the local weather forecast. There is more protection from potential storms on the Huckleberry Creek route.

Water is available almost all along the Huckleberry Creek route. In contrast, although there are several areas on the Tempest Mountain plateau where there is some flat ground and some water is available, it may be necessary to melt snow to obtain the water required. It may be advisable to carry an extra day's supply of water when using the Froze-to-Death Plateau routes.

Although the national forest roads are gravel, they are maintained and are normally suitable for any type of vehicle. Information, hiking guide sheets, and the national forest map can be obtained from Custer National Forest, Beartooth Ranger District, HC49, Box 3420, Red Lodge, MT 59068 (406/446-2103).

Historical Notes

The first recorded ascent of Granite Peak was made on August 29, 1923, by a party led by Elers Koch, who was superintendent of Lolo National Forest at the time. Granite Peak was the last of the 50 state highpoints to be climbed. The dam and powerhouse at Mystic Lake were completed in 1924 by the Montana Power Company. The dam is 300 feet long and 45 feet high. The powerhouse contains two 11,500-kilowatt generators and still produces electricity for the power company.

Natural History Notes

Approximately 35 million years ago a massive block of Precambrian granitic rock uplifted to form the Beartooth Mountains. Over the aeons, water and ice have etched the massive peaks, created rock-strewn plateaus and glaciated U-shaped valleys, and left gemlike lakes that characterize the Absaroka-Beartooth Wilderness. There are more than 25 peaks that exceed 12,000 feet in height, of which Granite Peak is the highest. In fact, Granite Peak is named for the massive granite formations in the region.

At the higher elevations, mountain goats are commonly seen. Marmots and pikas also inhabit the area. Mule deer and black bear are found near the trailheads in the summer months.

The Beartooth Scenic Highway, U.S. Hwy 212, between Red Lodge and Yellowstone National Park via Cooke City, has been rated by Charles Kuralt as one of the ten most scenic highways in the United States. Breathtaking, magnificent mountain scenery is at every turn.

Guides/Outfitters

Jackson Hole Mountain Guides and Climbing School, P.O. Box 7477, 165 N. Glenwood Street, Jackson, WY 83002 (800/239-7642).

Nebraska

Panorama Point

5,424 Feet

County
   Kimball

Location
   Approximately 26 miles sw of Kimball.

Hiking
   Primary Route: Drive-up.
   Alternate Route 1: Drive-up.
   Alternate Route 2: 2.4 miles, round trip, cross-country.

Gain
   Primary Route: Drive-up.
   Alternate Route 1: Drive-up.
   Alternate Route 2: 100 feet, Class 1, easy.

Maps
   Topographic: Pine Bluffs SE, Wyo.-Nebr.-Colo., 7½ minute.

Primary Route
   Approach ▲ From the Pine Bluffs, Wyoming, interchange on I-80 (Exit 401), just w of the Nebraska-Wyoming state line, proceed to 8th Street, which is immediately N of I-80. Turn right (E) on 8th Street and proceed 0.6 miles to Beech Street. Turn right (s) on Beech Street, which becomes County Road 164, and proceed 9.2 miles to the junction with a gravel road on the left, County Road 203. Proceed 0.9 miles E on County Road 203, which bears right at 0.7 miles, then 0.6 miles s on County Road 1, then 2.0 miles E on County Road 6, then 2.0 miles s on County Road 5, passing a farmhouse on the right at 1.4 miles, to a signed dirt road on the right (w)

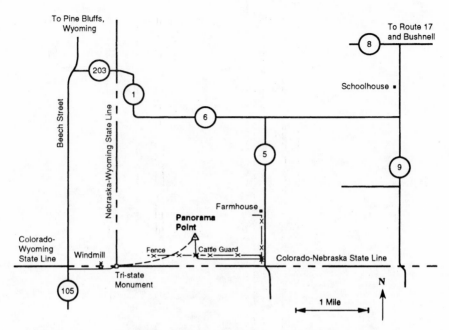

Panorama Point, Nebraska - 5,424 Feet

with a cattle guard. The sign reads, "Panorama Point, Highest Point in Nebraska." Turn right and continue 1.0 miles w on the dirt road to a second cattle guard on the right. Turn right (N) across the cattle guard and continue 0.3 miles to the highpoint.

Route ▲ There is a monument and a register on the highpoint. There is no USGS benchmark.

Alternate Route I

Approach ▲ From the Bushnell interchange on I-80 (Exit 8) approximately 12 miles w of Kimball, proceed s on the gravel road, County Road 17, 10.0 miles to where it dead-ends on another gravel road, County Road 8. Proceed 4.2 miles w on County Road 8, then 1.0 miles s on County Road 9, passing an old schoolhouse on the right, then 2.0 miles w on County Road 6, then 2.0 miles s on County Road 5, passing a farmhouse on the right at 1.4 miles, to a signed dirt road on the right (w) with a cattle guard. The sign reads, "Panorama Point, Highest Point in Nebraska." Turn right and continue 1.0 miles w on the dirt road to a second cattle guard on the right. Turn right (N) across the cattle guard and continue 0.3 miles to the highpoint.

Stone monument marks the indistinct highpoint of Nebraska.

Route ▲ There is a monument and a register on the highpoint. There is no USGS benchmark.

Alternate Route 2

Approach ▲ From the Pine Bluffs, Wyoming, interchange on I-80 (Exit 401), just W of the Wyoming-Nebraska state line, proceed to 8th Street, which is immediately N of I-80. Turn right (E) on 8th Street and proceed 0.6 miles to Beech Street. Turn right (S) on Beech Street and proceed 12.0 miles to the Colorado-Wyoming state line. Immediately S of the state line, turn left (E) onto a farm road and proceed 0.7 miles, passing a windmill, to a monument marking the Colorado-Nebraska-Wyoming tri-state intersection.

Route ▲ From the Tri-State Monument, hike 1.2 miles ENE across the pasture on a bearing of 71 degrees, true, to Panorama Point. There are a monument and a register on the highpoint. There is no USGS benchmark.

Special Conditions

Panorama Point is on private property, but it is open to the public. Please respect the rights of the property owner. Although some of the Primary Route and all of Alternate Route 1 are on gravel roads, the roads are very well maintained and suitable for any type of vehicle.

The Kimball Chamber of Commerce has a nice certificate available to commemorate one's visit to Panorama Point. For information, contact the Kimball–Banner County Chamber of Commerce, 119 E. Second Street, Kimball, NE 69145 (308/235-3782).

Historical Notes

The highpoint of Nebraska was located in 1951 by Art Henrickson and Claude Alden, both from Kimball, Nebraska. In 1971 the Kimball Chamber of Commerce erected a sandstone marker. The name, Panorama Point, was proposed in 1989 by Mr. Henrickson. To quote Mr. Henrickson from a letter written in 1989: "I think the Nebraska Legislature is going to give it [the highpoint] a name this next session. I think they will choose my suggestion, Panorama Point. It isn't a peak or mountain, but it does have a good view over the surrounding terrain, even to the Rockies in Colorado, almost 120 miles away." To date, the Nebraska Legislature has taken no action to adopt the name officially. Nevertheless, based on information supplied by Mr. Henrickson, the Nebraska Department of Roads has included Panorama Point on the official Nebraska State Highway Map beginning with the 1991–92 edition.

Nevada

Boundary Peak

13,140 Feet

County
Esmeralda

Location
Approximately 62 miles wsw of Tonopah in the Boundary Peak Wilderness Area of Inyo National Forest.

Hiking
7.4 miles, round trip, cross-country.

Gain
4,400 feet, Class 2, strenuous.

Maps
Topographic: Boundary Peak, Nev.-Calif.; Volcanic Hills East, Nev.; Volcanic Hills West, Nev.; and Mt. Montgomery, Nev., all 7½ minute.
National Forest: Inyo N.F.

Guidebooks
Hiking Nevada, by Bruce Grubbs, Falcon Press Publishing Co., Inc., Helena, Montana, 1998.
Hiking the Great Basin: The High Desert Country of California, Nevada, and Utah, by John Hart, Sierra Club Books, San Francisco, California, revised edition, 1992.

Primary Route
Approach ▲ From the N end of Big Pine, California, proceed E on California State Route 168 for 37.6 miles to the junction with California State Route 266. Turn N on State Route 266, which becomes Nevada State

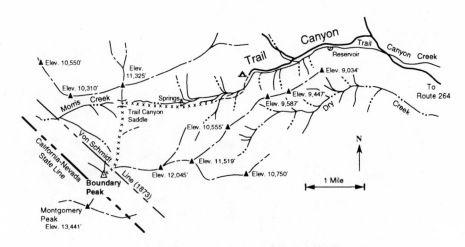

Boundary Peak, Nevada - 13,140 Feet

Route 264 after crossing the California-Nevada state line, and continue 32.4 miles, passing through Dyer at 15.3 miles, to a dirt road on the left. This point is approximately 200 yards s of the junction of Nevada State Routes 264 and 773. Turn left (sw) on the dirt road (see Special Conditions for additional information regarding dirt road conditions), staying on the main track at several junctions, and proceed 14.7 miles to the trailhead in Trail Canyon. Some significant junctions are as follows: Go straight at a crossroads at 2.0 miles, continue sw at a junction at 2.4 miles, go right then immediately left at 10.8 miles passing the B & B Mine, bear right at a Y-intersection at 12.2 miles, pass a reservoir at 12.9 miles, and bear left at a fork at 13.5 miles, continuing to the end of the road in Trail Canyon at 14.7 miles. (For an alternate approach from Bishop, California, see Special Conditions.)

Route ▲ Hike w for 2.3 miles up Trail Canyon to Trail Canyon Saddle on the use trail beginning at the end of the road. The trail, which is faint and fades out about halfway to Trail Canyon Saddle, soon crosses to the s side of the stream and continues near or on the bank above the wide streambed. At Trail Canyon Saddle, turn left (s) on the ridge and continue 1.4 miles over an intermediate peak up to the summit. There is a register and the USGS benchmark on the summit.

Special Conditions

Boundary Peak is in the newly established Boundary Peak Wilderness. Unlike in the other wilderness areas within Inyo National Forest, hiking

The California-Nevada border passes through the saddle to the right of Boundary Peak (center).

in Boundary Peak Wilderness does not require a wilderness permit. However, if a campfire is planned, a campfire permit is required.

The dirt road is maintained by the Forest Service for almost the entire route to the trailhead but is subject to flooding, washouts, and rerouting. The last 1.2 miles have not been graded. There is an alternate dirt road that can be used for the first portion of the route. It begins between Mileposts 26 and 27 on State Route 264, approximately 1.1 miles N of the junction of State Routes 264 and 773. It joins the dirt road of the route described above in 2.3 miles. If using a vehicle without high clearance, one must exercise care in order not to get stuck in the poorer parts of the road. Only the Boundary Peak, Nev.-Calif., topographic map is necessary for the route to the summit of Boundary Peak; however, the other listed topographic maps are useful in following the correct dirt road on the approach.

Occasionally, there is water in the stream in Trail Canyon, but it is usually fouled by livestock. Otherwise, except for melting snow, there is no water source on Boundary Peak. Carry all the water required. This climb can be done as a backpack. There are suitable campsites along the stream and near Trail Canyon Saddle. The usual climbing season for Boundary Peak is June through mid-October; the peak can be a nice snow climb earlier in the year.

An alternate approach from Bishop, California, to the dirt road turnoff north of Dyer, Nevada, is as follows: From the junction of U.S. Hwy 395 and U.S. Hwy 6 at the N end of Bishop, California, proceed N on U.S. Hwy 6 for approximately 58 miles to the junction with Nevada State Route 264 on the right. Turn right (SE) on Route 264 and continue 8.2 miles to the dirt road on the right. This point is approximately 200 yards S of the junction of State Routes 264 and 773.

Information, maps, hiking guide sheets, and campfire permits can be obtained from Inyo National Forest, White Mountain Ranger District, 798 N. Main Street, Bishop, CA 93514 (760/873-2500).

Maps, trail guides, and other books and items of interest can be obtained from the Eastern Sierra Inter-agency Visitor Center, P.O. Drawer R, U.S. Hwy 395 at State Route 136, Lone Pine, CA 93545 (760/876-6222).

Historical Notes

Boundary Peak derives its name from its proximity to the California-Nevada border. It was likely named by surveyors who were working in the West in the mid-1800s. In fact, the exact location of the entire California-Nevada border, including the Boundary Peak region, has had a long and varied history. It was finally legally settled in 1980. Part of the controversy stems from a survey done in 1873 by Alexey Von Schmidt. The California-Nevada border between Lake Tahoe and the Colorado River, as surveyed by Von Schmidt, is askew, with the current border established by the United States Coast and Geodetic Survey between 1893 and 1899. The effect of the Von Schmidt survey was to place the oblique boundary line east of Boundary Peak, thus putting Boundary Peak in California. If the border had not been changed by the USGS survey, Wheeler Peak in Great Basin National Park on the east side of Nevada, elevation 13,063 feet, would have the distinction of being the highest point in the state. The approximate location of the Von Schmidt survey line is shown on the Boundary Peak, Nev.-Calif., topographic map.

Natural History Notes

In addition to coyotes and numerous small mammals, wild horses are occasionally seen in Trail Canyon. Many species of birds also visit the area. Numerous wildflowers, including columbine, Indian paintbrush, wild iris, and mule's ears, are common in the spring and early summer.

Boundary Peak is located at the northern end of the White Mountains, which encompass the Ancient Bristlecone Pine Forest. Designated in 1958, the Ancient Bristlecone Pine Forest contains the world's oldest living trees, the Great Basin bristlecone pine, *Pinus longaeva*. Some of the trees are well over 4,000 years old. Limber pines are also found in the area.

Recorded information on the Bristlecone Pine Forest is available by calling 760/873-2573.

Guides/Outfitters

Jackson Hole Mountain Guides and Climbing School, P.O. Box 7477, 165 North Glenwood Street, Jackson, WY 83002 (800/239-7642).

Mammoth Mountaineering School, P.O. Box 7299 (located at Sandy's Ski and Sports on Main Street), Mammoth Lakes, CA 93546 (760/924-9100).

New Hampshire

Mount Washington

6,288 Feet

County
 Coos

Location
 Approximately 12 miles E of Twin Mountain in White Mountain National Forest.

Hiking
 Primary Route: Ride-up.
 Alternate Route 1: Drive-up.
 Alternate Route 2: 8.6 miles, round trip, on old dirt road and trail.
 Alternate Route 3: 9.0 miles, round trip, on trail.

Gain
 Primary Route: Ride-up.
 Alternate Route 1: Drive-up.
 Alternate Route 2: 4,270 feet, Class 1, strenuous.
 Alternate Route 3: 3,800 feet, Class 1, strenuous.

Maps
 Topographic: Mt. Washington, New Hampshire, 7½ x 15 minute.
 National Forest: White Mountain N.F.
 Other: Mount Washington and the heart of the Presidential Range, New Hampshire, Appalachian Mountain Club, Boston, Massachusetts.
 Trail Map & Guide to the White Mountain National Forest, DeLorme Publishing Co., Freeport, Maine.

Guidebooks
 AMC Guide to Mount Washington and the Presidential Range, Appalachian Mountain Club, Boston, Massachusetts, 5th edition, 1992.

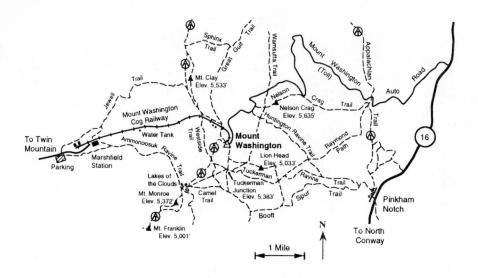

Mount Washington, New Hampshire - 6,288 Feet

AMC *White Mountain Guide*, edited by Gene Daniell and Jon Burroughs, Appalachian Mountain Club, Boston, Massachusetts, 1998.

Appalachian Trail Guide to New Hampshire–Vermont, edited by Jim Barnes, Appalachian Trail Conference, Harpers Ferry, West Virginia, 4th edition, 1985.

50 Hikes in the White Mountains, by Daniel Doan and Ruth Doan MacDougall, Backcountry Publications/The Countryman Press, Woodstock, Vermont, 5th edition, 1997.

High Huts of the White Mountains, by William Reifsnyder, Appalachian Mountain Club, Boston, Massachusetts, 2d edition, 1993.

Hiking Guide to Mount Washington and the Presidential Range, compiled by Gene Daniell and edited by Jon Burroughs, The Globe Pequot Press, Old Saybrook, Connecticut, 1998.

Hiking New Hampshire, by Larry B. Pletcher, Falcon Press Publishing Co., Inc., Helena, Montana, 2d edition, 1996.

Primary Route: Mount Washington Cog Railway

Approach ▲ From the junction of U.S. Hwys 3 and 302 in Twin Mountain, proceed E on Hwy 302 for 4.5 miles to Base Road on the left with signs indicating the route to the Cog Railway Marshfield Base Station. Turn left (NE) and continue 6.1 miles to the Marshfield Station. Park in the large lot near the station. Ride the Cog Railway to the summit.

The old steam engine pushes one car every trip to the summit of Mount Washington.

This is a three-hour round trip, allowing approximately 20 minutes at the summit.

Route ▲ The USGS benchmark is approximately 15 yards S of the Summit House.

Alternate Route 1: Mount Washington Auto Road
Approach ▲ From North Conway, proceed N on U.S. Hwy 302/State Route 16 for 5 miles to the point where U.S. Hwy 302 turns W. Continue N on Route 16 approximately 16 miles to the Mount Washington Auto Road. Turn left, pay toll, and proceed 8 miles to the summit. It requires 30 to 45 minutes for the one-way trip.

Route ▲ The USGS benchmark is approximately 15 yards S of the Summit House.

Alternate Route 2: Tuckerman Ravine Trail/Lion Head Trail
Approach ▲ From North Conway, proceed N on U.S. Hwy 302/State Route 16 for 5 miles to the point where U.S. Hwy 302 turns W. Continue N on Route 16 for 12 miles to Pinkham Notch Camp on the left. There is ample parking available.

Route ▲ From Pinkham Notch Camp, hike W on the Tuckerman Ravine Trail for 2.3 miles to a trail junction with the Lion Head Trail and

Don Holmes at the summit of Mount Washington.

the Boott Spur Link. This point is 0.1 miles before reaching the Hermit Lake. At the crossroads, bear right (N) onto the Lion Head Trail and continue 1.6 miles to where the Lion Head Trail again meets the Tuckerman Ravine Trail. Bear right (N) on the Tuckerman Ravine Trail and hike 0.4 miles to the summit. The USGS benchmark is approximately 15 yards S of the Summit House.

Note: Instead of the Lion Head Trail, an alternate summer route is to stay on the Tuckerman Ravine Trail to Tuckerman Junction at 3.6 miles, then continue N on the Tuckerman Ravine Trail for 0.6 miles to the summit.

Alternate Route 3: Ammonoosuc Ravine Trail/Crawford Path

Approach ▲ From the junction of U.S. Hwys 3 and 302 in Twin Mountain, proceed E on Hwy 302 for 4.5 miles to Base Road on the left with signs indicating the route to the Cog Railway Marshfield Base Station. Turn left (NE) and continue 5.5 miles to a parking area and the trailhead on the right.

Route ▲ From the parking area, hike nominally E on the Ammonoosuc Ravine Trail along the Ammonoosuc River for 3.1 miles to the Lakes of the Clouds Hut and the Crawford Path. From the hut, hike generally NE along the Crawford Path for 1.4 miles to the summit. The USGS benchmark is approximately 15 yards S of the Summit House.

Special Conditions

The Mount Washington Cog Railway operates on a seasonal basis, May through mid-October, and advance reservations are strongly recommended. For information, current fares, operating dates and times, and reservations, contact the Mount Washington Cog Railway, Route 302, Bretton Woods, Mount Washington, NH 03589 (800/922-8825).

The Mount Washington Auto Road is also open on a seasonal basis, mid-May through late October, weather permitting. Summer hours are 7:30 A.M. to 6:00 P.M. with shorter hours early and late in the season. Guided tours to the summit are also available. Hikers can also sign up for a ride down the mountain via the auto road. For information, hours of operation, and rates, contact the Mount Washington Auto Road, Pinkham Notch, P.O. Box 278, Gorham, NH 03581 (603/466-3988).

Including the trails noted above, there is an extensive trail system in the White Mountains, over 1,400 miles, maintained by the Appalachian Mountain Club. If the trails are combined, with or without a car shuttle, several one-way trips or loop trips can be created. The summit of Mount Washington can also be reached via the Appalachian Trail from the north or the south. The Appalachian Trail traverses New Hampshire for approximately 161 miles in generally a northeast-southwest direction and passes over the summit of Mount Washington. The entire Appalachian Trail is marked for travel in both directions with white paint blazes on trees or poles and rocks, about 2 inches wide and 6 inches high. Two blazes, one above the other, are a signal of an important trail feature such as an obscure turn or a change in route. Side trails from the Appalachian Trail are usually blazed in blue. This includes the trails listed above.

Lodging and meals are available at the Pinkham Notch Lodge. Reservations are required. In addition to the Pinkham Notch Visitor Center and Lodge and the Crawford Hostel, the Appalachian Mountain Club owns, operates, and maintains eight backcountry huts. The huts are a day's hike apart over a 56-mile route. All but one offer breakfast and dinner, on a seasonal basis, in addition to lodging.

Information, books, maps of the trails, and lodge and hut reservations in the Mount Washington area can be obtained from the Appalachian Mountain Club, Pinkham Notch Camp, P.O. Box 298, Gorham, NH 03581 (603/466-2727). Additional information on the Appalachian Trail can be obtained by contacting the Appalachian Trail Conference, P.O. Box 807, 799 Washington Street, Harpers Ferry, WV 25425-0807 (304/535-6331).

The national forest map and information on the White Mountain National Forest can be obtained from White Mountain National Forest, 719 Main Street, Laconia, NH 03246 (603/528-8721).

In order to simplify the map included here for Mount Washington, several connecting routes and secondary trails have been omitted. Maps listed provide additional detailed information on the Mount Washington trail system.

The weather on Mount Washington has a well-deserved reputation for producing some of the most severe conditions in the United States. Severe wintry storms with hurricane-force wind, dense fog, and driving snow and rain occur frequently, even in the summer months. The weather can undergo sudden changes, and storms may increase in intensity rapidly. If the weather begins to turn bad, seek shelter or come down off the mountain. Hikers have lost their lives by not heeding the weather warnings and getting caught in a storm.

Historical Notes

During the first scientific expedition to Mount Washington, led by the Reverend Manasseh Cutler in July 1784, the peak was named in honor of General George Washington (1732–99), who had recently retired from the Continental Army to Mount Vernon. Subsequently, of course, Washington became the first president of the United States. In July 1820 a party led by Adino N. Brackett and John W. Weeks ascended Mount Washington for the stated purpose of naming the high peaks. Since Mount Washington was now named for a president of the United States, they decided to continue the theme and named peaks in the region for Presidents Adams, Jefferson, Madison, and Monroe. The peak naming was a grand event, and the party had brought an adequate supply of "O-be-joyful" to toast the naming of each peak properly. When they ran out of presidents, they named Mount Franklin for Benjamin Franklin and called the next peak Mount Pleasant, a name it facetiously has been suggested was inspired by the O-be-joyful. Accordingly, the mountain range became known as the Presidential Range. Mount Pleasant was renamed Mount Eisenhower in 1969. The first recorded ascent of Mount Washington was accomplished by Darby Field in 1642.

The Primary Route affords the opportunity to ride the Mount Washington Cog Railway, the world's first mountain-climbing cog railway, completed in 1869. Its locomotives are still 100 percent steam-powered and coal-fired. On the three-mile journey to the summit, each locomotive consumes a ton of coal and a thousand gallons of water while pushing a single passenger car to the highpoint of New Hampshire. The train ascends Mount Washington almost entirely on trestles with an average grade of 25 percent. One trestle, called "Jacob's Ladder," climbs a steep, 34.7 percent grade. As many as seven locomotives can be in operation at any time. The original locomotive, "Old Peppersass," which first reached the summit on July 3, 1869, is on display at the Marshfield Base Station.

Construction on the Mount Washington Auto Road, Alternate Route 1, began in 1854 and was completed to the summit in 1861. The first transportation to the summit was provided by specially built mountain wagons drawn by four horses. The first motorized ascent was on August 31, 1899, by Freelan O. Stanley, driving a Stanley Steamer. The average grade of the road is 12 percent, and it is mostly paved. Summer events on the auto road include the Mount Washington Hillclimb (America's oldest motorsports event), the Mount Washington Bicycle Hillclimb, and the Mount Washington Foot Race.

At the highpoint, there is the Summit Stage Office, built in 1878; the Sherman Adams State Park building; the Mount Washington Observatory; and the fully restored Tip Top House.

The Appalachian Trail, completed in 1937, extends over 2,150 miles from Mount Katahdin, the highpoint of Maine, to Springer Mountain in northern Georgia.

Natural History Notes

The Presidential Range, which includes Mount Washington, exhibits visible evidence of recent glaciation. Valley glaciers once cut cirques and U-shaped valleys such as Tuckerman Ravine, King Ravine, and the Great Gulf, perhaps as recently as 50,000 years ago.

The weather at the summit of Mount Washington is notorious. The highest wind velocity ever recorded—231 mph—occurred here in April 1934. Winds exceed hurricane force (75 mph) over one hundred days a year. An average wind velocity of 35 mph, coupled with an average temperature of 27.1 degrees F, makes for extreme wind chill conditions.

New Jersey

High Point

1,803 Feet

County
Sussex

Location
Approximately 4 miles sse of Port Jervis, N.Y., in High Point State Park.

Hiking
Primary Route: Drive-up.
Alternate Route 1: 13.4 miles, round trip, on trail.

Gain
Primary Route: Drive-up.
Alternate Route: 2,030 feet, Class 1, moderate.

Maps
Topographic: Port Jervis South, N.J.-N.Y.-Pa., 7½ minute.
Other: High Point State Park, Division of Parks and Forestry, New Jersey State Park Service.

Guidebooks
Appalachian Trail Guide to New York–New Jersey, Appalachian Trail Conference, Harpers Ferry, West Virginia, 14th edition, 1998.
50 Hikes in New Jersey, by Bruce C. Scofield et al., Backcountry Publications/The Countryman Press, Woodstock, Vermont, 2d edition, 1997.

Primary Route
Approach ▲ From the junction of I-84 and State Route 23 in the extreme NW corner of New Jersey, proceed s on Route 23 for 4.5 miles to

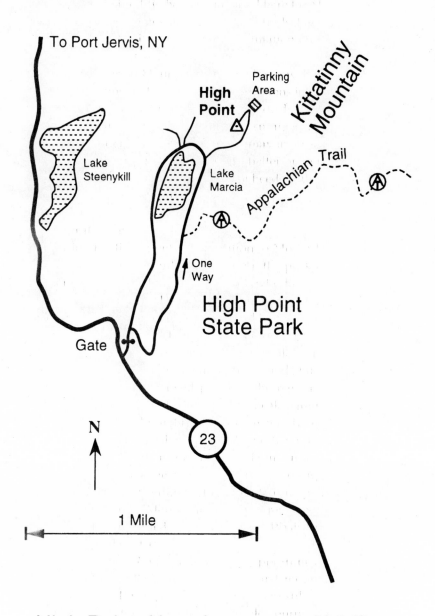

To Port Jervis, NY

Kittatinny Mountain

Parking Area

High Point

Lake Steenykill

Lake Marcia

Appalachian Trail

One Way

High Point State Park

Gate

N

23

1 Mile

High Point, New Jersey - 1,803 Feet
(Primary Route)

the High Point State Park entrance on the left. Turn left (N) into the park and follow the park road to the summit monument parking area.

Route ▲ Walk to the monument on the summit.

Alternate Route: Appalachian Trail

Approach ▲ From the junction of I-84 and State Route 23 in the extreme NW corner of New Jersey, proceed S on Route 23 for 4.1 miles to Sawmill Road on the right. Turn right (S) on Sawmill Road and continue 4.5 miles, passing Sawmill Pond at 1.8 miles, to Deckertown Turnpike, County Route 650. Turn left (E) on Deckertown Turnpike and proceed 1.5 miles to the Appalachian Trail crossing and a parking area on the left (N).

Route ▲ From the parking area, hike N on the white-blazed Appalachian Trail for 6.5 miles to a blue-blazed trail at a saddle S of the highpoint, where the Appalachian Trail bears downhill to the right. While on the Appalachian Trail, be alert for the white blazes, as the Appalachian Trail crosses several other trails within High Point State Park. Continue N on the blue-blazed trail for 0.2 miles to the monument on the summit. **Note:** This can be done as a one-way hike with a car shuttle.

Special Conditions

There is a daily parking fee during the summer season, which is from Memorial Day through Labor Day ($5.00 on weekdays and $7.00 on weekends and holidays). Several campsites and a few cabins are available within the park. The top of the monument affords a panoramic view of the surrounding area. Information and a park map can be obtained from High Point State Park, 1480 Route 23, Sussex, NJ 07461 (201/875-4800).

The portion of the Appalachian Trail in High Point State Park is hilly, as evidenced by the gross elevation gain on the round trip. The entire Appalachian Trail is marked for travel in both directions with white paint blazes on trees or poles and rocks, about 2 inches wide and 6 inches high. Two blazes, one above the other, are a signal of an important trail feature such as an obscure turn or a change in route. Side trails from the Appalachian Trail are usually blazed in blue. Information on hiking the Appalachian Trail can be obtained from the Appalachian Trail Conference, P.O. Box 807, 799 Washington Street, Harpers Ferry, WV 25425-0807 (304/535-6331).

In addition to the Appalachian Trail, which traverses the entire park in a north-south direction, there are 14 miles of marked trails within High Point State Park. The trails vary in length from 0.5 miles to 3 miles and range from easy walking to difficult hiking. Approximately 74 miles of the Appalachian Trail are in New Jersey.

Historical Notes

High Point was aptly named probably around 1888, when Charles St. John and family built the High Point Inn, a plush resort at the time. When the St. Johns went bankrupt in 1909, Anthony R. Kuser and John L. Kuser purchased the inn and surrounding property. In 1911 Anthony Kuser reconstructed the High Point Inn as a summer home now known as the Lodge. High Point State Park was created in 1923 with land donated to the state of New Jersey by Colonel and Mrs. Anthony R. Kuser. The 220-foot monument at the summit, also provided by the Kusers, is dedicated to New Jersey's wartime heroes and was completed in 1930. It is 34 feet square at the base and is faced with New Hampshire granite and local quartzite. The original monument lighting system, out of use since World War II, was refurbished in 1989, and on July 4 of that year the lights were again turned on.

The Alternate Route affords the opportunity to hike along a portion of the Appalachian Trail. This trail, completed in 1937, extends over 2,150 miles from Mount Katahdin, the highpoint of Maine, to Springer Mountain in northern Georgia.

Natural History Notes

Immediately north of the highpoint is the Dryden Kuser Natural Area. This area is practically virgin woodland containing an old-growth Atlantic white cedar swamp that supports a variety of conifers, including large hemlocks, white pine, black spruce, and a stand of mature southern white cedar. The undergrowth is largely rhododendron interspersed with deciduous shrubs and other plants.

Mammals that may be sighted here include white-tailed deer, black bear, bobcat, gray fox, red fox, raccoon, and some smaller animals. More than eighty species of birds have been observed in the park.

New Mexico

Wheeler Peak

13,161 Feet

County
Taos

Location
Approximately 13 miles NE of Taos in the Wheeler Peak Wilderness Area of Carson National Forest.

Hiking
Primary Route: 6.2 miles, round trip, on trail and cross-country.
Alternate Route: 14.2 miles, round trip, on old dirt road and trail.

Gain
Primary Route: 3,250 feet, Class 1, strenuous.
Alternate Route: 4,700 feet, Class 1, strenuous.

Maps
Topographic: Wheeler Peak, N.Mex., 7½ minute.
National Forest: Carson N.F.; Latir Peak and Wheeler Peak Wildernesses, Carson N.F.

Guidebooks
50 Hikes in New Mexico, by Harry Evans, Gem Guides Book Co., Pico Rivera, California, revised edition, 1988.
Hiking New Mexico, by Laurence Parent, Falcon Press Publishing Co., Inc., Helena, Montana, 1998.
Hiking the Southwest: Arizona, New Mexico, and West Texas, by Dave Ganci, Sierra Club Books, San Francisco, California, 1983.
Hiking the Wilderness, by Kay Matthews, Acequia Madre Press, Chamisal, New Mexico, 1999.

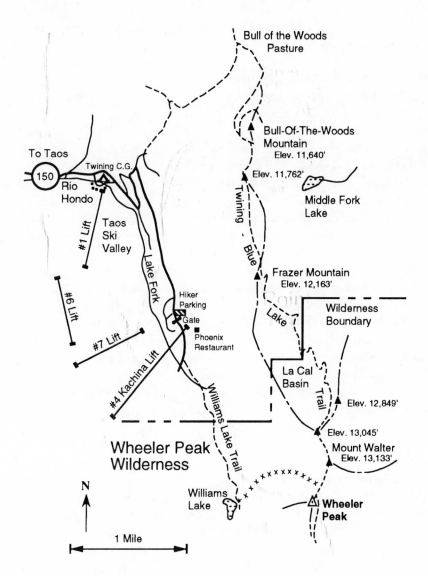

Bull of the Woods
Pasture

To Taos

150

Twining C.G.

Rio
Hondo

Taos
Ski
Valley

#1 Lift

#6 Lift

#7 Lift

#4 Kachina Lift

Lake Fork

Hiker
Parking

Gate

Phoenix
Restaurant

Williams Lake Trail

Bull-Of-The-Woods
Mountain
Elev. 11,640'

Elev. 11,762'

Twining - Blue

Lake

Middle Fork
Lake

Frazer Mountain
Elev. 12,163'

Wilderness
Boundary

La Cal
Basin

Trail

Elev. 12,849'

Elev. 13,045'

Mount Walter
Elev. 13,133'

Wheeler Peak
Wilderness

N

Williams
Lake

x x x x x x x x x x

Wheeler
Peak

1 Mile

Wheeler Peak, New Mexico - 13,161 Feet

75 Hikes in New Mexico, by Craig Martin, The Mountaineers, Seattle, Washington, 1995.

Primary Route: Williams Lake Trail

Approach ▲ From Taos, proceed NW on State Route 522 for 4 miles to State Route 150 on the right. Turn right on Route 150 and continue 14.7 miles to the Taos Ski Valley. Continue through the ski valley parking area for 0.3 miles to the E end of the parking area. Turn left (N) at the end of the parking area, and the small Twining Forest Service Campground will be on the right. At the N end of the campground, turn right onto Twining Road. Continue up Twining Road for 0.5 miles and make a hard left onto Phoenix Switchback. Proceed 0.3 miles on Phoenix Switchback, make a hard right uphill, and continue 1.4 miles to a "Hikers Parking" area on the left. Park here.

Route ▲ From the SW corner of the parking area, hike generally S along a dirt road, which becomes a trail approximately 0.3 miles after passing the lower terminal of the Kachina Chair Lift. The distance from the chairlift to Williams Lake is 2.0 miles. While on the dirt road, stay on the left (E) side of Lake Fork Creek, bearing left at a fork approximately 0.2 miles S of the chairlift. From the NE corner of Williams Lake, climb E up the steep gully and steep slope, following a climbers' trail, 0.9 miles to the saddle at the ridge between Mount Walter and Wheeler Peak. Turn right (S) on the ridge and continue 0.2 miles along the ridge to the summit. There is a metal plaque on a 3-foot monument at the highpoint. The USGS benchmark is on the summit.

Alternate Route: Wheeler Peak Trail

Approach ▲ From Taos, proceed NW on State Route 522 for 4 miles to State Route 150 on the right. Turn right on Route 150 and continue 14.7 miles to the Taos Ski Valley. Continue through the ski valley parking area for 0.3 miles to the E end of the parking area. Turn left (N) at the end of the parking area, and the small Twining Forest Service Campground will be on the right. Park next to the campground.

Route ▲ From Twining Campground, the signed trailhead is across Twining Road. Hike NE 2.1 miles on a trail and an old dirt road, which follows the NE-SW trending canyon of the Bull-of-the-Woods Fork of the Rio Hondo to Bull-of-the-Woods Pasture and the intersection with the Gold Hill Trail, leading NW. At this point the Wheeler Peak Trail turns SW and follows an old road that ascends toward Bull-of-the-Woods Mountain. The trail skirts Bull-of-the-Woods Mountain and continues 5.0 miles up to and generally S along the ridge to the highpoint. Follow the trail as it goes over Frazer Mountain, down into La Cal Basin, over Mount Walter, and

Wheeler Peak summit register.

onto the summit of Wheeler Peak. There is a metal plaque on a 3-foot monument at the highpoint. The USGS benchmark is on the summit.

Special Conditions

Wheeler Peak is in the 19,150-acre Wheeler Peak Wilderness, but wilderness permits are not required. The usual climbing season for Wheeler Peak is June through mid-September.

Although Wheeler Peak is on public land, the initial part of the Primary Route passes through private property of the Taos Ski Valley complex. Permission to cross the property is not required. However, hikers should be cautious about parking. Taos Ski Valley has provided a "Hikers Parking" area specifically for hikers. The general area is patrolled by a security officer, who will issue citations to cars incorrectly parked in other areas. Cars parked too long are subject to being towed to Taos at the owner's expense. Please respect the rights of the property owner. For information on Taos Ski Valley, contact Taos Ski Valley at 505/776-2291 or the Taos Valley Resort Association at 800/776-1111.

Information, hiking guide sheets, and national forest maps can be obtained from Carson National Forest, Questa Ranger District (2 miles E of Questa, on NM 38), P.O. Box 110, Questa, NM 87556 (505/586-0520). Additional trail information may be obtained from the Forest Service website, www.fs.fed.us/r3/, and search for "Wheeler Peak."

During the summer and early fall, sudden afternoon thunderstorms occur frequently in the Wheeler Peak area. They may be accompanied by rain or hail, high winds, low visibility, and lightning. Take care not to get caught on the peaks or exposed ridges during one of these storms.

The routes may be combined to form a loop trip.

Historical Notes

Wheeler Peak was named for Major George Montague Wheeler (1842–1905). In 1871 First Lieutenant Wheeler was selected to lead the survey of the territory of the United States west of the 100th meridian. This was an awesome undertaking. The 100th meridian extends through the middle of North Dakota down through the middle of Texas: nearly half the land area of the contiguous 48 states is to the west of the meridian. The primary objective of the survey was the topographic mapping of the country, which was still largely unexplored. The scope of the survey was eventually expanded to include geological, zoological, and ethnological investigations as well. In 1869–70 Wheeler led a surveying expedition into the Wheeler Peak area. Wheeler's organization lost its identity in 1879 when the new United States Geological Survey was created. Wheeler spent the next nine years completing reports and supervising publication of the eight-volume definitive *Report upon United States Geographical Surveys West of the One Hundredth Meridian*, published between 1875 and 1889. He retired in June 1888 and, in 1890, by an act of Congress, was retroactively promoted to the rank of major, effective July 23, 1888.

There are several historic sites surrounding Wheeler Peak, including the town of Taos, which is a National Historic Landmark.

Natural History Notes

The plant life in the Wheeler Peak area is subalpine vegetation mixed with Engelmann spruce, corkbark fir, aspen, and bristlecone pine. Above timberline, the alpine tundra contains plants not usually found at lower elevations, such as the purplish Indian painted cup, nailwort, moss-pink campion, blue bells, mouse ear, alpine willows, and stonecrop. The plants are usually less than one foot high and have small but colorful flowers. Wildlife includes mule deer, elk, antelope, black bear, mountain lion, and bighorn sheep. Once prominent in the region, bighorn sheep were reintroduced in 1993 and are thriving in the alpine meadow habitat. Marmot, pika, and marten are chief among the smaller mammals. Many species of birds are to be found, including golden eagle, magpie, woodpecker, blue grouse, and, occasionally, ptarmigan, in addition to songbirds.

New York

Mount Marcy

5,344 Feet

County
Essex

Location
Approximately 12 miles SSE of Lake Placid in the Adirondack Forest Preserve.

Hiking
Primary Route: 14.8 miles, round trip, on trail.
Alternate Route 1: 18.2 miles, round trip, on trail.
Alternate Route 2: 20.6 miles, round trip, on trail.

Gain
Primary Route: 3,200 feet, Class 1, strenuous.
Alternate Route 1: 4,000 feet, Class 1, strenuous.
Alternate Route 2: 3,900 feet, Class 1, strenuous.

Maps
Topographic: Mount Marcy, New York; Keene Valley, New York; and Santanoni Peak, New York, all 7½ x 15 minute.
Other: Trails of the Adirondack High Peaks Region, The Adirondack Mountain Club, Inc., Lake George, New York.

Guidebooks
50 Hikes in the Adirondacks, by Barbara McMartin, Backcountry Publications/The Countryman Press, Woodstock, Vermont, 3d edition, 1997.
Guide to Adirondack Trails, Volume 1: High Peaks Region, edited by Tony Goodwin, The Adirondack Mountain Club, Inc., Lake George, New York, 12th edition, 1992.

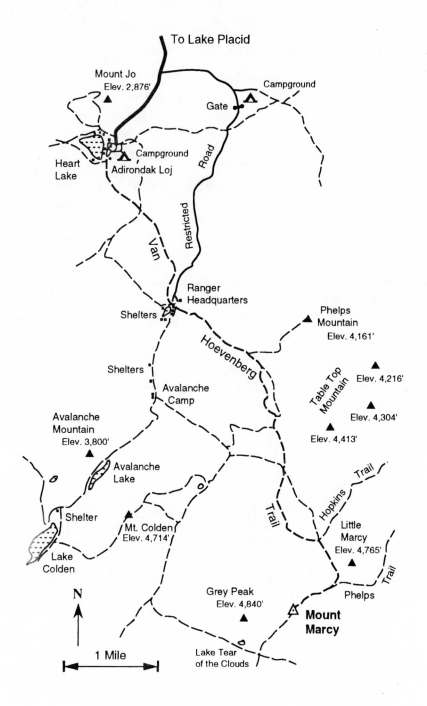

To Lake Placid

Mount Jo
Elev. 2,876'

Campground

Gate

Heart
Lake

Campground
Adirondak Loj

Road

Restricted

Van

Ranger
Headquarters

Shelters

Phelps
Mountain
Elev. 4,161'

Hoevenberg

Shelters

Table Top Mountain

Elev. 4,216'

Avalanche
Camp

Elev. 4,304'

Avalanche
Mountain
Elev. 3,800'

Elev. 4,413'

Avalanche
Lake

Trail

Hopkins

Trail

Shelter

Mt. Colden
Elev. 4,714'

Little
Marcy
Elev. 4,765'

Trail

Lake
Colden

Trail

N

Grey Peak
Elev. 4,840'

Phelps

Mount
Marcy

1 Mile

Lake Tear
of the Clouds

Mount Marcy, New York - 5,344 Feet
(Primary Route)

150

Hiking New York, by Rhonda Ostertag and George Ostertag, Falcon Press Publishing Co., Inc., Helena, Montana, 1996.

Primary Route: Van Hoevenburg Trail

Approach ▲ From Lake Placid, proceed E on State Route 73 for 3.3 miles to the junction with Adirondak Loj Road on the right. Turn right (S) and continue 4.8 miles to the Adirondak Loj area entrance booth. Just beyond the entrance booth, turn left into the parking area near the High Peaks Information Center.

Route ▲ From the E end of the parking area, hike S on the well-signed Van Hoevenburg Trail, following the round blue markers placed by the New York Department of Environmental Conservation (DEC) for 7.4 miles to the summit. On the summit is a USGS benchmark, and just below the summit is a large plaque noting the first recorded ascent.

Alternate Route 1: Phelps Trail/Van Hoevenburg Trail

Approach ▲ From the junction of I-87 (Adirondack Northway) and State Route 73 approximately 1 mile SE of Underwood (I-87 Exit 30), proceed N on State Route 73 for approximately 11 miles to Adirondack Road on the left in the middle of the village of Keene Valley. There is a sign indicating the direction to the High Peaks trails. Turn left (W) on Adirondack Road, which becomes Interbrook Road in 0.5 miles, and follow the yellow markers 1.6 miles to a large parking area at the Garden. Be sure to park in the designated parking area.

Route ▲ From the register at the W end of the Garden, hike generally SW on the well-signed Phelps Trail (also called the Johns Brook Trail), following the yellow markers to the junction with the Hopkins Trail at 5.1 miles and passing Johns Brook Lodge at 3.5 miles. At this junction, bear left on the Phelps Trail, now following red markers (the yellow markers continue on the Hopkins Trail), and continue to the junction with the Van Hoevenburg Trail at 8.5 miles. Turn left on the Van Hoevenburg Trail and follow the blue markers 0.6 miles to the summit. Along the Phelps Trail, there are additional trail junctions to note: At 0.5 miles bear right at the Southside Trail junction; bear right at a junction with the trail to the DEC Interior Outpost at 3.1 miles; bear left at a junction at 3.2 miles; go straight at the junction with the State Range and Klondike Trails just beyond Johns Brook Lodge; bear right at the Slant Rock Trail junction at 6.8 miles; and bear right at the State Range Trail junction at 7.8 miles. On the summit is a USGS benchmark, and just below the summit is a large plaque commemorating the first recorded ascent.

Alternate Route 2: Calamity Brook Trail

Approach ▲ From the junction of I-87 (Adirondack Northway) and County Road 2 (Blue Ridge Road), approximately 2.5 miles E of Blue

Ridge (I-87 Exit 29), proceed w on County Road 2 for approximately 17.5 miles to County Road 25 on the right. This point is 1.6 miles before County Road 28N is reached. Turn right (N) on County Road 25 and continue approximately 9.3 miles, bearing left at junctions at 0.5 miles and 5.8 miles, to a parking area at the Upper Works.

Route ▲ From the Upper Works, hike N on the trail, following red and yellow markers. At a trail junction at 0.4 miles, bear sharp right on the Calamity Brook Trail, following red markers. Cross Calamity Brook on a suspension bridge at 1.3 miles. At the junction with a trail from the Indian Pass Trail at 1.8 miles, bear right, now following blue markers, to a trail junction at 4.7 miles, passing Calamity Pond at 4.3 miles. Bear sharp left, once again following red markers, to a trail junction at 5.7 miles near the E end of Lake Colden Dam. Cross the dam, following the red markers, to a register and trail junction at 5.8 miles. Bear right at the register, soon crossing the Opalescent River on a suspension bridge, and continue following the red markers to a junction with the abandoned Twin Brook Trail at 7.4 miles. Continue along the trail, from this point following yellow DEC markers, to a junction with the Lake Arnold Trail at 8.0 miles. Turn right and continue to a junction with the blue-marked trail from Elk Lake at 9.5 miles, passing Lake Tear of the Clouds at 9.2 miles. Turn left and continue on the yellow-marked trail to the summit of Mount Marcy at 10.3 miles. On the summit is a USGS benchmark, and just below the summit is a large plaque commemorating the first recorded ascent.

Special Conditions

Practically all the trails in the High Peaks Region are well signed and marked with round colored disks bearing the insignia of the organization responsible for the trails. The three organizations that maintain the trails are the Adirondack Mountain Club, Inc. (ADK), the Department of Environmental Conservation (DEC), and the Adirondack Trail Improvement Society (ATIS).

There is an extensive trail system in the Adirondack Mountains in addition to the one in the High Peaks Region. The guidebook listed above, which includes a complete map of the High Peaks Region, is an excellent reference for hiking the trails to Mount Marcy. Its companion guides, Volumes 2 through 7, cover other areas of the Adirondack Mountains. Volume 8 covers the Catskill Mountains. Information, maps, and books on hiking in the Adirondack Mountains and the Catskill Mountains can be obtained from the Adirondack Mountain Club, Inc., 814 Goggins Road, Lake George, NY 12845-4117 (518/668-4447).

There is a fee for parking at the Adirondak Loj ($2.00 per day for ADK members and $7.00 per day for nonmembers). Lodging and meals are available at the Adirondak Loj and at Johns Brook Lodge. Both lodges are owned and operated by the Adirondack Mountain Club, Inc. Information about reservations and rates for both lodges can be obtained from the Adirondak Loj, P.O. Box 867, Lake Placid, NY 12946 (518/523-3441).

The High Peaks Information Center provides trail and hiking information, basic supplies, limited groceries, pay showers, restrooms, and pay phones. There are also backcountry displays, maps, and weather information. The center is open from 8:00 A.M. to 8:00 P.M. every day during the summer season and on weekends during the fall and spring.

Historical Notes

Mount Marcy was named in honor of Governor William Learned Marcy (1786–1857) in 1837 by Ebenezer Emmons, chief geologist of the Second District of the New York Geological Survey. William Marcy served as governor of New York from 1833 to 1838, and during his administration the first geological survey of New York's fifty-six counties was organized. In the course of this survey, Mount Marcy, the highest peak in the Adirondack Mountains, was named for Governor Marcy. Ebenezer Emmons led the group that made the first recorded ascent of Mount Marcy, on August 5, 1837. After his three terms as governor, William Marcy served as secretary of war under President Polk and as secretary of state under President Pierce.

The unusual spelling of Adirondak Loj resulted because its builder was Melvil Dewey, who championed the concept of "simplified spelling."

Adirondack State Park, created by the New York Legislature in 1892, encompasses more than 6 million acres of both private and state-owned lands. The 2.5 million-acre Adirondack Forest Preserve is state-owned land within the state park.

In 1901 Vice President Theodore Roosevelt was descending Mount Marcy when he learned that President McKinley had been shot and was near death. As Roosevelt rushed to return to civilization, word came that McKinley had died and Roosevelt had become president.

Natural History Notes

The Nature Museum at Adirondak Loj contains specimens of mosses, lichens, birds' nests, rocks, and other Adirondack features.

The High Peaks region supports a wide variety of flora and fauna. More than 100 species of wildflowers and approximately 95 species of trees and shrubs are found in the area. In addition to numerous small mammals, the High Peaks Region is home to moose, white-tailed deer, black bear, bobcat, coyote, raccoon, beaver, red fox, gray fox, and cottontail rabbit. More than 150 species of birds are also found in the High Peaks Region.

North Carolina

Mount Mitchell

6,684 Feet

County
Yancey

Location
Approximately 30 miles NE of Asheville in the Mount Mitchell State Park area of Pisgah National Forest.

Hiking
Primary Route: 0.1 miles, round trip, on trail.
Alternate Route 1: 11.2 miles, round trip, on trail.
Alternate Route 2: 14.4 miles, round trip, on trail.

Gain
Primary Route: 100 feet, Class 1, easy.
Alternate Route 1: 3,700 feet, Class 1, strenuous.
Alternate Route 2: 5,900 feet, Class 1, strenuous.

Maps
Topographic: Mt. Mitchell, N.C.; Montreat, N.C.; Celo, N.C.; and Old Fort, N.C., all 7½ minute.
National Park Service: Blue Ridge Parkway.
National Forest: Pisgah N.F.; Grandfather, Toecane, and French Broad Ranger Districts; South Toe River Trail Map.
Trails Illustrated: #780, Pisgah National Forest, North Carolina.
Other: Mount Mitchell State Park.

Guidebooks
50 Hikes in the Mountains of North Carolina, by Elizabeth W. Williams and Robert L. Williams III, Backcountry Publications/The Countryman Press, Woodstock, Vermont, 1995.

Parking
Area

Mount
Mitchell

Campground

Service
Area

Park Boundary

Mount Mitchell
State Park

Restaurant

Park
Office

Gate

Stepps
Gap

Mt. Gibbs ▲
Elev. 6,520'

Clingmans ▲
Peak
Elev. 6,530'

128

Potato Knob ▲
Elev. 6,420'

To
Asheville

Blue Ridge Parkway

Gate

Black Mountain
Gap

N
↑

Bald Knob ▲
Elev. 5,410'

|← 1 Mile →|

Mount Mitchell, North Carolina - 6,684 Feet
(Primary Route)

Hiking North Carolina, by Randy Johnson, Falcon Press Publishing Co., Inc., Helena, Montana, 1996.

North Carolina: A Guide to Backcountry Travel and Adventure, by James Bannon, Out There Press, Asheville, North Carolina, 1996.

North Carolina Hiking Trails, by Allen de Hart, Appalachian Mountain Club Books, Boston, Massachusetts, 3d edition, 1996.

Primary Route

Approach ▲ From the junction of the Blue Ridge Parkway and U.S. Hwy 70 E of Asheville, proceed N on the Blue Ridge Parkway for 27.2 miles to State Route 128 on the left (Blue Ridge Parkway Milepost 355.4). Turn left (N) on Route 128 and continue 4.7 miles to the Mount Mitchell State Park parking area at the end of the road.

Route ▲ From the parking area, hike up to the observation tower, which is on the highpoint. The USGS benchmark is immediately s of the tower.

Alternate Route 1: Mount Mitchell Trail

Approach ▲ From the junction of the Blue Ridge Parkway and U.S. Hwy 70 E of Asheville, proceed N on the Blue Ridge Parkway for 38.6 miles to State Route 80 (Blue Ridge Parkway Milepost 344). Turn left (w) on Route 80 and continue 2.3 miles to Forest Route 472 on the left; it is a paved road at this point. Turn left (s) on Forest Route 472, which becomes a gravel road in 1.0 miles, and proceed 2.9 miles, staying hard right at 2.3 miles, to the Black Mountain Campground. (This point can also be reached by proceeding 4.8 miles N on Forest Route 472 from the Blue Ridge Parkway, Milepost 351.9. See Special Conditions for additional information.) The trailhead is on the left just across the bridge into the campground.

Route ▲ From the Black Mountain Campground, hike generally w on the blue-blazed Mount Mitchell Trail for 5.6 miles to the observation tower, which is on the highpoint. At the 1.5 and 2.7 milepoints, keep right at intersections with the Higgins Bald Ground Trail, a side trail to the Higgins Bald Ground cabin site. The Mount Mitchell Trail crosses the Buncombe Horse Range Trail at 4.0 miles. At 5.4 miles, bear left on the Mount Mitchell Tower Trail and continue 0.2 miles to the observation tower. The USGS benchmark is immediately s of the tower.

Alternate Route 2: Colbert Ridge Trail/Black Mountain Crest Trail

Approach ▲ From the junction of the Blue Ridge Parkway and U.S. Hwy 70 E of Asheville, proceed N on the Blue Ridge Parkway for 38.6 miles to State Route 80 (Blue Ridge Parkway Milepost 344). Turn left (w) on Route 80 and continue 5.7 miles W then N, passing Carolina Hemlocks Recreation Area at 5.4 miles, to Colbert Creek Road on the left. This point is 0.1 miles N of the bridge across the South Toe River. Turn hard left onto Colbert Creek Road and continue 0.3 miles to a small parking area on the right and the obscure trailhead.

Route ▲ Hike generally WNW on the white-blazed Colbert Ridge Trail for 3.7 miles to the junction with the Black Mountain Crest Trail at Deep Gap. Stay left, uphill, at a minor trail junction at 0.2 miles. Turn left on the unblazed Black Mountain Crest Trail and continue S along the crest for 3.5 miles to the Mount Mitchell State Park parking area. From the parking area, hike up to the observation tower, which is on the highpoint. The USGS benchmark is immediately S of the tower.

Special Conditions

The Blue Ridge Parkway is a 469-mile throughway joining Shenandoah National Park and Great Smoky Mountains National Park. Most facilities and services along the parkway are open May 1 through October. The parkway is subject to closure for repair. From November through mid-April it is often cold and icy atop the mountains, and sections of the parkway are frequently closed to travel. Forest Route 472 from the Blue Ridge Parkway, Milepost 351.9 (see Alternate Route 1), is gated at the parkway and near the Black Mountain Campground entrance. It is usually open during the spring and summer months. Information can be obtained from the National Park Service, Blue Ridge Parkway, 400 BB&T Building, Asheville, NC 28801 (828/298-0398), or the Blue Ridge Parkway website, www.nps.gov/blri/.

Mount Mitchell State Park is usually open year-round, weather permitting. The gate across State Route 128 is opened at 8:00 A.M. and is closed at times ranging from 6:00 P.M. to 8:00 P.M., depending on the time of year. Information can be obtained from Mount Mitchell State Park, Route 5, Box 700, Burnsville, NC 28714 (828/675-4611).

The national forest maps may be obtained by contacting Pisgah National Forest, Toecane Ranger District, P.O. Box 128, U.S. Hwy 19E By-Pass, Burnsville, NC 28714 (828/682-6146).

There is no water available along the trails. Carry all that you will require. The trail routes can be done as one-way hikes with a car shuttle. They may also be combined with a car shuttle to provide a one-way loop trip. The Black Mountain Crest Trail continues N from Deep Gap 8.5 miles along the crest to a trailhead at Bowlen's Creek Road, State Secondary Route 1109.

Mount Mitchell lookout tower.

Historical Notes

The Black Mountains receive their name from the evergreen forest of spruce and fir that covers the peaks of the range.

Mount Mitchell, the most prominent peak in the Black Mountains, is the highest mountain E of the Mississippi River. It was named in honor of Dr. Elisha Mitchell (1793–1857), a clergyman and University of North Carolina professor who explored the mountain. On trips during 1835, 1838, and 1844, Dr. Mitchell, using barometric pressure readings, determined the height of the mountain to be 6,672 feet.

In 1855 North Carolina senator Thomas L. Clingman, for whom Clingmans Dome, the highpoint of Tennessee, is named and a former student of Dr. Mitchell's, stated that he, not Dr. Mitchell, was the first to measure the height of the tallest peak in the Black Mountains. Further, Senator Clingman said that Dr. Mitchell had measured another peak.

In June 1857 Dr. Mitchell returned to the Black Mountains to verify his measurements and support his claim. During this trip he decided to visit William Riddle and Big Tom Wilson on the other side of the mountain. While hiking across the mountain, he fell to his death from a cliff above a 40-foot waterfall. When Dr. Mitchell did not return to his camp at the appointed time, a search was instituted. Big Tom Wilson, whose uncle had guided Dr. Mitchell in 1835 and who was a famous hunter and mountaineer, led the search. Dr. Mitchell's body was found in a deep pool at the base of the waterfall.

Dr. Mitchell was buried at the First Presbyterian Church Cemetery in Asheville. A year later he was reburied on the mountain that now bore his name. His grave is at the base of the observation tower.

As a matter of interest, there is a lesser peak in the Black Mountains approximately 2.3 miles s of Mount Mitchell called Clingmans Peak, presumably named for Senator Clingman.

Natural History Notes

The Black Mountains are the highest range in the eastern United States, with nine peaks above 6,000 feet. Although the Black Mountains are higher than the nearby Blue Ridge of the Great Smoky Mountains, the length and breadth of the Black Mountains do not equal those of the Blue Ridge.

Before extensive logging operations in the early 1900s, the slopes of the Black Mountains were covered with a forest of red spruce, and Fraser fir dominated the peaks. Logging operations and fires destroyed much of the coniferous forest. Today fire cherry, oak, hickory, and mountain maple have become established where the spruce and fir forest was disturbed. Plants such as blueberry, mountain raspberry, red elder, and bush honeysuckle and wildflowers such as ox-eye daisy, white snakeroot, purple-fringed orchid, and purple turtlehead are abundant. Some plants and animals found on Mount Mitchell, such as the boomer (red squirrel), Fraser fir, and red spruce, represent relict species from an era when the climate was significantly colder.

The fauna of Mount Mitchell is also diverse. More than 90 species of birds have been recorded in the park. Mammals include white-tailed deer, black bear, bobcat, gray fox, and striped skunk.

North Dakota

White Butte

3,506 Feet

County
Slope

Location
Approximately 7 miles s of Amidon.

Hiking
2.0 miles, round trip, cross-country.

Gain
400 feet, Class 1, easy.

Maps
Topographic: Amidon, N.Dak., 7½ minute.

Primary Route
   Approach ▲ From junction of U.S. Hwy 85 and Main Street in the center of Amidon, proceed E on Hwy 85 for 2.0 miles to a gravel road. Turn
right (s) on the gravel road and continue 5.0 miles to a gravel road on the
right. Turn right (w) and proceed 1.0 miles to a farmhouse off to the left.
Turn into the farm driveway and park. This is the farm of Joseph and
Angeline Van Daele, who own the property surrounding White Butte. Ask
permission of the Van Daeles to cross their property to hike to White
Butte. Once permission is granted, proceed back out the driveway and
immediately turn right (s) on a farm road (two tire tracks) along the E side
of the fence line. Continue s approximately 0.7 miles and park beyond an
old house on the right.
   Route ▲ Hike s on the farm road along the fence approximately 350
yards to a gate. Cross over to the w side of the N-S fence line and continue

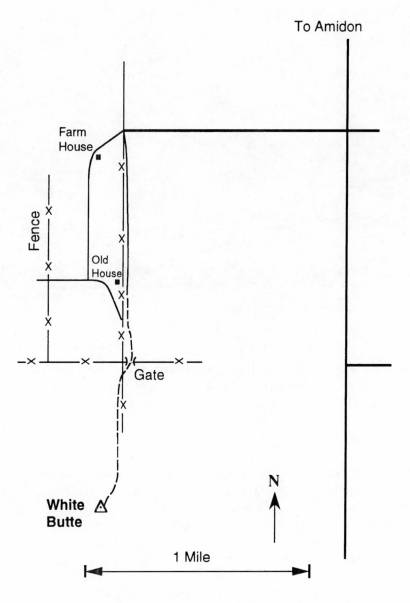

To Amidon

Farm House

Fence

Old House

Gate

X

N

White Butte

1 Mile

White Butte, North Dakota - 3,506 Feet

The view from the summit of White Butte.

along the fence line to a faint trail, which leads to the highpoint. The one-way distance is approximately 1 mile. The USGS benchmark is mounted on a pipe at the highpoint.

Special Conditions

The Van Daeles would prefer that permission be obtained to cross their property. It can be done in person or by telephone. The Van Daeles' phone number is 701/879-6236. However, in the event no one is home to grant permission, it is not mandatory. Remember, White Butte is on private property. Please respect the rights of the property owner.

There is a highway sign along U.S. Hwy 85 approximately 0.8 miles E of the center of Amidon that indicates White Butte. It points S to the high-point.

Be alert for rattlesnakes in the area. They are very common, and close encounters occur frequently.

Historical Notes

The name, White Butte, is descriptive of the white rock and soil con-taining bentonite, which constitutes strata of the buttes in the region. North Dakota's Badlands feature buttes ranging in color from putty gold to blazing red.

Old Indian burial grounds have been found on White Butte.

Natural History Notes

The region around White Butte supports a variety of birds and mammals, including sage grouse, sharptailed grouse, ruffed grouse, golden eagle, prairie falcon, pheasant, dove, mule deer, antelope, prairie dog, and rabbit. Lizards and rattlesnakes are common reptiles in the area.

Ohio

Campbell Hill

1,549 Feet

County
Logan

Location
Approximately 2 miles ENE of Bellefontaine.

Hiking
Drive-up.

Gain
Drive-up.

Maps
Topographic: Zanesfield, Ohio, 7½ minute.

Guidebooks
50 Hikes in Ohio: Day Hikes and Backpacks throughout the Buckeye State, by Ralph Ramey, Backcountry Publications/The Countryman Press, Woodstock, Vermont, 2d edition, 1997.

Primary Route
Approach ▲ From the junction of U.S. Hwy 33 and State Route 540 approximately 1.5 miles E of Bellefontaine, proceed E on Route 540 for 0.6 miles to the Ohio Hi-Point Career Center on the right. Enter the fenced facility and follow the road to the obvious highpoint, which has a flagpole that can be seen from Route 540. Park in the area near the flagpole.

Route ▲ The USGS benchmark is immediately s of the flagpole.

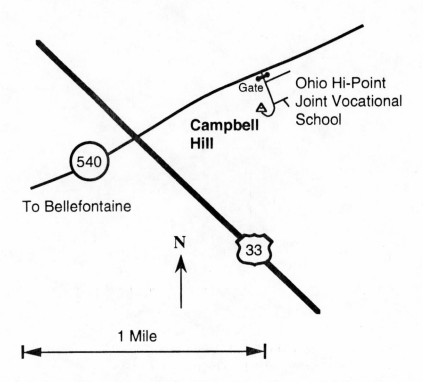

Campbell Hill, Ohio - 1,549 Feet

Special Conditions

The Campbell Hill complex is currently occupied by the Ohio Hi-Point Career Center. This is the Ohio Hi-Point Joint Vocational School, which is operated by the Joint Vocational School District and serves five adjacent counties. Permission to enter the property is not required during normal operating hours. The gate is open from 7:00 A.M. to 11:00 P.M. Monday through Friday during the normal school year, nominally September through May. The summer hours are 7:00 A.M. to 10:00 P.M. Monday through Friday. The facility is usually closed on Saturday and Sunday. Permission is required to enter the facility during the closed hours. For permission and/or information, contact the Ohio Hi-Point Career Center, 2280 State Route 540, Bellefontaine, OH 43311 (937/599-3010).

The highpoint of Ohio was once a Nike missile site.

Historical Notes

Campbell Hill was named for Edward Campbell, who once owned the land. Before it became the Ohio Hi-Point Joint Vocational School, this site was occupied by the Bellefontaine Air Force Station. Now the various buildings surrounding the highpoint are used by the school.

Oklahoma

Black Mesa

4,973 Feet

County
Cimarron

Location
Approximately 35 miles NW of Boise City in Black Mesa Nature Preserve.

Hiking
8.6 miles, round trip, on an old dirt road and cross-country.

Gain
775 feet, Class 1, moderate.

Maps
Topographic: Kenton, Okla.-Colo., 7½ minute.

Primary Route
Approach ▲ From the small grocery store in Kenton, proceed E on County Road 325 for 0.6 miles to a paved road on the left with a sign indicating the way to Colorado. Turn left (N) and continue 5.0 miles to the Black Mesa Preserve parking area on the left. Turn left (SW) into the parking area and park near the trailhead.

Route ▲ Hike generally W on the trail, an old ranch road, for 2.2 miles to the point where the trail turns sharply S. Continue 1.0 miles as the trail approaches and then winds up to the top of the mesa. Once on top of Black Mesa, continue 1.1 miles S then SW to the 9-foot native granite monument at the highpoint. There is also a USGS benchmark at the highpoint.

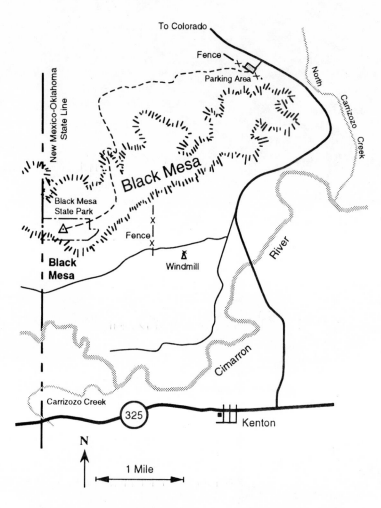

Black Mesa, Oklahoma - 4,973 Feet

Special Conditions

Most of the land that the trail passes over was acquired by the Nature Conservancy in January 1991. The 1,500 acres north of and on Black Mesa have been deeded to the Oklahoma Tourism and Recreation Department. Black Mesa Preserve is operated jointly by the Nature Conservancy and Black Mesa State Park, which is a part of the Oklahoma Tourism and Recreation Department. The preserve is open from dawn to dusk. One should allow about four hours for the round trip from the parking area. This is rattlesnake country. Be alert when hiking and climbing around and on Black Mesa.

Monument at Oklahoma's highpoint.

Kenton Mercantile, the combination grocery store/post office/restaurant/gas station in Kenton, is owned and operated by Allan Griggs. It is worth a stop for the good food and conversation. A nice certificate is available to commemorate one's climb of Black Mesa. For information, contact Kenton Mercantile, HC-1, Box 54, Kenton OK 73946 (580/261-7447).

For information on Black Mesa Preserve, contact the Nature Conservancy Oklahoma Field Office, 23 West 4th Street, Suite 200, Tulsa, OK 74103 (918/585-1117), or Black Mesa State Park, HC-1, Box 8, Kenton, OK 73946 (580/426-2222).

Historical Notes

During the mid-1800s Black Mesa was a part of No Man's Land, a favorite outlaw hideout. The tracks of settlers' wagon trains are still visible near Kenton.

Black Mesa's name is derived from the color of the volcanic ash found in the region.

Natural History Notes

Black Mesa is one of the largest mesas in the world, extending over 40 miles into New Mexico and Colorado. It is a basalt-capped plateau formed by the flow of an ancient volcano. Dakota sandstone underlies the basalt. Both rocks erode vertically, resulting in steep, talus-strewn slopes that merge abruptly with the plains below.

Black Mesa supports 31 state rare species—23 plants and 8 animals—and 4 vegetation community types. The Black Mesa area is where the Rocky Mountains meet the short-grass prairie. Some of the birds found here are golden eagle, scaled quail, black-billed magpie, and pinyon jay. Black bear, bobcat, mule deer, and antelope are some of the mammals frequently seen. Look out for rattlesnakes, which may be active at any time, particularly during the morning and afternoon.

Oregon

Mount Hood

11,239 Feet

County
Clackamas–Hood River

Location
Approximately 50 miles ESE of Portland in the Mount Hood Wilderness
Area of Mount Hood National Forest.

Hiking
8.0 miles, round trip, on trail, cross-country, and on snow and glaciers.

Gain
5,300 feet, Class 4, strenuous.

Maps
Topographic: Mount Hood South, Oreg., 7½ minute.
National Forest: Mount Hood N.F.; Mount Hood Wilderness, Mount
Hood N.F.
Other: Mount Hood Wilderness Map and Columbia Gorge/Mt. Hood
Recreation Map, Geo-Graphics, Beaverton, Oregon.

Guidebooks
*Hikes and Walks on Mt. Hood: Government Camp and Timberline Lodge
Area*, by Sonia Buist and Emily Keller, Lolits Press, Portland, Oregon,
1995.
Hiking Oregon, by Donna Lynn Ikenberry, Falcon Press Publishing Co.,
Inc., Helena, Montana, revised edition, 1997.
100 Hikes in Oregon, by Rhonda Ostertag and George Ostertag, The
Mountaineers, Seattle, Washington, 1992.

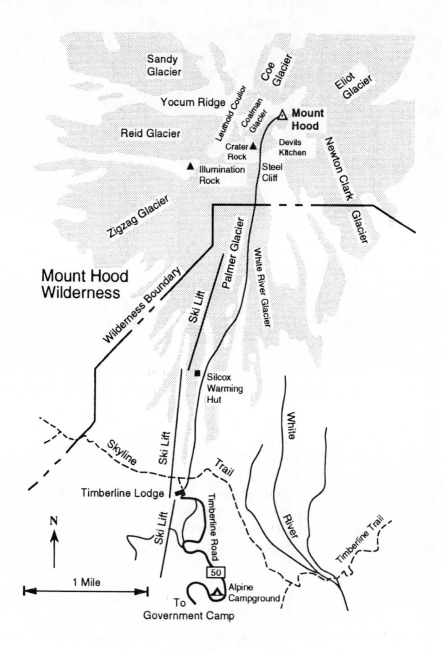

Sandy
Glacier

Coe
Glacier

Eliot
Glacier

Yocum Ridge

Leuthold Couloir

Coalman
Glacier

Mount
Hood

Reid Glacier

Crater
Rock

Devils
Kitchen

Newton Clark

△ Illumination
Rock

Steel
Cliff

Glacier

Zigzag Glacier

Palmer Glacier

White River Glacier

Mount Hood
Wilderness

Wilderness Boundary

Ski Lift

■ Silcox
Warming
Hut

White

Skyline

Ski Lift

Trail

Timberline Lodge

Timberline Road

River

Timberline Trail

N

Ski Lift

50

Alpine
Campground

1 Mile

To
Government Camp

Mount Hood, Oregon - 11,239 Feet

The Pacific Crest Trail, Volume 2: Oregon and Washington, by Jeffrey P. Schaffer et al., Wilderness Press, Berkeley, California, 5th edition, 1990.

Timberline Trail #600—A Brief Guide (brochure), by the U.S. Forest Service, Mount Hood National Forest, Sandy, Oregon, 1992.

Primary Route: Hogsback, South Side

Approach ▲ From Portland, proceed E on U.S. Hwy 26 approximately 53 miles to Timberline Road, 0.5 miles E of the village of Government Camp. Turn left (N) and continue 6 miles to Timberline Lodge.

Route ▲ From Timberline Lodge (6,000 feet), hike up the snowfield along the E edge of the ski area to Silcox Hut (6,950 feet). From Silcox Hut continue up the Palmer Glacier to the upper terminal of the Palmer Express Chair Lift (8,540 feet). Continue up past the E face of Crater Rock to the Devils Kitchen (10,400 feet), also known as "the lower hot rocks." Climb the Hogsback, a high ridge of snow that extends from the N side of Crater Rock to the crater wall. A large crevasse across the wall has to be crossed, either to the right or to the left, depending on conditions. Above the crevasse, climb directly to the summit ridge and the summit. If it is not covered by snow, a register may be found approximately 20 feet NE of the summit.

Special Conditions

Mount Hood is in the Mount Hood Wilderness, and wilderness permits are required. Climbers are required to register and pick up a self-issue permit at the Wy'east Day Lodge across from Timberline Lodge before starting the climb. Be sure to check out on return. Mount Hood is usually climbed in one day with a very early (12:00 A.M. to 2:00 A.M.) start in order to be off the summit by early morning. The usual climbing season is May through early July to minimize the danger from avalanches and rock fall. In fact, the Forest Service discourages climbing after July 4. Climbing on the snow and glaciers requires roped travel and the use of an ice ax and crampons. There is no water available on Mount Hood. It is necessary to melt snow or carry all the water required.

Most climbing injuries and deaths on Mount Hood have occurred when inexperienced and ill-equipped climbers were hit by falling rock, ice, or snow; fell down steep slopes or into crevasses; or became disoriented owing to poor weather conditions. Weather on Mount Hood is extremely changeable, and summer storms are not uncommon. Snowstorms can occur in any month of the year. Before starting the climb, be aware of the local weather forecast. If the ski lifts are in operation and skiing is in progress, climbers should ascend and descend along the E edge of the patrolled ski area between Timberline Lodge and the upper terminal of the Palmer Express Chair Lift.

Mount Hood.

A Snocat is available for hire that will transport climbers from Timberline Lodge to the upper terminal of the Palmer Express Chair Lift. This saves approximately 2,500 feet of elevation gain during the climb. The Snocat can carry 8 to 10 climbers, depending on the amount of equipment (the 2000 fare is $90.00 for the one-way trip). If the Snocat is used, each party is required to carry a Mountain Locator Unit or a cellular phone. For information and reservations, contact the Mountain Department of the Timberline Lodge (503/272-3311).

Information on Timberline Lodge and the available accommodations can be obtained from the Timberline Lodge and Ski Resort, Timberline Lodge, OR 97028 (503/272-3311). For lodge reservations, call 800/547-1406.

Information on recreation in the Mount Hood region, hiking guide sheets, and the national forest maps can be obtained from the Mount Hood Information Center, Mount Hood National Forest, P.O. Box 819, 65000 East Highway 26, Welches, OR 97067 (888/622-4822 or 503/622-7674). The Mount Hood website, www.fs.fed.us/r6/mthood, also has current information.

In addition to the technical climbs of Mount Hood, there is an extensive trail system in the Mount Hood region. Two major trails that are near the base of Mount Hood are the Timberline Trail and the Pacific Crest National Scenic Trail. The Timberline Trail is almost 41 miles long and circles Mount

Hood. It was constructed primarily by the Civilian Conservation Corps during the 1930s. The trail is generally snow-free from mid-July until September, except for a few persistent snowbanks on the northeast side. On the south and west side of the mountain, the Timberline and Pacific Crest Trails share tread for approximately 17 miles. The Pacific Crest National Scenic Trail extends some 2,640 miles from Mexico to Canada along the Pacific Crest through California, Oregon, and Washington. Approximately 461 miles of the trail are in Oregon. In 1968 Congress passed the National Trails System Act, which made the Pacific Crest and the Appalachian Trails the first two National Scenic Trails.

Historical Notes

On October 29, 1792, Lt. William Robert Broughton, a member of Captain George Vancouver's British expedition to the Northwest, sighted and named Mount Hood in honor of Rear Admiral Samuel Hood (1724–1816), of the British Royal Navy. In 1780 Hood was sent with a squadron of ships to reinforce the Royal Navy's presence in the West Indies. He remained second in command in American waters until the peace of 1773. In 1788 Rear Admiral Hood was made a member of the Board of Admiralty, and while in this position he signed the original instructions for Captain Vancouver's voyage.

Mount Hood is the most frequently climbed glaciated peak in North America and, with the possible exception of Mount Fuji in Japan, may be the most climbed glaciated peak in the world. It is estimated that more than ten thousand people climb the mountain every year.

Timberline Lodge was built by hand in 1935–37 from native materials: stone from quarries in nearby canyons, and giant timbers from the surrounding forest. The lodge timbers were hand-hewn with a broadax and then smoothed with an adze. Skilled stonemasons chiseled carefully selected stones into shape and lifted them into place by hand with the aid of a block and tackle. The unique gates, light fixtures, ornaments, andirons, and furniture were hand wrought under the direction of a master blacksmith. The U.S. Forest Service and a private architectural consultant were responsible for the design and engineering. The roof, which rises to a central point, was designed to complement the shape of Mount Hood and its ridges. What began as a Roosevelt-era Work Projects Administration project has become a unique National Historic Landmark.

Natural History Notes

Mount Hood is a stratovolcano, a peak composed of loosely consolidated ash, pumice, and rock fragments interbedded with thin flows of lava and mud. Stratovolcanoes grow explosively to considerable heights but are easily eroded. Mount Hood was last active in August 1907, when a dense column of smoke was observed rising from near Crater Rock.

Douglas fir is the dominant tree species on Mount Hood, followed, as elevation increases, by western hemlock, Pacific silver fir, noble fir, mountain hemlock, subalpine fir, and whitebark pine. The ground cover includes huckleberry, vinemaple, Oregon grape, and rhododendron.

Nearly 150 species of birds have been observed around Mount Hood, ranging from hummingbirds to bald eagles. Mammals living on the slopes of Mount Hood include marmot, weasel, coyote, bear, mountain lion, deer, and elk.

Timberline is the highest elevation at which trees will grow and is marked by an abrupt change in vegetation. Above this line of dwarf trees, the land is bare and intensely lighted. These stunted trees, often hundreds of years old, are called krummholz, a German word meaning "elfin timber" or "crooked wood." Many plants and animals live at or near timberline. Short, cool summers; sandy, rocky soil; winds greater than 60 miles per hour; and winter snow depths of more than 20 feet create an extremely severe environment. Plants have adapted to these conditions by hugging the ground in compact ball-like forms to reduce the effects of wind and cold, regrowing from the same root stalk each year, and having either thick waxy leaves or small hairy ones to retard water evaporation. The small animals at timberline spend considerable time eating or storing food for the long winter, during which they hibernate, eat their stored food, or tunnel underground for roots and tubers. Ears, nose, feet, and tail are usually small or fur-coated in order to expose less surface area to the bitter cold.

Guides/Outfitters

Art of Adventure, Inc., P.O. Box 250, Government Camp, OR 97028 (503/662-0202).

Northwest School of Survival, Inc., P.O. Box 1465, Sandy, OR 97055 (503/668-8264).

Timberline Mountain Guides, Inc., P.O. Box 19, Powell Butte, OR 97753 (800/464-7704 or 541/548-2799).

Pennsylvania

Mount Davis

3,213 Feet

County
Somerset

Location
Approximately 8 miles wnw of Salisbury in the Forbes State Forest.

Hiking
Primary Route: Drive-up.
Alternate Route: Drive-up.

Gain
Primary Route: Drive-up.
Alternate Route: Drive-up.

Maps
Topographic: Markleton, Pa., and Meyersdale, Pa., both 7½ minute.
State Forest: Forbes State Forest Public Use Map.

Guidebooks
50 Hikes in Western Pennsylvania: Walks and Day Hikes from the Laurel Highlands to Lake Erie, by Tom Thwaites, Backcountry Publications/The Countryman Press, Woodstock, Vermont, 3d edition, 2000.
Mount Davis (booklet), by the Bureau of Forestry, Forbes State Forest, Laughlintown, Pennsylvania, 1997.
Pennsylvania Hiking Trails, edited by David Raphael, The Keystone Trails Association, Cogan Station, Pennsylvania, 11th edition, 1993.

Primary Route
Approach ▲ From the intersection of U.S. Hwy 219 and Broadway Street in Meyersdale, proceed w on Broadway Street, bearing right onto

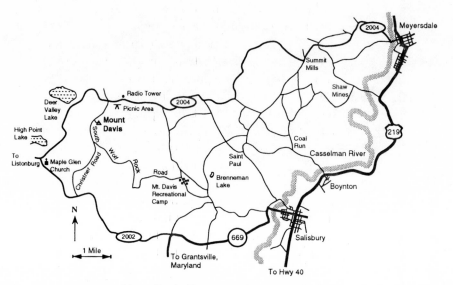

Mount Davis, Pennsylvania - 3,213 Feet

State Secondary Route 2004 shortly after crossing the railroad tracks, for 9.6 miles to South Wolf Rock Road on the left. South Wolf Rock Road is 0.4 miles w of the Mount Davis picnic area and the large microwave relay station that is across the road from the picnic area. Turn left (s) on South Wolf Rock Road and continue 0.7 miles to the Mount Davis parking area on the left.

Route ▲ A large boulder a few yards w of the observation tower is the highpoint. The usgs benchmark is on this boulder.

Alternate Route

Approach ▲ From the intersection of U.S. Hwy 219 and State Route 669 in Salisbury, proceed w on Route 669 for 3.9 miles. Route 669 turns left (s) immediately after crossing the Casselman River. At the 3.9 mile-point, Route 669 turns s, and State Secondary Route 2002 continues w. Proceed w on Route 2002 for 3.2 miles to Christner Road, a gravel road, on the right. Turn right (N) on Christner Road and continue 2.3 miles, keeping left at a junction at 1.7 miles, to the Mount Davis parking area on the right.

Route ▲ A large boulder a few yards w of the observation tower is the highpoint. The usgs benchmark is on this boulder.

Special Conditions

The Primary Route approach to Mount Davis is well marked with brown and white "Point of Interest" signs at every decision point. The Mount Davis Natural Area is open year-round, weather permitting.

There is a small trail system in the Mount Davis Natural Area and the surrounding territory. The trails range from ¼ mile to 3 miles in length. The trails may be combined to provide several interesting loop hikes in the area. Information, maps, and the Mount Davis booklet may be obtained by contacting the Bureau of Forestry, Forbes State Forest, P.O. Box 519, Laughlintown, PA 15655 (724/238-1200).

There are several trail systems in western Pennsylvania described in the guidebooks listed above. One nearby trail of note is the Laurel Highlands Hiking Trail, located approximately 15 miles west of Mount Davis. This 70-mile hiking and backpacking trail extends from Ohiopyle to near Johnstown in Laurel Ridge State Park. For information and a map, contact Laurel Ridge State Park, RD #3, Box 246, Rockwood, PA 15557 (814/455-3744).

Historical Notes

The Mount Davis Natural Area, within Forbes State Forest, comprises 581 acres surrounding the highpoint on Negro Mountain. There are plaques on boulders at the highpoint depicting the history and flora of the area. Most of the 5,685 acres in the area making up a portion of Forbes State Forest were purchased in 1929. Additional small parcels were purchased from the heirs of John N. Davis in 1931 and 1942.

In 1921 the U.S. Geological Survey determined that the crest of Negro Mountain was the highest point in Pennsylvania. On June 18, 1921, the crest was officially named Mount Davis for John Nelson Davis (1835–1913). Mr. Davis served in the Civil War in 1862 and 1863 and was an educator in Pennsylvania for 22 years, a land surveyor who laid out and constructed additions to the town of Salisbury, a naturalist, and a former owner of the Mount Davis area.

An interesting historical note regarding Negro Mountain is that in 1753 Lieutenant George Washington, only 21 years old at the time, explored the Casselman River and climbed Negro Mountain. Lieutenant Washington was with Christopher Gist, who, in 1751, had explored the area looking for a route between Will's Creek and the Monongahela River area. Later, during the French and Indian War (1754–59), troops under the command of Colonel Washington and General Braddock occasionally used the route until the end of the war.

The observation tower at the highpoint was constructed in 1935 by the Civilian Conservation Corps. Several of the area trails and roads, the pic-

Pennsylvania's highpoint.

nic area, and the buildings now used as the Forest Headquarters were built by the ccc between June 1933 and July 1937.

Natural History Notes

The trees of the highpoint area include black birch, yellow birch, quaking aspen, black cherry, fire cherry, black gum, red maple, chestnut oak, red oak, scarlet oak, sassafras, serviceberry, and pitch pine.

Unusual patterns of small concentric stone rings formed by frost heaving over thousands of years occur near the base of the observation tower.

Rhode Island

Jerimoth Hill

812 Feet

County
Providence

Location
Approximately 20 miles W of Providence.

Hiking
Drive-up (see Special Conditions).

Gain
Drive-up.

Maps
Topographic: East Killingly, Conn.-R.I., 7½ minute.

Guidebooks
AMC *Massachusetts and Rhode Island Trail Guide*, edited by Jeff Wulfson, Appalachian Mountain Club, Boston, Massachusetts, 7th edition, 1995.
Hiking Southern New England, by George Ostertag et al., Falcon Press Publishing Co., Inc., Helena, Montana, 1997.

Primary Route
Approach ▲ From the point where State Route 101 crosses the Connecticut–Rhode Island state line, proceed E on Route 101 for 0.8 miles to a point where the road starts downhill and there is a sign on the N side of the road reading, "Jerimoth Hill, State's Highest Point, 812 Feet." This point is 5.5 miles W of the junction of State Routes 101 and 102. Park along the side of the road.

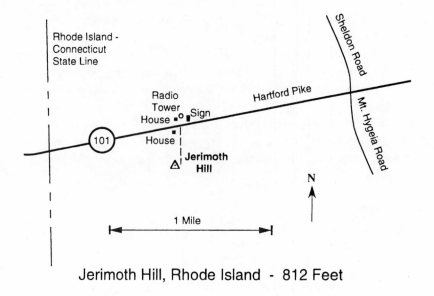

Jerimoth Hill, Rhode Island - 812 Feet

Route ▲ Except as stated in Special Conditions below, the Highpointers Club recognizes the sign on the N side of State Route 101 as the highpoint of Rhode Island.

Special Conditions

There have been serious access problems associated with Jerimoth Hill. Recently, members of the Highpointers Club have been successful in gaining permission to cross private land to get to the highpoint. However, permission to cross is granted only on specific dates. For 2000, the permitted access dates are February 20, May 28, July 2, and September 3. If you visit the Rhode Island highpoint other than on the listed dates, do not attempt to go to the actual highpoint. The Highpointers Club recognizes the sign on the N side of State Route 101 as the official highpoint if you are visiting the highpoint at other times of the year. Please respect the rights of the property owner and do not abuse the access privilege. The Highpointers Club will continue to try to improve the access situation, and the cooperation of all Highpointers is necessary to ensure that the Rhode Island highpoint remains open to the public, if only on specified dates. Access dates beyond those listed above will be posted on the official Highpointers website, www.highpointers.org. When it is permissible to go to the actual highpoint, the route is as follows: On the s side of State Route 101 and a few yards w of the sign, there is a leaf-covered road leading s. There is a brown house immediately w of the dirt road. Hike s along the dirt road approximately 235 yards to the highpoint on the right, which is a boulder with a small rock cairn on top.

The area where the highpoint is actually located is the property of Brown University. Again, please respect the rights of the property owner. There are three USGS benchmarks in the immediate area, none of which is on the highpoint.

In the event of problems with access to Jerimoth Hill, remember that the Highpointers Club has since 1993 recognized the sign on the N side of Route 101 as an acceptable alternative to the actual highpoint and continues to do so.

Historical Notes

The name Jerimoth Hill is derived from Jerimoth, a biblical name and a Hebrew word meaning "elevation."

South Carolina

Sassafras Mountain

3,560 Feet

County
Pickens

Location
Approximately 14 miles N of Pickens.

Hiking
Primary Route: Drive-up.
Alternate Route: 18.4 miles, round trip, on trail.

Gain
Primary Route: Drive-up.
Alternate Route: 4,200 feet, Class 1, strenuous.

Maps
Topographic: Eastatoe Gap, S.C.-N.C., and Table Rock, S.C.-N.C., both 7½ minute.
Other: Foothills Trail Map, Duke Power Company.

Guidebooks
Guide to the Foothills Trail, edited by Karen LaFleur, The Foothills Trail Conference, Greenville, South Carolina, 2d edition, 1988.
Hiking South Carolina, by John F. Clark and John Dantzler, Falcon Press Publishing Co., Inc., Helena, Montana, 1998.
Hiking South Carolina Trails, by Allen de Hart, The Globe Pequot Press, Old Saybrook, Connecticut, 4th edition, 1998.

Primary Route
Approach ▲ From the center of Pickens where U.S. Hwy 178 turns N, proceed N on Hwy 178 for 15.6 miles to the hamlet of Rocky Bottom and

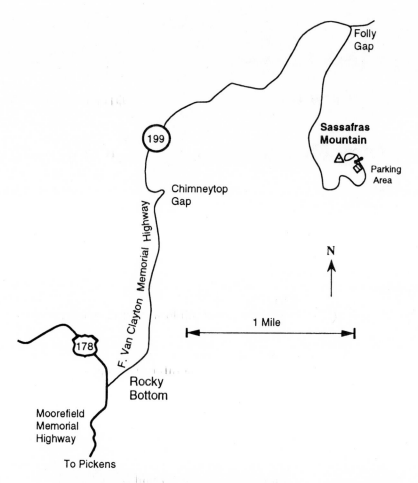

Sassafras Mountain, South Carolina - 3,560 Feet

(Primary Route)

the F. Van Clayton Memorial Hwy (County Road 199) on the right. (This point is 3.3 miles s of the North Carolina–South Carolina state line via Hwy 178.) Turn right (NE) on County Road 199 and continue 4.7 miles to a locked gate. Park in the large parking area on the left.

Route ▲ Walk up the road approximately 100 yards to the highpoint. The USGS benchmark is at the E end of the cleared area within the loop at the end of the road. The actual highpoint appears to be next to a tree that is in front of a Foothills Trail sign approximately 25 yards w of the benchmark.

Alternate Route: Pinnacle Trail/Foothills Trail

Approach ▲ From the center of Pickens where U.S. Hwy 178 turns N, proceed N on U.S. Hwy 178 for 8.5 miles to State Route 11. Turn right (E) on Route 11 and continue 4.1 miles to the west gate of Table Rock State Park. Enter the west gate of the park and proceed 1.3 miles to the Pinnacle Lake parking area on the right across from the nature center.

Route ▲ From the nature center, hike generally W along the yellow-blazed Pinnacle Trail for 3.1 miles, bearing left at trail junctions at 0.2 miles, 0.8 miles, and 2.4 miles, to the junction with the Foothills Trail. Bear left onto the white-blazed Foothills Trail and continue 6.1 miles along the Foothills Trail to the road to the summit. Turn right and walk up the road approximately 150 yards to the highpoint. The USGS benchmark is at the E end of the cleared area within the loop at the end of the road. The actual highpoint appears to be next to a tree that is in front of a Foothills Trail sign approximately 25 yards W of the benchmark.

Special Conditions

Table Rock State Park is open year-round. The entrance gates are open from 7:00 A.M. to 10:00 P.M. during Daylight Saving time, and they close at 9:00 P.M. the remainder of the year. There is a daily fee of $1.50 per person over 15 years of age. There are cabins and campgrounds in the park. No camping is allowed in Table Rock State Park except in the established campgrounds. Wilderness camping is permitted outside the park boundaries. In addition to the cabins and camping sites, park facilities include a picnic area, a restaurant, a meeting building, playground equipment, and a nature center. Activities include nature/history programs, lake fishing, nature and hiking trails, and seasonal activities such as swimming and canoeing. If a stay at the park is planned, reservations are strongly recommended. For trail and other information, and cabin or camping reservations, contact Table Rock State Park, 158 E. Ellison Lane, Pickens, SC 29671 (864/878-9813).

Three trails begin at the nature center. Initially, the trees are marked with three colored blazes: red, yellow, and green. The Pinnacle Trail is marked with yellow blazes, and the Foothills Trail is marked with white blazes. From the Pinnacle Trail/Foothills Trail junction, it is 0.2 miles to the summit of Pinnacle Mountain. At 3,425 feet, Pinnacle Mountain is the second highest peak in South Carolina. Water availability along the trails is seasonal. Inquire at the park office about current water availability and be sure to carry enough water to meet your needs. The Pinnacle Trail/Foothills Trail route can be done as a one-way hike with a car shuttle.

In addition to the Pinnacle Trail, there is an extensive trail system within Table Rock State Park. This trail system has been designated a

National Recreation Trail. Beyond Sassafras Mountain, the Foothills Trail, which is the longest trail in South Carolina, extends another 65 miles to Oconee State Park. Development of the Foothills Trail, which began in 1968, has been primarily a joint effort of the U.S. Forest Service, the Duke Power Company, the Sierra Club, and the Foothills Trail Conference. Information on the Foothills Trail can be obtained from the Foothills Trail Conference, P.O. Box 3041, Greenville, SC 29620 (864/232-2681).

Additional information on the Foothills Trail can be obtained from the Duke Power Company, Shoreline Management, P.O. Box 33189, Charlotte, NC 28242 (704/382-8575)

Historical Notes

Sassafras Mountain was named for the sassafras tree, *Sassafras albidum*, which is abundant in the region. The roots and root bark supply oil of sassafras (used to perfume soap) and sassafras tea and have been used to flavor root beer. Explorers and colonists thought the aromatic root bark was a panacea and shipped quantities to Europe.

This area was once dotted with Cherokee Indian villages. The Cherokee gave upper South Carolina a descriptive name—*Sah-ka-na-ga*, or "Great Blue Hills of God." Table Rock Mountain, being a prominent feature, was used as a natural landmark.

Table Rock State Park, consisting of more than 3,000 acres surrounding Table Rock Mountain, was developed in 1935 by the Civilian Conservation Corps. The quality of the work and the lasting importance of the CCC's contribution were recognized in 1989 when Table Rock State Park was placed on the National Register of Historic Places.

Once known as Cherokee Path, the 130-mile Cherokee Foothills Scenic Highway, SC State Route 11, was the route used by the Cherokee and the English and French fur traders. It now offers a scenic alternative to driving I-85 through South Carolina's Upcountry.

Natural History Notes

Mammals found in the area include black bear, white-tailed deer, raccoon, opossum, gray and red fox, bobcat, and spotted skunk. Wild turkey and ruffed grouse roam the forest floor. Two common poisonous snakes in the area are the copperhead and the timber rattlesnake.

Shrubs and trees include mountain laurel, rhododendron, oak, pine, hickory, and hemlock.

South Dakota

Harney Peak

7,242 Feet

County
Pennington

Location
Approximately 8 miles NNE of Custer in the Black Elk Wilderness Area of Black Hills National Forest.

Hiking
Primary Route: 6.8 miles, round trip, on trail.
Alternate Route 1: 5.8 miles, round trip, on trail.
Alternate Route 2: 10.8 miles, round trip, on trail.

Gain
Primary Route: 1,600 feet, Class 1, moderate.
Alternate Route 1: 1,500 feet, Class 1, moderate.
Alternate Route 2: 2,500 feet, Class 1, strenuous.

Maps
Topographic: Custer, S.Dak., and Hill City, S.Dak., both 7½ minute.
Trails Illustrated: #238, Black Hills Southeast, South Dakota.
National Forest: Black Hills N.F.; Trail Guide to Your Black Hills National Forest, Black Hills N.F.
Other: Hiking Map of the Norbeck Wildlife Preserve, The Black Hills Group, Sierra Club, Rapid City, South Dakota.

Guidebooks
Exploring the Black Hills and Badlands, by Hiram Rogers, Johnson Books, Boulder, Colorado, revised edition, 1999.
Hiking South Dakota's Black Hills Country, by Bert Gildart and Jane Gildart, Falcon Press Publishing Co., Inc., Helena, Montana, 1996.

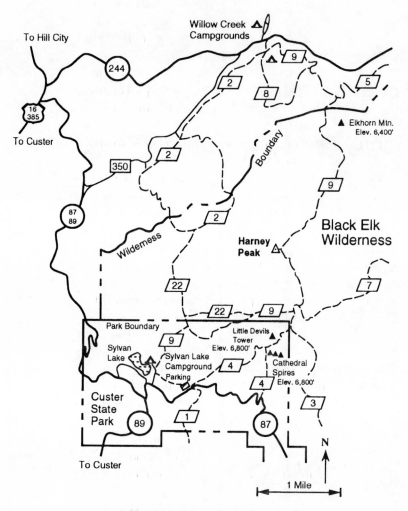

Harney Peak, South Dakota - 7,242 Feet

Primary Route: Harney–Sylvan Lake Trail (Southern Approach)

   Approach ▲ From the junction of U.S. Hwy 16 Alt. and State Route 89 approximately 1 mile E of Custer, proceed N on Route 89 for 6 miles to a junction with State Route 87, immediately S of Sylvan Lake. Turn right on Route 87 (Needles Highway), almost immediately arriving at the Custer State Park entrance, and proceed N and then E 0.3 miles to the Sylvan Lake Day Use Parking Area across from Sylvan Lake.

Route ▲ From the Sylvan Lake trailhead, hike NE on the well-signed Harney–Sylvan Lake Trail for 3.4 miles to the summit. The Harney–Sylvan Lake Trail is Trail No. 9 and is blazed with the number 9. Be alert for the number 9 blazes at trail junctions at 0.7 miles, 2.4 miles, and 2.6 miles. The summit is several yards w of the trail location on Harney Peak. A lookout tower is at the highpoint. The actual highpoint is a natural rock at the base of the tower on the SE side. This point is below the tower "balcony." There is no USGS benchmark on the summit.

Alternate Route 1: Cathedral Spires Trail/Harney–Sylvan Lake Trail

Approach ▲ From the junction of U.S. Hwy 16 Alt. and State Route 89 approximately 1 mile E of Custer, proceed N on Route 89 for 6 miles to a junction with State Route 87 immediately s of Sylvan Lake. Turn right on Route 87 (Needles Highway), almost immediately arriving at the Custer State Park entrance, and proceed N and then E 2.5 miles to the Cathedral Spires Trailhead Parking Area on the left. (This is the third trailhead for the Cathedral Spires Trail along Route 87. See Special Conditions for additional information.)

Route ▲ Hike N on the well-signed Cathedral Spires Trail for 1.9 miles to the junction with the Harney–Sylvan Lake Trail, bearing right at the junction at 0.7 miles with the Cathedral Spires Trail coming from the Little Devils Tower Trailhead, and bearing left at the junction with the Norbeck Trail. The Cathedral Spires Trail is Trail No. 4 and is blazed with the number 4. Similarly, the Harney–Sylvan Lake Trail is Trail No. 9 and is blazed with the number 9. Continue N on the Harney–Sylvan Lake Trail for 1.0 miles to the summit. The summit is several yards w of the trail location on Harney Peak. A lookout tower is at the highpoint. The actual highpoint is a natural rock at the base of the tower on the SE side. This point is below the tower "balcony." There is no USGS benchmark on the summit.

Alternate Route 2: Harney–Sylvan Lake Trail (Northern Approach)

Approach ▲ From Hill City, proceed s on U.S. Hwy 16/385 approximately 3 miles to State Route 244 on the left. Turn left (E) on Route 244 and continue 3.1 miles to Willow Creek Horse Camp on the right. Turn right (s) into the camp and proceed to the day-use parking area just before reaching the horse camp.

Route ▲ From the horse camp, hike initially NE then s on the well-signed Harney–Sylvan Lake Trail for 5.4 miles to the summit. The Harney–Sylvan Lake Trail is Trail No. 9 and is blazed with the number 9. Bear right at the junction with the Willow Creek–Rushmore Trail at 1.8 miles. The summit is several yards w of the trail location on Harney Peak. A lookout tower is at the highpoint. The actual highpoint is a

Harney Peak lookout tower, built in the 1930s.

natural rock at the base of the tower on the SE side. This point is below the tower "balcony." There is no USGS benchmark on the summit.

Special Conditions

Harney Peak is in the Black Elk Wilderness, but wilderness permits are not required.

Near the highpoint there is a pillar approximately 100 yards NW of the tower. This pillar may look higher than the rock at the base of the tower. Nevertheless, a recent survey indicates that the rock at the tower is slightly more than 2 feet higher than the pillar.

Relative to Alternate Route 1, there are three trailheads that provide access to the Cathedral Spires Trail along Route 87. One is located at the farthest SE corner of the Sylvan Lake Day Use Parking Area; a second, called the Little Devils Tower Trailhead, is located approximately 1 mile E along Route 87; and the third is as described in the Alternate Route 1 approach.

The Harney Range Trail System consists of 55 miles of trails that wind their way through the Black Hills and approach Harney Peak from several directions. The trails are numbered and are blazed with the trail number. The trails can be combined in several ways, with and without a car shuttle, to create one-way or loop routes. In addition to the trails in the Harney

Range Trail System, the Centennial Trail passes through the region. This trail, officially opened in June 1989 to commemorate the one hundredth anniversary of South Dakota statehood, spans some 111 miles in a north-south direction from Wind Cave National Park to Bear Butte State Park northeast of Sturgis. The Centennial Trail is blazed with a combination of brown fiberglass posts and gray diamonds fastened to trees. Maps and other information on the Harney Range Trail System and the Centennial Trail can be obtained by contacting Black Hills National Forest, Custer–Elk Mountain Ranger District, 330 Mount Rushmore Road, Custer, SD 57730-1928 (605/673-4853), or Black Hills National Forest, Pactola-Harney Ranger District, 23939 Highway 385, Hill City, SD 57745-6516 (605/574-2534).

The trailheads for the Primary Route and Alternate Route 1 are within Custer State Park. There is an entrance fee to Custer State Park. Camping, cabins, and lodge facilities are available. For information and rates, contact Custer State Park, HC 83, Box 70, Custer, SD 57730 (605/255-4515). For lodging or camping reservations, call 800/658-3530 or 800/710-2267, respectively.

Historical Notes

Harney Peak was named in 1857 by Lt. Gouverneur Kemble Warren for his commanding officer, Gen. William Selby Harney (1800–1889). In 1855, Lieutenant Warren was a topographical engineer with the punitive expedition of General Harney. In 1857, he was making a topographical survey of the southern Black Hills region. General Harney had conducted military operations throughout the region at various times and may have sighted the peak in 1855. Harney was commander of the military district of the Black Hills in 1878.

The name Black Hills comes from the Lakota Sioux name *Paha Sapa*, which roughly translates as "hills that are black," a reference to the dark green, almost black, color of the ponderosa pine–covered hills when seen from a distance. The Black Hills are a relatively small forested oasis in stark contrast with the surrounding grassland.

The stone lookout tower on the summit was constructed by the Civilian Conservation Corps in 1938–39 and is a testament to the excellent work done during that program. The tower was manned as a fire lookout from 1938 to 1967. In 1982 the lookout tower, along with the adjacent dam and pumphouse, was placed on the National Registry of Historic Places. One can ascend the tower for a magnificent view of the surrounding area.

Members of the Custer Black Hills Expedition of 1874 attempted to climb Harney Peak. Darkness fell, and the expedition failed to reach the summit. It is generally accepted that the first white man to reach the summit was Dr. Valentine T. McGillycuddy on July 5, 1875. At the time, Dr.

McGillycuddy was an army surgeon with the Jenney Scientific Expedition. After leaving the army, he became the first Indian agent at Pine Ridge, from 1879 to 1886. From 1894 to 1897, Dr. McGillycuddy served as the first president of the South Dakota School of Mines. At his request, after his death, his ashes were placed in a crypt in the stone stairway leading to the lookout tower. A plaque embedded in the base of the tower steps marks the location of the crypt.

Mount Rushmore, with the carved faces of Presidents Washington, Jefferson, Lincoln, and Theodore Roosevelt, is approximately 5 miles E of Harney Peak.

Natural History Notes

Harney Peak lies within the 35,000-acre Norbeck Wildlife Preserve. The 9,824-acre Black Elk Wilderness, named for Black Elk, the Oglala Sioux holy man, is completely contained within the preserve. The preserve is home to a variety of wildlife, including elk, deer, bison, mountain goat, antelope, bighorn sheep, coyote, and bobcat. Among the small mammals are raccoon, skunk, marmot, prairie dog, squirrel, chipmunk, and mole. Birds frequently seen include turkey, various hawks, golden eagle, prairie falcon, mountain bluebird, red crossbill, and western tanager. Reptiles, including the prairie rattlesnake, and amphibians also inhabit the area.

Tennessee

Clingmans Dome

6,643 Feet

County
Sevier

Location
Approximately 22 miles s of Gatlinburg in Great Smoky Mountains National Park.

Hiking
Primary Route: 1.0 miles, round trip, on paved trail.
Alternate Route: 15.8 miles, round trip, on trail.

Gain
Primary Route: 330 feet, Class 1, easy.
Alternate Route: 2,370 feet, Class 1, moderate.

Maps
Topographic: Clingmans Dome, N.C.-Tenn., 7½ minute.
Trails Illustrated: #229, Great Smoky Mountains National Park, Tennessee–North Carolina.
National Park: Great Smoky Mountains, Great Smoky Mountains National Park; Great Smoky Mountains Trail Map.
Other: Hiking Map and Guide, Great Smoky Mountains National Park, Earthwalk Press, La Jolla, California.

Guidebooks
Appalachian Trail Guide to Tennessee–North Carolina, edited by Nancy Shoffner, Appalachian Trail Conference, Harpers Ferry, West Virginia, 11th edition, 1995.

196

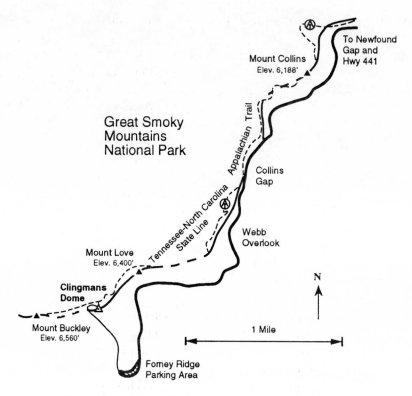

Clingmans Dome, Tennessee - 6,643 Feet

Hiking Great Smoky Mountains, by Rodney Albright and Priscilla Albright, The Globe Pequot Press, Old Saybrook, Connecticut, 4th edition, 1999.

Hiking Tennessee, by Kelley Roark, Falcon Press Publishing Co., Inc., Helena, Montana, 1996.

Hiking Tennessee Trails, by Evan Means et al., The Globe Pequot Press, Old Saybrook, Connecticut, 5th edition, 1998.

Hiking Trails of the Smokies, edited by Don DeFoe et al., Great Smoky Mountains Natural History Association, Gatlinburg, Tennessee, revised edition, 1995.

Primary Route

Approach ▲ From the Sugarlands Visitor Center on the w edge of Great Smoky Mountains National Park, proceed s on U.S. Hwy 441 for 13.2 miles to Clingmans Dome Road. (This point is 16.1 miles N of the junction of the Blue Ridge Parkway and U.S. Hwy 441 N of Cherokee, N.C., also via U.S. Hwy 441.) Turn right (W) on Clingmans Dome Road and continue 7.0 miles to the Forney Ridge parking area. Ample parking is available.

Route ▲ From the W end of the parking area, hike 0.5 miles N on the well-signed paved trail to the lookout tower at the summit.

Alternate Route: Appalachian Trail

Approach ▲ From the Sugarlands Visitor Center on the W edge of Great Smoky Mountains National Park, proceed S on U.S. Hwy 441 for 13.0 miles to Newfound Gap. (This point is 16.3 miles N of the junction of the Blue Ridge Parkway and U.S. Hwy 441 N of Cherokee, N.C., also via U.S. Hwy 441.) Park in the Newfound Gap parking area on the left.

Route ▲ From the parking area, cross U.S. Hwy 441 and hike SW along the white-blazed Appalachian Trail for 7.9 miles to the Clingmans Dome Trail. Follow the Clingmans Dome Trail 50 yards to the lookout tower at the summit. **Note:** This can be done as a one-way hike with a car shuttle.

Special Conditions

There is no entrance fee to the Great Smoky Mountains National Park. Clingmans Dome Road is usually open from April through November unless winter conditions dictate otherwise. For current conditions and national park information and maps, contact Superintendents Office, Great Smoky Mountains National Park, 107 Park Headquarters Road, Gatlinburg, TN 37738 (865/436-1200).

The Appalachian Trail extends for 278 miles in Tennessee. About 210 miles of the trail are shared with North Carolina since the track follows or runs close to the North Carolina–Tennessee state line. The entire Appalachian Trail is marked for travel in both directions with white paint blazes on trees or poles and rocks, about 2 inches wide and 6 inches high. Two blazes, one above the other, are a signal of an important trail feature such as an obscure turn or a change in route. Side trails from the Appalachian Trail are usually blazed in blue. Information on hiking the Appalachian Trail can be obtained from the Appalachian Trail Conference, P.O. Box 807, 799 Washington Street, Harpers Ferry, WV 25425-0807 (304/535-6331).

In addition to the Appalachian Trail, which traverses almost the entire park in an east-west direction, there is an extensive backcountry trail system in Great Smoky Mountains National Park. There are several campsites and shelters in the backcountry. A backcountry use permit is required for all overnight camping. The permits are free and may be obtained at any ranger station. Some of the campsites are rationed, that is, the number

Lookout tower atop Clingman's Dome.

of occupants is limited, and these campsites must be reserved in advance. To reserve a site or shelter, call 865/436-1231. For an official backcountry map that lists all regulations and the locations of campsites and shelters, stop at any park visitor center or call 865/436-0120.

Historical Notes

Originally known as Smoky Dome, Clingmans Dome was renamed for Thomas Lanier Clingman (1812–97), who was a United States senator representing North Carolina from 1858 until the beginning of the Civil War. During the Civil War he attained the rank of brigadier general.

Thomas Clingman devoted his life to politics and the development of the mountain region of North Carolina. In his later years much of his activity was directed toward exploiting the resources of western North Carolina, an area he had explored during the 1850s. Although it is the highpoint of Tennessee, Clingmans Dome is situated astride the North Carolina–Tennessee state line and is, therefore, part of North Carolina.

An interesting sidelight regarding Thomas Clingman is the 1855 controversy he initiated over measuring the height of Mount Mitchell, the highpoint of North Carolina. He stated that he, and not Dr. Elisha Mitchell, was the first to measure the elevation of the highest point in the Black Mountains. Trying to resolve the controversy in 1857 cost Dr. Mitchell his life. (See North Carolina Historical Notes for more information.)

The Alternate Route affords the opportunity to hike along a portion of the Appalachian Trail. This trail, completed in 1937, extends over 2,150 miles from Mount Katahdin, the highpoint of Maine, to Springer Mountain in northern Georgia.

There are a number of historic sites preserved throughout the park. Historic homes are found at Cades Cove, Cataloochee, and the Oconaluftee Mountain Farm Museum. Several other historic sites can be reached via short trails.

Small-scale mining was conducted at Alum Cave Bluff periodically from the early 1800s through the Civil War. The miners were likely looking for alum, epsom salts, and saltpeter.

Natural History Notes

The Great Smoky Mountains are a wildlands sanctuary supporting a wide variety of flora and fauna. The name "Smoky" comes from the smoke-like haze that envelops the mountains. Because of the fertile soils and abundant rain, more than 1,500 species of flowering plants are found in the park.

The fauna includes numerous small mammals, a wide variety of birds (both resident and migrating species), and large mammals such as deer and black bear. Various species of reptiles live in the Smokies, including the poisonous northern copperhead snake and the timber rattlesnake.

In 1991 the endangered red wolf was reintroduced to the park. This program has been successful in that three breeding pairs of red wolves are now roaming the park.

Texas

Guadalupe Peak
8,749 Feet

County
Culberson

Location
Approximately 110 miles E of El Paso in Guadalupe Mountains National Park.

Hiking
8.4 miles, round trip, on trail.

Gain
2,950 feet, Class 1, moderate.

Maps
Topographic: Guadalupe Peak, Tex., 7½ minute.
Trails Illustrated: #203, Guadalupe Mountains National Park, Texas.
National Park: Guadalupe Mountains—Official Map and Guide, Guadalupe Mountains National Park.

Guidebooks
Hiking Carlsbad Caverns and Guadalupe Mountains National Parks, by Bill Schneider, Falcon Press Publishing Co., Inc., Helena, Montana, 1996.
Hiking Texas, by Laurence Parent, Falcon Press Publishing Co., Inc., Helena, Montana, 1996.
Hiking the Southwest—Arizona, New Mexico, and West Texas, by Dave Ganci, Sierra Club Books, San Francisco, California, 1983.
The Sierra Club Guides to the National Parks—Desert Southwest, by James V. Murfin et al., Random House, Inc., New York, New York, 1995.

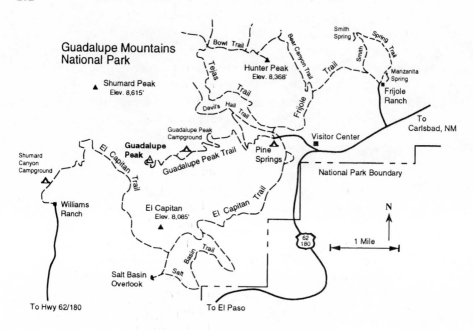

Guadalupe Peak, Texas - 8,749 Feet

Trails of the Guadalupes—A Hiker's Guide to the Trails of the Guadalupe Mountains National Park, by Don Kurtz and William D. Goran, Environmental Associates, Champaign, Illinois, 2d edition, 1982.

Primary Route: Guadalupe Peak Trail

Approach ▲ From the junction of U.S. Hwy 62/180 and State Route 54, proceed N on U.S. Hwy 62/180 for 3.0 miles to the Guadalupe Mountains National Park Visitor Center and Park Headquarters. Turn left (w) and proceed 0.5 miles to the Pine Springs Campground parking area. Park in the area designated for hikers.

Route ▲ From the w end of the parking area, follow the well-signed Guadalupe Peak Trail 4.2 miles to the summit, where a memorial monument will be found.

Special Conditions

The Guadalupe Peak Trail is a relatively new trail and is not shown on the topographic map. This is a desert peak; take sufficient water. There is no water available in the backcountry.

With more than 80 miles of trails and ten backcountry campgrounds, Guadalupe Mountains National Park offers excellent backpacking opportunities. All overnight backpackers must obtain a free backcountry use permit issued at the Visitor Center.

The Pine Springs Campground has twenty tent sites and eighteen RV sites (no hookups). The fee is $7.00 per night per site. The campground may be full; call ahead for current status.

Information, maps, and trail guides can be obtained from Guadalupe Mountains National Park, HC 60, Box 400, Salt Flat, TX 79847 (915/828-3251), or the Guadalupe Mountains National Park website, www.nps.gov/gumo/.

Historical Notes

The Pinery, a short walk from the visitor center, is the location of a station on the famous Butterfield Overland Mail Route. The first stagecoach arrived at this station on September 28, 1858. All that remains today are tumbled stone ruins and a granite historical marker.

The Guadalupe Mountains provided one of the last strongholds of the Mescalero Apache led by Geronimo and Victorio.

The memorial on the summit of Guadalupe Peak is a six-foot-high, stainless steel triangular pyramid. It was dedicated on September 28, 1958, as a tribute to pioneer pilots who traveled the early air routes over the Guadalupe Mountains. The three bronze plaques represent (1) the Great Seal of the Post Office Department, (2) the insignia of American Airlines, the only air carrier to serve all the terminals and many of the stations of the Butterfield Overland Mail route that eventually had airmail service, and (3) the pioneer pilot within a compass card.

The Guadalupe Mountains and Guadalupe Peak are named for Our Lady of Guadalupe, the patron saint of Mexico. The name occurs often in areas formerly belonging to Spain or Mexico.

Natural History Notes

The mountains making up Guadalupe Peak and El Capitan are part of an ancient marine fossil reef. The reef was formed about 250 million years ago, when a vast tropical ocean covered parts of Texas and New Mexico. Over millions of years, calcareous sponges, algae, and other lime-secreting marine organisms, along with lime precipitated from the seawater, built up to form the 400-mile-long, horseshoe-shaped Capitan Reef. After the sea evaporated and as the reef subsided, it was buried in a thick blanket of sediments and mineral salts. Millions of years later, a mountain-building uplift exposed part of the reef. This is the same limestone formation that has been eroded by underground water to form the Carlsbad Caverns in New Mexico.

From the Chihuahuan Desert to the conifer forest, the mountain's diverse ecosystems are home to more than 900 species of plants, 60 species

El Capitan from the summit of Guadalupe Peak.

of mammals, 289 species of birds, and 55 species of reptiles and amphibians. Wildlife includes jackrabbit, coyote, porcupine, gray fox, mule deer, mountain lion, and elk. Among the trees found in the canyons is the rare Texas madrone. It is easily identified by its smooth reddish bark and evergreen leaves.

Four of Texas's highest peaks are in Guadalupe Mountains National Park, as well as many unnamed peaks over 8,000 feet. The four highest are Guadalupe Peak, 8,749 feet; Bush Mountain, 8,631 feet; Shumard Peak, 8,615 feet; and Hunter Peak, 8,368 feet.

Utah

Kings Peak

13,528 Feet

County
Duchesne

Location
Approximately 42 miles N of Duchesne in the High Uintas Wilderness Area of the Ashley and Wasatch National Forests.

Hiking
28.8 miles, round trip, on trail and cross-country.

Gain
5,350 feet, Class 2, strenuous.

Maps
Topographic: Kings Peak, Utah; Gilbert Peak NE, Utah-Wyo.; Bridger Lake, Utah-Wyo.; and Mount Powell, Utah, all 7½ minute.
Trails Illustrated: #711, High Uintas Wilderness, Utah.
National Forest: Ashley N.F.; Wasatch N.F.; High Uintas Wilderness, Wasatch and Ashley N.F.

Guidebooks
High in Utah, by Michael R. Weibel and Dan Miller, University of Utah Press, Salt Lake City, Utah, 1999.
High Uinta Trails, by Mel Davis and John Vernath, University of Utah Press, Salt Lake City, Utah, 1993.
Hiking Utah, by Dave Hall, Falcon Press Publishing Co., Inc., Helena, Montana, revised edition, 1996.
Hiking Utah's Summits, by Paula Huff and Tom Wharton, Falcon Press Publishing Co., Inc., Helena, Montana, 1997.

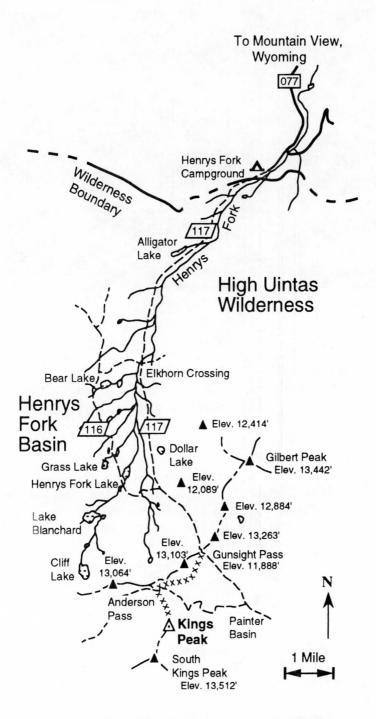

To Mountain View,
Wyoming

077

Henrys Fork
Campground

Wilderness
Boundary

117

Alligator
Lake

Henrys Fork

High Uintas
Wilderness

Bear Lake

Elkhorn Crossing

Henrys
Fork
Basin

116   117

▲ Elev. 12,414'

Dollar
Lake

Gilbert Peak
Elev. 13,442'

Grass Lake

Henrys Fork Lake

▲ Elev.
12,089'

▲ Elev. 12,884'

Lake
Blanchard

▲ Elev. 13,263'

Cliff
Lake

Elev.
13,064'

Elev.
13,103'

Gunsight Pass
Elev. 11,888'

Anderson
Pass

N

△ Kings
Peak

Painter
Basin

▲ South
Kings Peak
Elev. 13,512'

1 Mile

Kings Peak, Utah - 13,528 Feet

Summit of Kings Peak.

Primary Route: Henrys Fork Trail/Highline Trail

Approach ▲ From the junction of I-80 and Wyoming State Route 414 (I-80 Exit 40), 35 miles E of Evanston, Wyo., proceed s on Route 414 for 6.0 miles to Wyoming State Route 410 in Mountain View, Wyo. Route 414 turns w through Mountain View and becomes Route 410 as the road turns s at the w end of town. Continue on Route 410 toward Robertson, Wyo., for 6.7 miles to the point where Route 410 turns w. At this point, Uinta County Road 283, which soon becomes Forest Road 072, continues s. Proceed s on County Road 283 (Forest Road 072) toward Grahams Reservoir and Bridger Lake for 12.1 miles to Forest Road 017 on the left. Stay left at the junction with Forest Road 075 at 7.2 miles. Turn left on Forest Road 017 and continue s 6.8 miles to Forest Road 077. (This point can also be reached by proceeding 12 miles sw on Forest Road 077 from Lonetree, Wyo.) Proceed s on Forest Road 077 for 2.8 miles to the road to Henrys Fork Campground on the right. Turn right and continue 0.6 miles to Henrys Fork Campground.

Route ▲ From Henrys Fork Campground, hike generally s on the Henrys Fork Trail (Trail No. 117) for 9.6 miles to Gunsight Pass. At 5.2 miles, the trail crosses Henrys Fork at Elkhorn Crossing. There is a bridge approximately 150 yards downstream from the point where the trail breaks out of the forest and encounters a sign indicating Elkhorn Crossing. From Gunsight Pass, continue SE on the trail 1.6 miles to the Highline Trail. Turn right (w) on the Highline Trail and hike 2.6 miles to Anderson Pass. From

Anderson Pass, hike SE up the ridge 0.6 miles to the summit. The summit is marked with a plaque. There is no USGS benchmark.

Special Conditions

Kings Peak is in the High Uintas Wilderness, but wilderness permits are not required. Although the forest roads are gravel, they are very well maintained and suitable for any type of vehicle.

Kings Peak has been done as a very long dayhike. It is usually done as a 2- to 5-day backpack. There are numerous campsites available along the trail and near the many lakes in Henrys Fork Basin. The usual climbing season for Kings Peak is July through mid-September.

From Gunsight Pass to Anderson Pass, it is possible to contour near the 11,800-foot level across a boulder field intersecting the Highline Trail W to Anderson Pass. This saves over a mile each way.

Thunderstorms are common in the summer and early fall. Take care not to get caught on the peaks or exposed ridges during one of these storms.

Information and the national forest maps can be obtained from Wasatch-Cache National Forest, 8226 Federal Bldg., 125 S. State Street, Salt Lake City, UT 84128 (801/524-3900)

Historical Notes

Kings Peak was named in honor of Clarence King (1842–1901), an American geologist who helped open up the West with his survey of mineral resources along the route of the Union Pacific Railroad. King was director of the project, which lasted from 1867 to 1877. When Congress established the United States Geological Survey in 1878, King was named the director. He is commemorated on the plaque on the summit.

Natural History Notes

Henrys Fork Basin is a scenic alpine area with excellent trout fishing in the lakes. The forested areas of the High Uintas include lodgepole pine, Engelmann spruce, Douglas fir, and subalpine fir. Quaking aspen occur on the lower slopes. Alpine and subalpine plant communities cover about one-third of the area.

A variety of mammals, birds, fish, and a few reptiles occupy this area. The High Uintas are a summer habitat for elk, deer, and moose. Carnivores include black bear, mountain lion, bobcat, coyote, pine marten, fox, mink, and weasel. Other small mammals are squirrel, porcupine, hoary marmot, and pika.

Guides/Outfitters

North Slope Outfitters, c/o Ken Aimone, 35689 Business Loop 80, Fort Bridger, WY 82933 (307/782-3898).

Vermont

Mount Mansfield

4,393 Feet

County
Lamoille

Location
Approximately 8 miles ENE of Stowe in Mount Mansfield State Forest.

Hiking
Primary Route: 4.6 miles, round trip, on trail.
Alternate Route 1: 2.8 miles, round trip, on trail.
Alternate Route 2: 1.6 miles, round trip, on trail.

Gain
Primary Route: 2,800 feet, Class 2, moderate.
Alternate Route 1: 550 feet, Class 1, easy.
Alternate Route 2: 750 feet, Class 2, moderate.

Maps
Topographic: Mount Mansfield, Vt., 7½ minute.
Other: Trail Map of Mount Mansfield, The Green Mountain Club, Inc., Waterbury Center, Vermont.

Guidebooks
Appalachian Trail Guide to New Hampshire–Vermont, edited by Jim Barnes, The Appalachian Trail Conference, Harpers Ferry, West Virginia, 4th edition, 1985.

Day Hiker's Guide to Vermont, edited by Brian T. Fitzgerald and Robert P. Lindemann, The Green Mountain Club, Inc., Waterbury Center, Vermont, 3d edition, 1987.

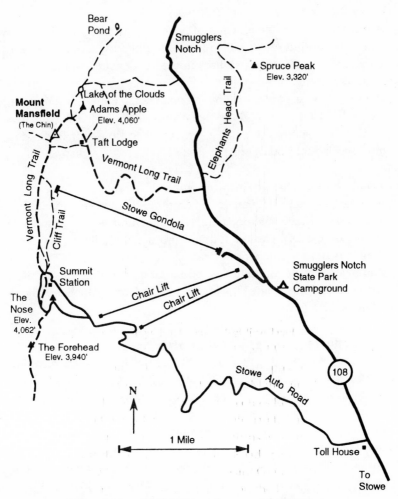

Mount Mansfield, Vermont - 4,393 Feet

50 Hikes in Vermont: Walks, Hikes, and Overnights in the Green Mountain State, by Bob Lindemann and Mary Deaett, Backcountry Publications/The Countryman Press, Woodstock, Vermont, 5th edition, 1997.

Hiking Vermont, by Larry B. Pletcher, Falcon Press Publishing Co., Inc., Helena, Montana, 1996.

Long Trail Guide, edited by Sylvia Plumb, The Green Mountain Club, Inc., Waterbury Center, Vermont, 24th edition, 1996.

Primary Route: Vermont Long Trail

Approach ▲ From the junction of State Routes 100 and 108 in Stowe, proceed NW on Route 108 for 8.2 miles to the point where the Long Trail meets Route 108 on the left (W). Park in the parking area on the left, just N of the trail crossing.

Route ▲ Hike 2.3 miles NW on the Long Trail, passing Taft Lodge at 1.7 miles, to the "Chin," the highpoint of Mount Mansfield. The USGS benchmark is on the summit. (For an alternate route from Taft Lodge to the "Chin," see Special Conditions.)

Alternate Route 1: Stowe Auto Toll Road

Approach ▲ From the junction of State Routes 100 and 108 in Stowe, proceed NW on Route 108 for 6.0 miles to the entrance to the Stowe Auto Toll Road on the left. Pay the toll and proceed 4.5 miles to the Summit Station. Park in the main parking area.

Route ▲ From the Summit Station parking area, hike N 1.4 miles on the Long Trail to the "Chin," the highpoint of Mount Mansfield. The USGS benchmark is on the summit.

Alternate Route 2: Stowe Gondola Skyride

Approach ▲ From the junction of State Routes 100 and 108 in Stowe, proceed NW on Route 108 for 7.5 miles to the Stowe Gondola Skyride entrance on the left. Turn left (NW) and continue 0.3 miles to the parking area at the lower gondola terminal. Ride the gondola to the upper terminal.

Route ▲ About 30 yards S of the upper gondola terminal (to the left of the terminal as viewed on the way up), there is a spur trail heading W up the wooded slope. Hike W along this spur trail for 0.1 miles to the Cliff Trail. Turn right (N) and hike along the Cliff Trail for 0.3 miles to the Long Trail. Bear right and hike N along the Long Trail 0.4 miles to the "Chin," the highpoint of Mount Mansfield. The USGS benchmark is on the summit.

Special Conditions

All hiking trails on the mountain are closed by the state of Vermont during the spring "mud season" (mid-April to Memorial Day). This is done to preserve the arctic-alpine tundra area during the rainy season. In addition to the Long Trail, there are several miles of other trails in the Mount Mansfield region. Like the Appalachian Trail, which was inspired by development of the Long Trail, the Long Trail is marked for travel in both directions with white paint blazes on trees or poles and rocks, about 2 inches wide and 6 inches high. Two blazes, one above the other, are a signal of an important trail feature such as an obscure turn or a change in route. Side trails from the Long Trail are usually blazed in blue. Information on hiking in the Mount Mansfield area and the Long Trail can be obtained from the Green Mountain Club, Inc., 4711 Waterbury-Stowe Road, Waterbury Center, VT 05677 (802/244-7037).

The Stowe Auto Toll Road is open from 10:00 A.M. to 5:00 P.M. on a seasonal basis, nominally from mid-May to mid-October. The actual opening and closing dates vary from year to year. The toll is currently $12.00 per vehicle. To obtain up-to-date rates, operating dates, and road condition information, contact the Stowe Auto Toll Road at 802/253-3000.

The Stowe Gondola Skyride is also open from 10:00 A.M. to 5:00 P.M. on a seasonal basis, nominally from mid-May to mid-October. The actual opening and closing dates vary from year to year. The round-trip fare (as of November 1999) is $10.00 per adult, $6.00 per child (6–12), and $8.00 for seniors over 65. The Skyride also offers a family fare of $25.00 (two adults and a maximum of two children). To obtain up-to-date rates and operating dates, contact the Stowe Gondola Skyride at 802/253-3000.

In bad weather, the half-mile Profanity Trail is a recommended alternative to the precipitous Long Trail route between Taft Lodge and the "Chin" (see Primary Route). Although the trail is steep, hence its name, it is sheltered and not as exposed as the Long Trail north of the "Chin." The route from Taft Lodge is as follows: From the s side of Taft Lodge, ascend w via the Profanity Trail for 0.5 miles to the Long Trail just s of the "Chin." Turn right (N) and hike 0.2 miles to the "Chin," the highpoint of Mount Mansfield. The USGS benchmark is on the summit.

The Long Trail and the Appalachian Trail follow the same track for some 100 miles in southern Vermont. The Appalachian Trail traverses Vermont for approximately 146 miles. The entire Appalachian Trail is marked for travel in both directions with white paint blazes on trees or poles and rocks, about 2 inches wide and 6 inches high. Two blazes, one above the other, are a signal of an important trail feature such as an obscure turn or a change in route. Side trails from the Appalachian Trail are usually blazed in blue. Information on hiking the Appalachian Trail can be obtained from the Appalachian Trail Conference, P.O. Box 807, 799 Washington Street, Harpers Ferry, WV 25425-0807 (304/535-6331).

For information on the Stowe area, including accommodations and reservations, contact the Stowe Area Association, Inc., P.O. Box 1320, Main Street, Stowe, VT 05672 (800/24-STOWE).

Historical Notes

Mount Mansfield was named for the township of Mansfield, which was between Stowe on the east and Underhill on the west. Mansfield, Underhill, and Stowe, along with other towns in the area, were granted township in 1763. Mansfield township was named after Lord Mansfield of

England, William Murray, who held the chief justiceship on the king's bench at the time. In 1776 William Murray was also created earl of Mansfield. Mansfield was mostly a mountainous area and had almost no land suitable for farming. In addition, because the Green Mountains run through the center of the township, it was impossible to go from one side to the other. In 1839 the western half of Mansfield was annexed by Underhill. Mansfield town ceased to exist when the eastern half was annexed by Stowe in 1848.

The Primary Route affords the opportunity to hike along a portion of the Long Trail. This 270-mile footpath, completed in 1930, traverses Vermont along the main ridge of the Green Mountains from Massachusetts to Canada. The Long Trail system includes another 175 miles of side trails.

The unusual names for the peaks on Mount Mansfield, such as the "Chin" and the "Nose," are derived from the unique shape of the ridgeline. When viewed from the east, with a little imagination, it resembles the profile of a man's face. The Abenaki Indians called the mountain *Moze-o-de-be-Wadso*, "mountain with the head of a moose."

The Appalachian Trail, completed in 1937, extends over 2,150 miles from Mount Katahdin, the highpoint of Maine, to Springer Mountain in northern Georgia.

Natural History Notes

The summit area of Mount Mansfield supports the largest community of arctic-alpine tundra in Vermont, about 250 acres. The plants in this community are normally found 1,500 miles to the north in Canada. At the lower elevations, the hardwood forests are predominantly maple, beech, yellow birch, and eastern hemlock mixed with other species such as white ash, aspen, and white pine. At higher elevations, the hardwood forest yields to the boreal forest, where balsam fir and red spruce dominate.

Many species of mammals are found in the region, including white-tailed deer, moose, black bear, beaver, and bobcat, in addition to smaller inhabitants. Among the birds, spring and summer visitors include warblers, thrushes, woodpeckers, flickers, and broadwinged hawks. Resident species include ruffed grouse, wild turkey, black-capped chickadee, white-breasted nuthatch, owls, and sharp-shinned hawk.

Virginia

Mount Rogers

5,729 Feet

County
Grayson-Smyth

Location
Approximately 14 miles E of Damascus in the Mount Rogers National Recreation Area of Jefferson National Forest.

Hiking
Primary Route: 8.6 miles, round trip, on trail.
Alternate Route: 8.6 miles, round trip, on trail.

Gain
Primary Route: 1,500 feet, Class 1, moderate.
Alternate Route: 1,500 feet, Class 1, moderate.

Maps
Topographic: Whitetop Mountain, Va., 7½ minute.
National Forest: Jefferson N.F. (South Half); Mount Rogers High Country and Wildernesses; Mount Rogers National Recreation Area.
Appalachian Trail Conference: Appalachian Trail Map 1, Mount Rogers National Recreation Area.

Guidebooks
Appalachian Trail Guide to Southwest Virginia, edited by Vaughn Thomas, Appalachian Trail Conference, Harpers Ferry, West Virginia, 2d edition, 1998.
Hiking Virginia, by Randy Johnson, Falcon Press Publishing Co., Inc., Helena, Montana, 2d edition, 1996.
Hiking Virginia's National Forests, by Karin Wuertz-Schaefer, The Globe Pequot Press, Old Saybrook, Connecticut, 6th edition, 1998.

216

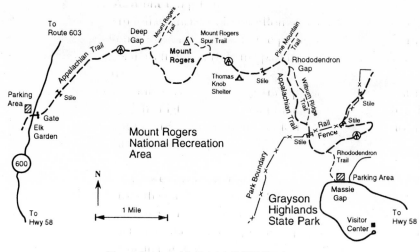

Mount Rogers, Virginia - 5,729 Feet

Trails in Southwest Virginia: James River to New River, by Bryan McDonald et al., Pocahontas Press, Inc., Blacksburg, Virginia, revised edition, 1993.

The Trails of Virginia: Hiking the Old Dominion, by Allen de Hart, University of North Carolina Press, Chapel Hill, North Carolina, revised edition, 1995.

Primary Route: Rhododendron Trail/Appalachian Trail

Approach ▲ From the junction of U.S. Hwy 58 and State Route 16 in Mouth of Wilson, proceed w on U.S. Hwy 58 for 11.5 miles to the Grayson Highlands State Park entrance on the right. (This point is 25.8 miles E of the junction of U.S. Hwy 58 and State Route 91 in Damascus via U.S. Hwy 58.) Turn right (N) and continue on the park road 3.5 miles to the hiker parking area at Massie Gap.

Route ▲ From the parking area, hike N 0.5 miles on the blue-blazed Rhododendron Trail to the Appalachian Trail. Turn left (W) on the white-blazed Appalachian Trail and continue 2.1 miles to Rhododendron Gap. From Rhododendron Gap, continue on the Appalachian Trail 1.2 miles to the signed Mount Rogers Spur Trail, also called the Susan Spillane Memorial Trail, on the right. Turn right (N) and hike up this blue-blazed trail 0.5 miles to the summit, where the USGS benchmark is found.

Alternate Route: Appalachian Trail

Approach ▲ From the junction of U.S. Hwy 58 and State Route 91 at the E end of Damascus, proceed s then immediately E on U.S. Hwy 58 for 10.6 miles to State Route 603, which goes straight ahead and U.S. Hwy 58 again turns s. Continue E on Route 603 for 2.7 miles to State Route 600. Turn right (s) on Route 600 and proceed 5.1 miles to Elk Garden. Park in the small parking area on the right (w). (See Special Conditions for an alternate route to Elk Garden from Mouth of Wilson.)

Route ▲ From the parking area at Elk Garden, cross Route 600, pass through a gate, bear left, and ascend NE across the field toward Mount Rogers via the white-blazed Appalachian Trail 1.8 miles to Deep Gap. Use care in route finding in this area. Be alert for the white blazes. A short distance beyond Deep Gap, the trail makes a sharp right uphill. Continue 2.0 miles from Deep Gap to the signed Mount Rogers Spur Trail, also called the Susan Spillane Memorial Trail, on the left. Turn left (N) and hike up this blue-blazed trail 0.5 miles to the summit, where the USGS benchmark is found.

Special Conditions

The summit of Mount Rogers is in the 5,730-acre Lewis Fork Wilderness. Lewis Fork is one of the most heavily used wilderness areas in Virginia; no permits are required, however.

An alternate approach to Elk Garden from Mouth of Wilson is as follows: From the junction of U.S. Hwy 58 and State Route 16 in Mouth of Wilson, proceed w on U.S. Hwy 58 for 18.9 miles to State Route 600 on the right. Turn right (N) on Route 600 and continue 2.9 miles to Elk Garden. Park in the small parking area on the left (w).

The Appalachian Trail was moved to the Mount Rogers area in 1972. The current alignment of the trail is not shown on the topographic map, and the route identified as the Appalachian Trail is now designated the Iron Mountain Trail. The Appalachian Trail traverses Virginia in a northeast-southwest direction for approximately 546 miles. This is the largest length of the trail in any state. The entire Appalachian Trail is marked for travel in both directions with white paint blazes on trees or poles and rocks, about 2 inches wide and 6 inches high. Two blazes, one above the other, are a signal of an important trail feature such as an obscure turn or a change in route. Side trails from the Appalachian Trail are usually blazed in blue. Information on the Appalachian Trail can be obtained from the Appalachian Trail Conference, P.O. Box 807, 799 Washington Street, Harpers Ferry, WV 25425-0807 (304/535-6331).

The Mount Rogers National Recreation Area was established by Congress on May 31, 1966. It offers a variety of campground and picnic

The trail to Mount Rogers from Grayson Highlands State Park.

areas. The facilities range from primitive to modern. With few exceptions, camping and picnicking is on a first-come, first-served basis. The busy season is nominally May through September. Information on the Mount Rogers National Recreation Area and the national forest maps can be obtained from the Area Ranger, Mount Rogers National Recreation Area, USDA Forest Service, 3714 Hwy 16, Marion, VA 24354 (800/628-7202).

Mount Rogers National Recreation Area covers more than 118,000 acres, and the three highest mountains in Virginia are within its borders. In addition to the Appalachian Trail, there is an extensive trail system with nearly 400 miles of trails in the Mount Rogers National Recreation Area and the surrounding region. Several loop trips or one-way trips, with a car shuttle, can be organized. The two routes listed above can be combined with a car shuttle to create a one-way route from Massie Gap to Elk Garden or vice versa.

Another interesting trail in the area is the 34-mile-long Virginia Creeper Trail. This trail connects Abingdon, Virginia, with the North Carolina–Virginia state line 1.1 miles E of Whitetop Station, Virginia. It began as an Indian footpath and was later used by European pioneers. A railroad was built along the path in the early 1900s. It got its nickname, Virginia Creeper, from the early steam engines that struggled up the steep grades hauling lumber, iron ore, supplies, and passengers. The last train ran on March 31, 1977. Once again a trail, the Virginia Creeper Trail is a multi-

Worn sign at the summit of Mount Rogers.

use trail and has been designated a National Recreation Trail. For more information on the Virginia Creeper Trail, contact the Abingdon Convention and Visitors Bureau, Cummings Street, Abingdon, VA 24210 (800/435-3440).

Grayson Highlands State Park was established in 1965 and covers more than 4,900 acres. There is a nominal fee for parking. Although the campground and visitor center are open on a seasonal basis, access to the Massie Gap parking area is open year-round. Information on Grayson Highlands State Park can be obtained from Grayson Highlands State Park, 829 Grayson Highland Lane, Mouth of Wilson, VA 24363 (540/579-7092).

Historical Notes

Mount Rogers was named for William Barton Rogers (1804–82). He was appointed the first Virginia state geologist in 1835 in the newly organized survey of the state. Along with his younger brother, Henry Darwin Rogers, he charted the geologic structure of the Appalachian Mountains. In 1853 he moved to Boston, and in 1861, largely owing to Rogers's efforts to establish a technical school, the Massachusetts Legislature incorporated the Massachusetts Institute of Technology. When it opened in 1862, Rogers was elected its first president. After his death in 1882, the state of Virginia changed the name of Balsam Mountain to Mount Rogers in his honor.

In the Mount Rogers area, some of the Appalachian Trail is on old tram and railroad lines used during the logging days of the early 1900s. Both routes afford the opportunity to hike along a portion of the Appalachian Trail. This trail, completed in 1937, extends over 2,150 miles from Mount Katahdin, the highpoint of Maine, to Springer Mountain in northern Georgia.

Natural History Notes

Mount Rogers is completely wooded, mostly with spruce and fir. Because of the unusual vegetation and the frequency of mist and rain, unique flora and fauna are found on the mountain. This is the southernmost range of many northern plants and animals and the northernmost range of many southern ones. The animals include white-tailed deer, wild turkey, grouse, squirrels, and many other species.

There is a herd of free-roaming ponies in Grayson Highlands State Park. The herd is owned and managed by a private nonprofit association.

Washington

Mount Rainier

14,410 Feet

County
Pierce

Location
Approximately 70 miles SE of Seattle in Mount Rainier National Park.

Hiking
16.0 miles, round trip, on trail, cross-country, and on snow and glaciers.

Gain
9,100 feet, Class 4, strenuous.

Maps
Topographic: Mt. Rainier West, Wash., and Mt. Rainier East, Wash., both 7½ minute.
Trails Illustrated: #217, Mount Rainier National Park, Washington.
National Park: Mount Rainier—Official Map and Guide, Mount Rainier National Park; Mount Rainier Wilderness Trip Planner, Mount Rainier National Park.
Other: Hiking Map and Guide—Mt. Rainier National Park, Earthwalk Press, La Jolla, California.

Guidebooks
Adventure Guide to Mount Rainier: Hiking, Climbing, and Skiing in Mount Rainier National Park, by Jeff Smoot, Chockstone Press, Evergreen, Colorado, 1997.
Cascade Alpine Guide: Climbing and High Routes, Volume 1: Columbia River to Stevens Pass, by Fred W. Beckey, The Mountaineers, Seattle, Washington, 2d edition, 1987.

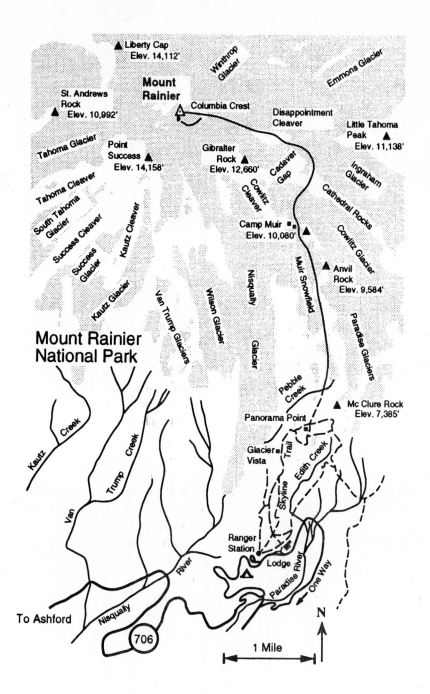

Liberty Cap
Elev. 14,112'

Mount
Rainier

Columbia Crest

Winthrop Glacier

Emmons Glacier

Disappointment
Cleaver

St. Andrews
Rock
Elev. 10,992'

Little Tahoma
Peak
Elev. 11,138'

Tahoma Glacier

Point
Success
Elev. 14,158'

Gibralter
Rock
Elev. 12,660'

Cadaver
Gap

Ingraham
Glacier

Tahoma Cleaver

Cowlitz
Cleaver

Cathedral Rocks

South Tahoma
Glacier

Success Cleaver

Camp Muir
Elev. 10,080'

Cowlitz Glacier

Success
Glacier

Kautz Cleaver

Anvil
Rock
Elev. 9,584'

Kautz Glacier

Nisqually Glacier

Van Trump Glaciers

Muir Snowfield

Paradise Glaciers

Wilson Glacier

Mount Rainier
National Park

Mc Clure Rock
Elev. 7,385'

Pebble
Creek

Panorama Point

Kautz
Creek

Van Trump Creek

Glacier
Vista

Edith Creek

Skyline Trail

Ranger
Station

Lodge

Paradise River

One Way

To Ashford

Nisqually River

706

N

1 Mile

Mount Rainier, Washington - 14,410 Feet

The Challenge of Rainier: A Record of the Explorations and Ascents, Triumphs and Tragedies, by Dee Molenaar, The Mountaineers, Seattle, Washington, 3d edition, 1979.

50 Hikes in Mount Rainier National Park, by Ira Spring and Harvey Manning, The Mountaineers, Seattle, Washington, 4th edition, 1999.

Hiking Washington, by Ron Adkison, Falcon Press Publishing Co., Inc., Helena, Montana, 2d edition, 1996.

100 Classic Hikes in Washington: North Cascades, Olympics, Mount Rainier and South Cascades, Alpine Lakes, Glacier Peak, by Ira Spring and Harvey Manning, The Mountaineers, Seattle, Washington, 1998.

100 Hikes in Washington's South Cascades and Olympics, by Ira Spring and Harvey Manning, The Mountaineers, Seattle, Washington, 3d edition, 1998.

Selected Climbs in the Cascades, by Jim Nelson, The Mountaineers, Seattle, Washington, 1993.

Primary Route: Ingraham Glacier/Disappointment Cleaver

Approach ▲ From Tacoma, proceed s on State Route 7 approximately 40 miles to State Route 706 in Elbe. Continue E on Route 706 approximately 31 miles to Paradise.

Route ▲ From the Paradise Ranger Station (5,420 feet), hike up Skyline Trail for 2.5 miles to Panorama Point (6,800 feet) via Alta Vista and Glacier Vista. From Panorama Point, continue over Pebble Creek (7,200 feet) and up the Muir Snowfield to Moon Rocks (9,200 feet) w of Anvil Rock and on to Camp Muir (10,080 feet), 2.7 miles beyond Panorama Point. Most or all of this route may be snow-covered until midsummer. Beware of steep cliffs to the E from Anvil Rock to Camp Muir. The compass bearing from Pebble Creek to Moon Rocks is 350 degrees, true, and the compass bearing from Moon Rocks to Camp Muir is 344 degrees, true. (The return bearings are 164 degrees, true, to Moon Rocks and 170 degrees, true, to Pebble Creek.)

From Camp Muir, the climb to the summit is 2.8 miles with an elevation gain exceeding 4,300 feet. Climb to the Ingraham Glacier by a near-level traverse of the upper Cowlitz Glacier and ascend the slope through the central gap in Cathedral Rocks (10,500 feet). At the gap, climb a snow or long scree slope to the ridge crest, then onto the Ingraham Glacier. Traverse across the glacier to the lower base of Disappointment Cleaver. Leave the glacier 200 to 300 feet above the cleaver's nose and continue up to the cleaver crest snowfield and onto the top of the cleaver (12,300 feet). Climb directly to the E summit crater rim. Continue across the summit crater to the western rim, Columbia Crest, which is the true summit. The register will be found in a three-rock outcrop about 300 feet inside the crater's NNE rim.

Special Conditions

Mount Rainier is usually climbed during a two-day trip. The first day is spent climbing to Camp Muir at the 10,080-foot level. With a very early start (usually 2:00 A.M.), the climb to the summit and return to Paradise is accomplished on the second day. The usual climbing season for Mount Rainier is June through mid-September. Registration with the Paradise Ranger Station is mandatory before starting the climb. For climbing above 10,000 feet, there is a $15.00 per person single-trip fee or a $25.00 per person annual fee. The minimum party size is two with a recommended minimum of three. Be sure to check out on return. Climbing on the snow and glaciers requires roped travel and the use of an ice ax and crampons.

Wilderness permits, available at hiking information centers, ranger stations, and visitor centers, are required year-round for all climbers who camp or bivouac on Mount Rainier. These free permits are issued on a first-come, first-served basis. No advance reservations for camping at Camp Muir are accepted, and the number of climbers at Camp Muir is limited. Camp Muir facilities include a ranger station–rescue cache, pit toilets, and a public shelter that will accommodate approximately 25 people on a space-available basis. Climbers must camp outside if the shelter is full.

Most climbing injuries and deaths on Mount Rainier have occurred when inexperienced and ill-equipped climbers were hit by falling rock, ice, or snow; fell down steep slopes or into crevasses; or became disoriented owing to poor weather conditions. Even the slightest climbing injury can result in tragedy because of the mountain's cold temperatures, high winds, and rapidly changing weather conditions. The long routes on Mount Rainier make rigorous demands on the speed and competence of climbers.

Weather is unpredictable since Mount Rainier bears the brunt of every ocean storm in addition to stirring up squalls of its own. Severe winter-like storms on the mountain are not uncommon during the summer months; snowstorms can occur in any month of the year. The formation of a cloudcap can create hazardous visibility problems. Cloudcaps can form very rapidly and envelop the upper mountain region, making progress up or down difficult. The appearance of lenticular clouds is a signal of a possible cloudcap and should not be ignored. Before starting the climb, be aware of the local weather and avalanche hazard forecasts. There is no water available on Mount Rainier. It is necessary to melt snow to obtain the water required.

There is a $10.00 fee for each automobile entering the park. A fee of $5.00 per person is charged for persons entering by foot or bicycle. There is a user fee of $10.00–$14.00 per night per campsite in the auto campgrounds.

There is an extensive trail system in Mount Rainier National Park, exceeding 240 miles. The 93-mile Wonderland Trail completely encircles the mountain, traversing through valley forests, alpine meadows, glacial streams, mountain passes, and occasional snow and rock.

Information, hiking guide sheets, and the national park map can be obtained from Mount Rainier National Park, Tahoma Woods, Star Route, Ashford, WA 98304 (360/569-2211), or the Mount Rainier website, www.nps.gov/mora/.

Information on accommodations at the Paradise Inn, open from mid-May to early October, and the National Park Inn in Longmire, open year-round, can be obtained from Mount Rainier Guest Services, P.O. Box 108, Ashford, WA 98304 (360/569-2275).

Books, maps, and other information may be obtained from the Branch Manager, Northwest Interpretive Association, Tahoma Woods, Star Route, Ashford, WA 98304 (360/569-2211, ext. 3320).

Historical Notes

Before the arrival of European explorers, Indian tribes lived in the low-lands surrounding Mount Rainier. Some tribes called the mountain *Takhoma*, others *Tahoma*, meaning "high mountain," "great snowy peak," or just "the mountain." On May 8, 1792, Captain George Vancouver, in command of a British government expedition exploring the Northwest coast, his ships at anchor in northern Puget Sound, named Mount Rainier in honor of his friend, British Rear Admiral Peter Rainier. Admiral Rainier never saw the mountain.

In August 1870 Sluiskin, a Yakima Indian, guided Hazard Stevens and Philemon Beecher Van Trump to the base of the mountain. Hazard and Van Trump accomplished the first recorded ascent to the summit on August 17, 1870.

On March 2, 1899, a national park bill was passed by Congress that made Mount Rainier the fifth national park in the United States. Paradise Inn, completed in 1917, was built to withstand heavy winter snowfalls of up to 25 feet. The architecture features classic wooden beam construction, stone fireplaces, and parquet wood floors. The inn is now a National Historic Landmark. The National Park Inn in Longmire is at the site of a mineral spring resort that James Longmire opened in 1884.

Natural History Notes

Mount Rainier is a volcano that is believed to be dormant but not extinct. It belongs to the class of exploding volcanoes, much like Mount St. Helens, and quite conceivably could one day erupt in a similar manner. The volcano began to grow between one million and half a million years ago. The slopes of lava flows on opposite sides of the mountain project a height more than 1,000 feet above the present summit. The upper portion of the cone was probably removed by explosions and landslides. The current summit, Columbia Crest, lies on the rim of the recent lava cone.

Mount Rainier is the most extensively glaciated volcanic peak and has the largest single peak glacial system in the contiguous United States. There are 25 named glaciers and approximately 50 small, unnamed glaciers and ice patches on its slopes. The largest glacier on the mountain is Emmons Glacier on the E side. The largest glacier seen from Paradise is the Nisqually Glacier.

Mount Rainier is often said to create its own weather. It reaches into the atmosphere and interrupts the flow of moist maritime air masses from the Pacific Ocean. This results in great amounts of rain and snowfall. The heavier rainfalls occur between October and May. During the winter of 1971–72, over 93 feet of snow fell at the Paradise weather station. The average snowfall at Paradise is 630 inches per year.

The forest surrounding the mountain is predominantly Douglas fir, western hemlock, red cedar, and several species of pine and true fir. The meadows above them are summertime celebrations of color as wildflowers bloom in July and August; more than 100 species of wildflowers are found in the park. In August tiny alpine ecosystems flourish at the toes of the icefields.

The largest mammal in Mount Rainier National Park is the elk, or wapiti. The bulls can weigh up to 800 pounds. Mountain goats are often found near the snowline. Mountain lion, black-tailed deer, black bear, raccoon, pine marten, porcupine, beaver, snowshoe hare, hoary marmot, pika, golden-mantled ground squirrel, and yellow pine chipmunk are among the other mammals found in the park.

There are approximately 30 species of birds that are commonly seen in the region. Several other transient species are occasionally seen.

Guides/Outfitters

Rainier Mountaineering, Inc., Paradise, WA 98398 (360/569-2227) (June through September), or Rainier Mountaineering, Inc., 535 Dock Street, Suite 209, Tacoma, WA 98402 (253/627-6242) (year-round).

West Virginia

Spruce Knob

4,861 Feet

County
Pendleton

Location
Approximately 13 miles ssw of Seneca Rocks in the Spruce Knob–Seneca Rocks National Recreation Area of Monongahela National Forest.

Hiking
Primary Route: Drive-up.
Alternate Route: 19.2 miles, round trip, on trail.

Gain
Primary Route: Drive-up.
Alternate Route: 4,100 feet, Class 1, strenuous.

Maps
Topographic: Spruce Knob, W.Va.; Circleville, W.Va.; and Whitmer, W.Va., all 7½ minute.
National Forest: Monongahela N.F.; Spruce Knob–Seneca Rocks National Recreation Area, Monongahela N.F.; Spruce Knob Area Guide, Monongahela N.F.; Seneca Creek Backcountry Hiking Guide, Monongahela N.F.

Guidebooks
Hiking Guide to the Allegheny Trail, edited by George L. Rosier, West Virginia Scenic Trails Association, Charleston, West Virginia, 2d edition, 1990.
Monongahela National Forest Hiking Guide, by Allen de Hart and Bruce Sundquist, West Virginia Highlands Conservancy, Charleston, West Virginia, 6th edition, 1993.

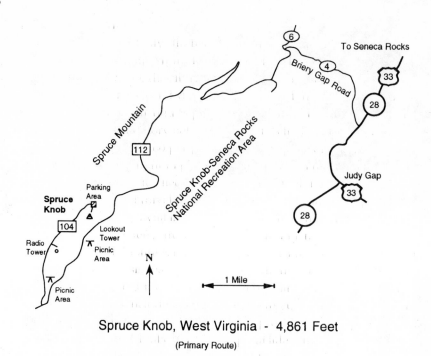

Spruce Knob, West Virginia - 4,861 Feet

(Primary Route)

West Virginia Hiking Trails: Hiking the Mountain State, by Allen de Hart, Appalachian Mountain Club Books, Boston, Massachusetts, 2d edition, 1997.

Primary Route

Approach ▲ From Seneca Rocks, proceed s on U.S. Hwy 33/State Route 28 for approximately 10 miles to County Road 4 on the right. This point is 2.5 miles s of Riverton. Turn right (w) on County Road 4 and proceed 1.8 miles to a junction with County Road 6. Keep left. At this point the road becomes Forest Route 112. Continue on Forest Route 112 for 8.2 miles, bearing right at an intersection at 0.6 miles, to Forest Route 104 on the right. Turn right (N) on Forest Route 104 and continue 1.9 miles to the Spruce Knob parking area.

Route ▲ Walk s to the observation tower on the highpoint. The usgs benchmark is immediately N of the observation tower.

Alternate Route: Horton Trail/Seneca Creek Trail/Huckleberry Trail

Approach ▲ From the village of Whitmer, proceed s on County Road 29 for 1.5 miles to the obscure trailhead with a hiker sign at a forest road on the left. This point is 0.1 miles s after crossing Lower Two Springs Run. There is parking on the forest road and nearby in a grove of trees.

Route ▲ From the trailhead, hike generally E on the Horton Trail (TR530) for 2.4 miles, taking the s fork beyond the parking area, bearing right at a fork at 1.5 miles, and bearing left at a fork at 1.9 miles, to the junction with the Allegheny Mountain Trail (TR532) at the top of the ridge. Cross the Allegheny Mountain Trail and continue downhill on the Horton Trail 1.1 miles to the Seneca Creek Trail (TR515) on the E side of Seneca Creek. Turn right (s) on the Seneca Creek Trail and continue 0.2 miles upstream to the junction with the Huckleberry Trail (TR533) on the left. This junction is near the Upper Seneca Creek Falls. Hike generally s on the Huckleberry Trail for 5.9 miles, passing the Judy Springs Trail (TR512) at 1.4 miles and the Lumberjack Trail (TR534) at 2.7 miles, to the Spruce Knob parking area. Continue s across the parking area to the observation tower on the highpoint. The USGS benchmark is immediately N of the observation tower. **Note:** This can be done as a one-way hike with a car shuttle.

Special Conditions

The Spruce Knob area is open year-round except when winter weather conditions dictate otherwise. Snow is not removed from Forest Route 112 in the winter.

There is an extensive trail system in the Spruce Mountain area. Nearly 70 miles of trails wind through stands of red spruce, across open meadows, and along mountain streams. Several trail combinations are possible, providing loop trips or one-way hikes when combined with a car shuttle. Information and maps for the Spruce Knob–Seneca Rocks National Recreation Area can be obtained by contacting Monongahela National Forest, Potomac Ranger District, HC59, Box 240, Petersburg, WV 26847-9502 (304/257-4488). Information can also be obtained from the Seneca Rocks Discovery Center, P.O. Box 13, Seneca Rocks, WV 26884 (304/567-2827).

In addition to the Spruce Mountain trail system, approximately 12 miles NW of Spruce Knob the Allegheny Trail passes through the village of Glady. When completed, the Allegheny Trail will extend over 300 miles from the Pennsylvania–West Virginia state line s to the Virginia–West Virginia state line, where it will join the Appalachian Trail. Currently, the trail extends almost 250 miles s from the Pennsylvania border. The southern part of the trail is in development and is not yet open to hikers. The entire Allegheny Trail is marked for travel in both directions with yellow paint blazes on trees, poles, and rocks, about 2 inches wide and 6 inches high. Two blazes, one above the other, are a signal of an important trail feature such as an obscure turn or a change in route.

The observation tower at Spruce Knob.

Information on the Allegheny Trail can be obtained from the West Virginia Scenic Trails Association, P.O. Box 4042, Charleston, WV 25364 or their website, www.wvonline.com/wvsta/.

West Virginia has a well-developed state park system that includes more than 35 facilities. One of particular note is the Cass Scenic Railroad State Park, located approximately 50 miles s of the Spruce Knob area. The Cass Scenic Railroad was once a major logging railroad. Now it climbs from the old lumber town of Cass to the summit of Bald Knob; at an elevation of 4,842 feet, it is the second highest peak in West Virginia. For information on schedules and fares, and to make reservations, contact the Cass Scenic Railroad State Park, P.O. Box 107, Main Street (Route 66), Cass, WV 24927 (304/456-4300). For information on parks in the West Virginia State Park System, including Cass Scenic Railroad State Park, contact the state parks office at 800/CALL WVA.

Historical Notes

Spruce Knob is named for the red spruce, *Picea rubens*, found on Spruce Mountain. This is the only spruce found this far south in the eastern mountains, its range extending south to western North Carolina and eastern Tennessee. It is often found in pure stands. Spruce gum, a forerunner of modern chewing gum made from chicle, was obtained commercially from resin from the red spruce trunks. The young leafy twigs were boiled with flavoring and sugar to make spruce beer.

In the mid-1800s settlers established hundreds of acres of high-elevation pasture in the area. Extensive logging occurred in the early 1900s, and remnants of old logging railroad grades can still be found. In fact, several of the old railroad grades have been incorporated into the trail system around Spruce Mountain.

The 100,000-acre Spruce Knob–Seneca Rocks National Recreation Area was established in 1965. It was the first National Recreation Area to be designated by the Forest Service.

Natural History Notes

The vegetation on Spruce Knob has adapted to a severe alpine climate. One-sided red spruce, deformed by strong westerly winds, and mountain ash occur on the high ridges. Blueberry and huckleberry plants hug the ground. In the spring the flowers of azaleas, mountain laurel, and rhododendron add color to the landscape. Hardwood forests of beech, birch, maple, and cherry cover the lower elevations.

Wisconsin

Timms Hill
1,951 Feet

County
> Price

Location
> Approximately 5 miles E of Ogema in Timm's Hill County Park.

Hiking
> Primary Route: 0.4 miles, round trip, on trail.
> Alternate Route: 18.8 miles, round trip, on trail.

Gain
> Primary Route: 130 feet, Class 1, easy.
> Alternate Route: 1,310 feet, Class 1, moderate.

Maps
> Topographic: Timms Hill, Wis., and Rib Lake, Wis., both 7½ minute.
> National Park Service: Ice Age Trail, National Scenic Trail, Wisconsin.

Primary Route
> **Approach** ▲ From the middle of Ogema, proceed E on State Route 86 for 4.1 miles to County Road C. (This point is 26.3 miles W of Tomahawk via State Route 86.) Turn right (S) on County Road C and proceed 0.9 miles to Rustic Road #62 on the left. Turn left (E) and proceed along Rustic Road #62 for 0.3 miles to the Timm's Hill County Park entrance on the left. Turn left (N) into the park entrance and continue 0.6 miles on the one-way road to the parking area.
>
> **Route** ▲ From the NW corner of the parking area, hike NW up the trail 0.2 miles to the observation tower. The USGS benchmark is 10 feet NW of the tower.

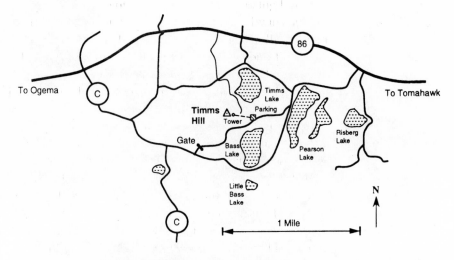

Timms Hill, Wisconsin - 1,951 Feet
(Primary Route)

Alternate Route: Timm's Hill National Trail

Approach ▲ From the middle of Rib Lake, proceed E on State Route 102 for 1.9 miles to County Road C. Turn left (N) on County Road C and continue 2.7 miles to the trailhead on the left. Turn left (W) into the trail-head parking area.

Route ▲ Hike a short distance W then generally N on the well-signed and red-blazed Timm's Hill National Trail for 8.9 miles to Timm's Hill County Park road. Turn right (E) and continue 0.3 miles to the parking area. From the NW corner of the parking area, hike NW up the trail 0.2 miles to the observation tower. The USGS benchmark is 10 feet NW of the tower. **Note:** This can be done as a one-way hike with a car shuttle.

Special Conditions

Timm's Hill County Park is usually open from 8:00 A.M. until dusk, year-round. When it is covered with snow, the one-way road in the park is closed to automobile traffic and is used for skiing and snowmobiling.

Timm's Hill National Trail is a nonmotorized trail connecting the Ice Age National Scenic Trail to Timms Hill. Except for the southernmost quarter mile, which is surfaced with limestone screenings, the trail is sod and is mowed annually. The entire trail is groomed for skiing in winter. The Timm's Hill Trail is a hilly trail, as evidenced by the gross elevation gain on the round trip. The trail is user-supported and maintained by volunteers.

The tower at Timms Hill. (Elizabeth Roherty)

The trail crosses County Road C at three locations as it goes N to Timms Hill. As measured N along County Road C from the southern trailhead, the crossings are located as follows: At 1.8 miles at the Spirit Wood Avenue–County Road C junction; at 2.4 miles just after County Road C turns right (E); at 5.9 miles N along County Road C. The trail is also approximately 0.1 miles S on Hultman Road from the Hultman Road–County Road C junction at the 5.0 milepoint. The trail can be accessed from any of these points to accommodate a shorter hike to Timms Hill. The one-way hiking distances are approximately 6.4 miles, 5.7 miles, and 2.9 miles from the respective County Road C trail crossings and 3.7 miles from the Hultman Road trail crossing. Information on the trail and an excellent trail map may be obtained from the Timm's Hill County Park caretakers, Lyle and Kathy Blomberg, at 715/767-5287.

At its southern terminus, the Timm's Hill National Trail connects to the Ice Age National Scenic Trail. Currently, the Ice Age National Scenic Trail leads for 475 miles through some of Wisconsin's most scenic glacial terrain. Eventually, it will extend over 1,000 miles in Wisconsin, essentially following the terminal moraine left by the last great glacier's farthest southerly advance about 10,000 years ago. Maps and information on the Ice Age National Scenic Trail can be obtained from the Ice Age Park and Trail Foundation, Inc., 207 East Buffalo Street, Suite 515, Milwaukee, WI 53202 (800/227-0046 or 414/278-8518). The Ice Age Trail website address is www.nps.gov/iatr/.

Information on Price County and the area surrounding Timms Hill can be obtained from the Price County Tourism Department, Price County Courthouse, Phillips, WI 54555 (800/269-4505).

Historical Notes

Timms Hill and Timms Lake were named for Timothy Gahan, who at one time owned the north half of Timms Lake and had a logging camp near the lake. There was a sawmill in operation on the E side of Bass Lake near Timms Hill from 1898 until 1907. Bass Lake was used to float logs to the sawmill. Owing to financial difficulties, the sawmill closed in 1907. The remaining logs that were on Bass Lake sank to the bottom. Around 1925, timber operations were resumed by the Heden Brothers of Ogema. Many of the logs retrieved from Bass Lake were found to be sound enough to be sawn into lumber. Timms Hill was last logged in 1944. Price County purchased 187 acres with the intent of converting it into a county park in 1978. Timm's Hill County Park was completed in November 1982 and was dedicated on June 4, 1983.

There are several points of historical interest along the Timm's Hill National Trail. Interpretive markers explain the history of the area.

View from the top of Wisconsin. (Bill Feeny)

Natural History Notes

Before logging, the timber around Timms Hill was white pine, hemlock, and hardwood. The area is now forested mainly with sugar maple, ash, basswood, white birch, and small areas of conifers. The fall colors can be spectacular.

Wyoming

Gannett Peak

13,804 Feet

County
Fremont-Sublette

Location
Approximately 25 miles NNE of Pinedale on the border of the Bridger Wilderness Area of Bridger National Forest and the Fitzpatrick Wilderness Area of Shoshone National Forest.

Hiking
Primary Route: 40.4 miles, round trip, on trail, cross-country, and on snow and glaciers.
Alternate Route 1: 49.8 miles, round trip, on trail, cross-country, and on snow and glaciers.
Alternate Route 2: 32.8 miles, round trip, on trail, cross-country, and on snow and glaciers.

Gain
Primary Route: 8,650 feet, Class 4, strenuous.
Alternate Route 1: 10,800 feet, Class 4, strenuous.
Alternate Route 2: 8,450 feet, Class 4, strenuous.

Maps
Topographic: Gannett Peak, Wyo.; Bridger Lakes, Wyo.; Fayette Lake, Wyo.; Fremont Lake North, Wyo.; Fremont Peak North, Wyo.; Ink Wells, Wyo.; Torrey Lake, Wyo.; and Hays Park, Wyo., all 7½ minute.
National Forest: Bridger Wilderness, Bridger-Teton N.F.; Shoshone National Forest—South Half, Shoshone N.F.
Other: Hiking Map and Guide, Northern Wind River Range, WY, Earthwalk Press, La Jolla, California; Hiking Map and Guide, Southern Wind River Range, WY, Earthwalk Press, La Jolla, California.

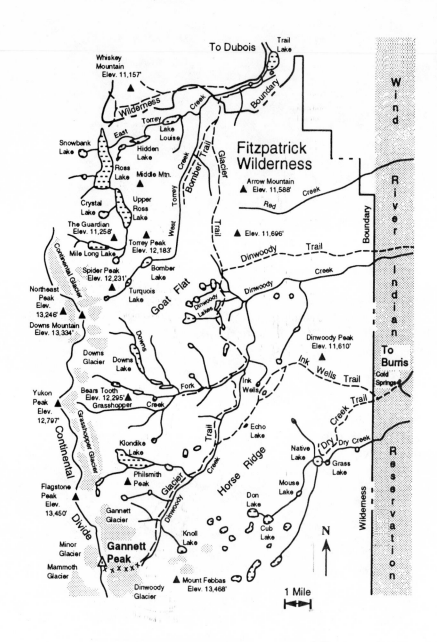

Gannett Peak, Wyoming - 13,804 Feet

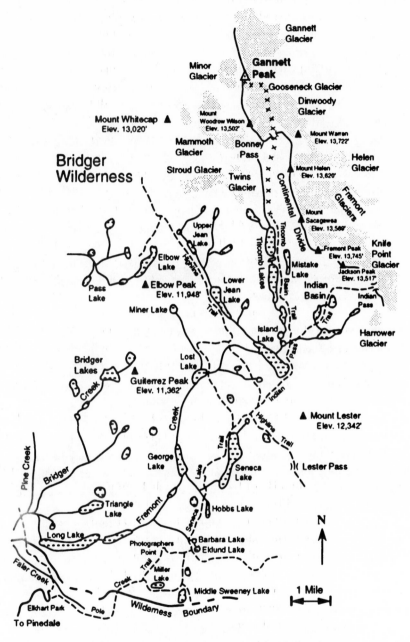

Gannett Glacier

Gannett Peak

Minor Glacier

Gooseneck Glacier

Dinwoody Glacier

Mount Woodrow Wilson
Elev. 13,502'

Mount Whitecap ▲
Elev. 13,020'

Mammoth Glacier

Bonney Pass

Stroud Glacier

Twins Glacier

Mount Warren
Elev. 13,722'

Helen Glacier

Mount Helen
Elev. 13,620'

Bridger Wilderness

Fremont Glaciers

Continental Divide

Upper Jean Lake

Mount Sacagawea
Elev. 13,569'

Elbow Lake

Thumb

Thumb Lakes

Fremont Peak
Elev. 13,745'

Knife Point Glacier

▲ Elbow Peak
Elev. 11,948'

Lower Jean Lake

Mistake Lake

Jackson Peak
Elev. 13,517'

Pass Lake

Miner Lake

Indian Basin

Indian Pass

Island Lake

Basin

Harrower Glacier

Lost Lake

Bridger Lakes

▲ Guiterrez Peak
Elev. 11,362'

Creek

Indian

▲ Mount Lester
Elev. 12,342'

Creek

George Lake

Highline Trail

Seneca Lake

Trail

)(Lester Pass

Triangle Lake

Hobbs Lake

N

Pine Creek

Long Lake

Bridger

Fremont

Seneca

Photographers Point

Barbara Lake

Eklund Lake

Faler Creek

Miller Lake

Middle Sweeney Lake

1 Mile

Elkhart Park

Pole

Wilderness Boundary

To Pinedale

Creek

Gannett Peak, Wyoming - 13,804 Feet

Guidebooks

Climbing and Hiking in the Wind River Mountains, by Joe Kelsey, Chockstone Press, Evergreen, Colorado, 1994.

Climbing Gannett Peak: A Wind River Adventure, by Donald B. Jacobs, Jacobs Enterprises, Vashon, Washington, 1990.

Guide to the Wyoming Mountains and Wilderness Areas, by Orrin H. Bonney and Lorraine G. Bonney, Swallow Press/Ohio University Press, Athens, Ohio, 3d revised edition, 1977.

Hiking Wyoming, by Bill Hunger, Falcon Press Publishing Co., Inc., Helena, Montana, revised edition, 1998.

Hiking Wyoming's Wind River Range, by Ron Adkison, Falcon Press Publishing Co., Inc., Helena, Montana, 1996.

Walking the Winds: A Hiking and Fishing Guide to Wyoming's Wind River Range, by Rebecca Woods, White Willow Publishing, Jackson, Wyoming, 1994.

Wind River Trails: A Hiking and Fishing Guide to the Many Trails and Lakes of the Wind River Range in Wyoming, by Finis Mitchell, University of Utah Press, Salt Lake City, Utah, 1999.

Primary Route: Pole Creek Trail/Seneca Lake Trail/Indian Pass Trail/Titcomb Basin Trail

Approach ▲ From the E end of Pinedale, where U.S. Hwy 191 bears S, proceed E then immediately N on Fremont Lake Road, which soon becomes Forest Road 101. There is a sign indicating "Fremont, Half Moon Lakes" at the turnoff in Pinedale. Continue for 14.3 miles to a large parking area and the trailhead for the Pole Creek Trail on the right, immediately beyond the Elkhart Park Ranger Station. On the way along Fremont Lake Road, stay right at the junction at 3.2 miles and left at the junction at 6.8 miles. The parking area is approximately 0.2 miles before reaching the end of the road.

Route ▲ From the parking area, hike E on Pole Creek Trail 5.3 miles to the junction with Seneca Lake Trail, immediately W of Eklund Lake. Turn N on Seneca Lake Trail and continue 5.1 miles to Indian Pass Trail (the last 0.5 miles is coincident with Highline Trail). Bear right on Indian Pass Trail and hike 2.4 miles to the junction with Titcomb Basin Trail. Turn left onto Titcomb Basin Trail and continue 5.5 miles to Bonney Pass. Note that Bonney Pass was formerly known as Dinwoody Pass (see Historical Notes). Be aware that the signs along the trails indicate destinations and not trail names. The destinations of interest are Seneca Lake, Island Lake, Indian Pass, and Titcomb Basin. It is 1.9 miles from Bonney Pass to the summit. From Bonney Pass, traverse across the Dinwoody Glacier to the lower portion of Gooseneck Pinnacle ridge and onto Gooseneck Glacier. Ascend on the S side of Gooseneck Glacier to the bergschrunds, then climb onto the

Gooseneck Pinnacle ridge. Pass Gooseneck Pinnacle on the N and continue to the summit ridge. Turn N on the summit ridge and cross the snowfield to the summit. There is a USGS benchmark and a register at the summit.

Alternate Route 1: Glacier Trail

Approach ▲ From the E end of Dubois where U.S. Hwy 26/285 makes a 90-degree turn, proceed E on U.S. Hwy 26/287 approximately 3.7 miles to Forest Road 411 (Trail Lake Road) on the right. Turn right (S) onto Forest Road 411, bearing immediately left toward Whiskey Basin after crossing a cattle guard, and continue 9.0 miles, bearing left at 2.4 miles and passing Torrey, Ring, and Trail Lakes, to a parking area at the end of the road.

Route ▲ From the parking area, hike up the N side of Torrey Creek to a bridge crossing a deep chasm. Cross the bridge and continue 3.0 miles to a junction where Glacier Trail bears to the left and the Bomber Trail bears to the right. (Glacier Trail is coincident with the Bomber Trail for the first 3 miles.) Continue S on the Glacier Trail approximately 20 miles to the Dinwoody Glacier moraine. It is another 1.9 miles to the summit. Ascend the moraine to the lower end of Gooseneck Pinnacle ridge and onto the Gooseneck Glacier. Continue ascending on the S side of Gooseneck Glacier to the bergschrunds, then climb onto the Gooseneck Pinnacle ridge. Pass Gooseneck Pinnacle on the N and continue to the summit ridge. Turn N on the summit ridge and cross the snowfield to the summit. There is a USGS benchmark and a register at the summit.

Alternate Route 2: Ink Wells Trail/Glacier Trail

Approach ▲ The approach to Cold Springs, the trailhead for the Ink Wells Trail, crosses through the Wind River Indian Reservation. See Special Conditions for travel restrictions on this route in the reservation.

Route ▲ Hike W on the Ink Wells Trail 8.5 miles to the Glacier Trail junction, keeping right at the Dry Creek Trail junction at 0.8 miles. Turn S on Glacier Trail and continue 6.0 miles to the Dinwoody Glacier moraine. It is another 1.9 miles to the summit. Ascend the moraine to the lower end of Gooseneck Pinnacle ridge and onto the Gooseneck Glacier. Continue ascending on the S side of Gooseneck Glacier to the bergschrunds, then climb onto the Gooseneck Pinnacle ridge. Pass Gooseneck Pinnacle on the N and continue to the summit ridge. Turn N on the summit ridge and cross the snowfield to the summit. There is a USGS benchmark and a register at the summit.

Special Conditions

Gannett Peak is on the border of the Bridger Wilderness and the Fitzpatrick Wilderness, but wilderness permits are not required.

A good campsite at Upper Titcomb Lakes on the way to Gannett Peak.

Gannett Peak is climbed during a multiday backpack trip. Usually, two or three days are spent getting to basecamp. The summit is ascended during a very strenuous one-day trip or a two-day trip with a high camp at Bonney Pass or on the Gooseneck Pinnacle ridge, depending on the route. In addition, one or two days are necessary for the return to the trailhead. Basecamp is usually set up at Upper Titcomb Lake or Wilson Meadows, depending on the route. Climbing on the snow and glaciers requires roped travel and the use of an ice ax and crampons. Ropes may also be necessary on Gooseneck Pinnacle ridge. The usual climbing season for Gannett Peak is July through mid-September.

Sudden storms with strong winds and subzero wind chill are common. Snow flurries can occur any month of the year. Thunderstorms often occur in the afternoons. Take care not to get caught on the peaks or exposed ridges during one of these storms. Be prepared with warm and windproof clothing and a tent sufficient to withstand high winds. Before starting the climb, be aware of the local weather forecast.

The Primary Route is within a special management area of Bridger Wilderness and has the following restrictions from July 1 through Labor Day: a maximum group size of 10, no open campfires, and no camping within sight of any lake or designated trail if within 200 feet.

Although the approach crosses the Wind River Indian Reservation, Alternate Route 2 is included here because it offers the shortest route to

Gannett Peak. The Tribal Fish and Game Department has established and enforces restrictions for crossing the reservation from U.S. Hwy 26/287 approximately 2 miles NW of Burris to Cold Springs. Two permits are required for each individual: one for the day going in and one for the day coming out ($10.00 per permit for residents and $20.00 per permit for non-residents). A Tribal Recreation Stamp is also required for each person ($10.00). Permits and the Tribal Recreation Stamp can be obtained from sporting goods stores in Lander, Riverton, and Dubois and at the Crowheart Store in Crowheart, Wyoming. In addition to the permits and recreation stamp, it is mandatory that transportation between Burris and the Cold Springs trailhead be provided by an outfitter authorized by the Tribal Council to use the Gannett Peak Road across the reservation. (See Guides/Outfitters for Alternate Route 2.) The outfitter's fee ranges from $150.00 (2 persons) to $200.00 (6 persons) each way (as of spring 2000).

Not all eight topographic maps listed are required for any one route. The first four topographic maps cover the Primary Route. "Gannett Peak" and the fifth through the seventh maps cover Alternate Route 1. Alternate Route 2 is covered by "Gannett Peak" and the fifth, sixth, and eighth topographic maps.

Information and the Bridger Wilderness map for the Primary Route can be obtained from Pinedale Ranger District, Bridger-Teton National Forest, P.O. Box 220, 29 E. Fremont Lake Road, Pinedale, WY 82941 (307/367-4326).

Information and the national forest map for Alternate Route 1 can be obtained from Wind River Ranger District, Shoshone National Forest, P.O. Box 186, 1403 W. Ramshorn Street, Dubois, WY 82513 (307/455-2466)

Information on the Wind River Indian Reservation requirements can be obtained from Tribal Fish and Game Office, Wind River Indian Reservation, Ft. Washakie, WY 82514 (307/332-7207).

Historical Notes

Gannett Peak was named in honor of the great American geographer Henry Gannett (1846–1914). Gannett was topographer for the Hayden Survey (1872–79) in Wyoming and Colorado. He was chief geographer of the U.S. Geological Survey from 1882 to 1914. Through Gannett's efforts, the U.S. Board on Geographic Names was established in 1890, and he was its chairman for twenty years. He was one of the founders of the National Geographic Society and served as its president from 1910 to 1914.

The first confirmed ascent of Gannett Peak occurred in 1922. Although the truth will never be known, U.S. Army Captain Benjamin L. E. Bonneville may have climbed Gannett Peak in September 1883. Bonneville's description of the view from the summit, as related in Washington Irving's

"The Adventures of Captain Bonneville," certainly could be that seen from Gannett Peak.

Bonney Pass was formerly known as Dinwoody Pass. In 1983 the pass was renamed in honor of Orrin Hanning Bonney (1904–79), who was a mountain climber, conservationist, and author of several guidebooks on the mountains of Wyoming, particularly the Wind River Range. The 1993 Gannett Peak, Wyo., topographic map identifies the pass as Bonney Pass. Maps dated before 1993 identify the pass as Dinwoody Pass.

Natural History Notes

Mosquitoes, deerflies, and horseflies are plentiful most of the summer, making insect repellent a must.

Gannett Peak is surrounded by five glaciers: Dinwoody, Gooseneck, Gannett, Mammoth, and Minor. This is one of the most extensively glaciated areas in the Rocky Mountains.

Lodgepole pine, Engelmann spruce, and alpine fir are found at the lower altitudes, and white bark pine and limber pine are found on higher slopes. The timberline averages about 10,600 feet.

Many species of birds, including the Canada jay, Clark's nutcracker, and ravens, are found in the Wind River Range. Mammals include elk, mule deer, moose, bear, mountain sheep, badger, beaver, marmot, and pika. There are six species of trout in the lakes and streams.

Guides/Outfitters
Primary Route
Exum Mountain Guides, Grand Teton National Park, P.O. Box 56, Moose, WY 83012 (307/733-2297).

Jackson Hole Mountain Guides and Climbing School, P.O. Box 7477, 165 North Glenwood Street, Jackson, WY 83001 (800/239-7642).

Skinner Brothers Wilderness Camps, 225 E. Magnolia Street, P.O. Box 859, Pinedale, WY 82941 (800/237-9138).

Alternate Route 1
Exum Mountain Guides, Grand Teton National Park, P.O. Box 56, Moose, WY 83012 (307/733-2297).

Larry Stetter, General Outfitter, P.O. Box 695, Dubois, WY 82513 (307/455-2725).

Clayton Voss, Lazy TX Outfitting, P.O. Box 482, Dubois, WY 82513 (307/455-2688).

Alternate Route 2
Monie O'Neal, P.O. Box 601, Crowheart, WY 82512 (307/486-2318).

State Highpoints List

Official List

This is the official list of state highpoints as recognized by the Highpointers Club. It largely adheres to the state highpoints as listed in the latest printing of the United States Geological Survey publication *Elevations and Distances in the United States,* and deviates only where updated data are available.

Location

Some peaks are not named on the USGS topographic maps, although most can be identified by the explicit summit elevation on the map. On other named peaks the actual highpoint may be difficult to identify. To aid in locating these peaks, the location is given on the Highpoint List by the standard six-digit convention, using the Universal Transverse Mercator (UTM) grid. This grid is defined by the numbered blue tick marks that are spaced one kilometer apart along the map edges. A location is designated by a six-digit number: the first three digits comprise the easterly coordinate, and the second three digits comprise the northerly coordinate, each to the nearest one hundred meters. The graphic scale on the map's lower boundary can be used for distances less than one kilometer. For example, Magazine Mountain, the highpoint of Arkansas, has the UTM location coordinates of 413916. This means Magazine Mountain is 300 meters east (third digit) of the north-south UTM grid line marked by "41" on the blue tick marks at the top and bottom of the map and 600 meters north (sixth digit) of the east-west UTM grid line marked "91" on the left and right edges of the map.

Summit Elevation

The highpoint elevation listed is that given in the U.S. Geological Survey publication. In some cases, the elevation given on the topographic map is different. In these cases, the topographic map elevation is shown in parentheses.

Climbing Difficulty

The class of a climb indicates the general difficulty of the most difficult part of the route to the highpoint. Usually, the majority of the route is one or two classes lower than that indicated. Please remember that ratings of this nature are always somewhat subjective. The classes are as follows:

Drive-up: A passenger car can be driven to the immediate vicinity of the highpoint.

Class 1: Hands-in-pockets hiking on trails or easy cross-country.

Class 2: Rough cross-country travel; may include boulder hopping and use of hands for balance.

Class 3: Handholds are necessary for climbing; some may wish rope belays because of exposure.

Class 4: More difficult climbing with considerable exposure or travel on glaciers or snowfields; ropes are required.

Highpoints of the United States

State	Highpoint	Elevation (Feet)	Class
Alabama	Cheaha Mountain	2,405	Drive-up
Alaska	Mount McKinley	20,320	4
Arizona	Humphreys Peak	12,633	1
Arkansas	Magazine Mountain (413916)	2,753	1
California	Mount Whitney	14,494	1
Colorado	Mount Elbert	14,433	1
Connecticut	Mount Frissell (South Slope)	2,380	1
Delaware	Ebright Azimuth (555095)	448 (442)	Drive-up
Florida	Lakewood Park (686282)	345	Drive-up
Georgia	Brasstown Bald	4,784 (4,788)	1
Hawaii	Mauna Kea	13,796	1
Idaho	Borah Peak	12,662	3
Illinois	Charles Mound	1,235	1
Indiana	Hoosier High Point (835298)	1,257	1
Iowa	Hawkeye Point (806153)	1,670	Drive-up
Kansas	Mount Sunflower	4,039	Drive-up
Kentucky	Black Mountain (312868)	4,139	Drive-up
Louisiana	Driskill Mountain (097873)	535	1
Maine	Mount Katahdin	5,267	1
Maryland	Backbone Mountain (309440)	3,360	1

Massachusetts	Mount Greylock	3,487	Drive-up
Michigan	Mount Arvon	1,979	1
Minnesota	Eagle Mountain	2,301	1
Mississippi	Woodall Mountain	806	Drive-up
Missouri	Taum Sauk Mountain (007605)	1,772	1
Montana	Granite Peak	12,799	4
Nebraska	Panorama Point (815398)	5,424	Drive-up
Nevada	Boundary Peak	13,140	2
New Hampshire	Mount Washington	6,288	Drive-up
New Jersey	High Point	1,803	Drive-up
New Mexico	Wheeler Peak	13,161	1
New York	Mount Marcy	5,344	1
North Carolina	Mount Mitchell	6,684	Drive-up
North Dakota	White Butte	3,506	1
Ohio	Campbell Hill	1,549	Drive-up
Oklahoma	Black Mesa	4,973	1
Oregon	Mount Hood	11,239	4
Pennsylvania	Mount Davis	3,213	Drive-up
Rhode Island	Jerimoth Hill	812	1
South Carolina	Sassafras Mountain	3,560 (3,554)	Drive-up
South Dakota	Harney Peak	7,242	1
Tennessee	Clingmans Dome	6,643	1
Texas	Guadalupe Peak	8,749	1
Utah	Kings Peak	13,528	2
Vermont	Mount Mansfield (736344)	4,393	2
Virginia	Mount Rogers	5,729	1
Washington	Mount Rainier	14,410	4
West Virginia	Spruce Knob	4,861	Drive-up
Wisconsin	Timms Hill	1,951	1
Wyoming	Gannett Peak	13,804	4

Highpoints of the United States by Region

Although the state highpoint guides are in alphabetical order, there is merit in grouping the highpoints by region. The highpoints in a given region usually all have something in common. Also, this is a convenient way to consider the highpoints if one is traveling in a particular part of the United States.

Northeast

From the rocky slopes of Maine's Mount Katahdin to Delaware's Ebright Azimuth at 442 feet at the edge of a highway, the summits of the northeastern states are a good introduction to the diversity of our nation's highpoints. Mount Katahdin in the wilds of Maine is the northern terminus of the Appalachian Trail and a strenuous climb of more than 4,000 vertical feet. The greatest danger on Delaware's highpoint is from passing automobiles. Between these extremes, a number of interesting summits await.

New Hampshire's Mount Washington is perhaps the most famous mountain east of the Mississippi. Although accessible by auto road and cog railroad as well as by trail, its summit is notorious for some of the most tempestuous weather on earth. Whether one is riding or hiking, Mount Washington is a mountain not to be taken lightly. Several generations of East Coast climbers have honed their technical snow and ice skills in Mount Washington's Tuckerman and Huntington ravines.

New York's Mount Marcy, the highpoint of the Adirondacks, is a strenuous hike of fifteen miles and 3,200 vertical feet, past the spot where young Vice President Theodore Roosevelt learned that the responsibility of the White House was to be thrust upon him. Vermont's Mount Mansfield, the highpoint of Vermont's storied Green Mountains, is a more moderate hike, particularly if done amid the splendor of a colorful New England fall. For the highpoint seeker stuck in New York City, New Jersey's nearby highpoint, named appropriately enough "High Point," offers a pleasant respite.

Connecticut - Mount Frissell (South Slope)

Massachusetts - Mount Greylock

New Hampshire - Mount Washington

Rhode Island - Jerimoth Hill

Vermont - Mount Mansfield

Maine

▲ Mount Katahdin

VT ▲

▲ Mount Marcy

NH

▲ **MA**

New York

▲ **CT**

RI

▲ High Point

Pennsylvania

▲ Mount Davis

New Jersey

Backbone Mountain ▲

Maryland

Delaware

Ebright Azimuth

▲ Spruce Knob

West Virginia

Northeast

Some obvious combination trips might involve visiting the highpoints of Massachusetts (Mount Greylock), Connecticut (Mount Frissell's south slope), and Rhode Island (Jerimoth Hill) or the summits of Mount Davis (Pennsylvania), Backbone Mountain (Maryland), and Spruce Knob (West Virginia). Mount Davis is a drive-up, but just getting there by auto will test your route-finding skills.

Highpoints of the Northeast

State	Highpoint	Elevation (Feet)	Class
Maine	Mount Katahdin	5,267	1
New Hampshire	Mount Washington	6,288	Drive-up
Vermont	Mount Mansfield (736344)	4,393	2
Massachusetts	Mount Greylock	3,487	Drive-up
Rhode Island	Jerimoth Hill	812	1
Connecticut	Mount Frissell (South Slope)	2,380	1
New York	Mount Marcy	5,344	1
New Jersey	High Point	1,803	Drive-up
Delaware	Ebright Azimuth (555095)	448	Drive-up
Pennsylvania	Mount Davis	3,213	Drive-up
Maryland	Backbone Mountain (309440)	3,360	1
West Virginia	Spruce Knob	4,861	Drive-up

South

The South is also a land of contrasting highpoints, from the rolling beauty of the peaks of the southern Appalachians to Lakewood Park, at 345 feet the lowest highpoint, in Florida. There are probably hotels in Miami that would tower above this highpoint, but thankfully, manmade objects don't count. In contrast, Mount Mitchell (North Carolina) has the distinction of being the highest point east of the mighty Mississippi River.

Driskill Mountain, note "Mountain," at 535 feet is the highpoint of Louisiana. This highpoint, when combined with a trip to Magazine Mountain (Arkansas), affords an excellent opportunity to tour the hills and mountains of those two states. This is a beautiful area in the fall when the leaves are turning.

Woodall Mountain (Mississippi) is located in the extreme northeast corner of Mississippi. Cheaha Mountain (Alabama) is located in Cheaha State Park and has a motel and restaurant near the highpoint. Cheaha State Park is part of the Alabama State Park System, which includes scenic areas throughout the state.

Probably the most scenic and enjoyable peaks in this region are the six summits in the southern Appalachians. They are Mount Rogers (Virginia),

South

Highpoints of the South

State	Highpoint	Elevation (Feet)	Class
Virginia	Mount Rogers	5,729	1
Kentucky	Black Mountain (312868)	4,139	Drive-up
North Carolina	Mount Mitchell	6,684	Drive-up
Tennessee	Clingmans Dome	6,643	1
South Carolina	Sassafras Mountain	3,560	Drive-up
Georgia	Brasstown Bald	4,784	1
Florida	Lakewood Park (686282)	345	Drive-up
Alabama	Cheaha Mountain	2,405	Drive-up
Mississippi	Woodall Mountain	806	Drive-up
Arkansas	Magazine Mountain (413916)	2,753	1
Oklahoma	Black Mesa	4,973	1
Louisiana	Driskill Mountain (097873)	535	1
Texas	Guadalupe Peak	8,749	1

Black Mountain (Kentucky), Mount Mitchell (North Carolina), Clingmans Dome (Tennessee), Sassafras Mountain (South Carolina), and Brasstown Bald (Georgia). These highpoints offer a number of possibilities for combining two or more highpoints in a grand tour of the southern Appalachians. Their geographical proximity is similar to that of the highpoints of the Northeast. It is interesting that, with the exception of Mount Rogers, they are all drive-ups or short, easy hikes. Because of the age of the Appalachian Mountains, the rolling character of these highpoints is in stark contrast to the rugged peaks in the West, where the mountains are much younger and less erosion has occurred.

The Texas and Oklahoma highpoints offer an interesting contrast. Guadalupe Peak, the highpoint of Texas, is an ancient reef. It was once on the edge of a large sea. This reef continues north and is the same formation that holds the Carlsbad Caverns, which were etched out by underground water that dissolved the limestone deposits. Guadalupe Peak is one of the two "desert" peaks among the fifty state highpoints (the other being Boundary Peak, Nevada). Black Mesa (Oklahoma), in the far western edge of the panhandle, is on a mesa that extends for forty miles. The surrounding land is several hundred feet below.

Midwest

The rolling, open nature of the Midwest's highpoints is readily apparent from some of their names—Campbell **Hill** (Ohio), Charles **Mound** (Illinois), Panorama **Point** (Nebraska), and Timms **Hill** (Wisconsin). With the exception of the four westernmost states, the elevations of the highpoints in this region range between 1,000 feet and 2,500 feet, illustrating the glacier-planed nature of the area. On the north, the area is bounded by the Great Lakes, remnants of the last great advance and retreat of the glacier cap from the north. In fact, Charles Mound is thought to be a drumlin—a long, narrow or oval rounded hill of unstratified glacial drift.

Eagle Mountain (Minnesota), Mount Arvon (Michigan), and Timms Hill (Wisconsin) are in areas populated with lakes. This also leads to a profuse population of mosquitoes. With minimal topographical relief and the wooded nature of the areas, the highpoints can be hard to find. This is especially true of Michigan, where the highpoint seems to change every time the U.S. Geological Survey updates its maps and elevations.

Six of the highpoints in this region—Illinois, Indiana, Iowa, Kansas, Nebraska, and North Dakota—are on private property. All six are surrounded by farmland. It is important to consider the rights of the property owners when visiting these highpoints.

The westernmost highpoints of the Midwest illustrate the character of the high plains. Here is dramatic evidence of the rise in the plains from the

Midwest

Highpoints of the Midwest

State	Highpoint	Elevation (Feet)	Class
Ohio	Campbell Hill	1,549	Drive-up
Indiana	Hoosier High Point (835298)	1,257	1
Illinois	Charles Mound	1,235	1
Michigan	Mount Arvon	1,979	1
Wisconsin	Timms Hill	1,951	1
Minnesota	Eagle Mountain	2,301	1
North Dakota	White Butte	3,506	1
South Dakota	Harney Peak	7,242	1
Iowa	Hawkeye Point (806153)	1,670	Drive-up
Nebraska	Panorama Point (815398)	5,424	Drive-up
Missouri	Taum Sauk Mountain (007605)	1,772	1
Kansas	Mount Sunflower	4,039	Drive-up

Mississippi Valley west toward the foothills of the Rockies. Each of the four highpoints lies in the extreme western part of its state along a north-south line between the 102d and 105th meridians.

A general characteristic of Mount Sunflower (Kansas), Panorama Point (Nebraska), and Hawkeye Point (Iowa) is that, for miles around, the area is characterized by low rolling hills with little elevation change. If they were not surveyed and marked, the highpoints would be hard to determine. The hill or "bump" nearby always looks "a little higher."

Because of massive rock outcroppings, both White Butte (North Dakota) and Harney Peak (South Dakota) are much more distinct than the other midwestern highpoints. Nevertheless, they illustrate the westward rise of the plains.

West

The highpoints of the thirteen western states are unique mountains, each of which has distinct characteristics. Although about half are only strenuous dayhikes, all should be approached with proper outdoor equipment, USGS topographic maps, and proven wilderness experience. Weather on these mountains can be exceptionally fickle and is generally predictable only in that it is certain to change. The blue-sky calm of early morning frequently gives way to powerful thunderstorms and even summer snow squalls. Be prepared for any extreme.

The West's distances make combination trips less likely, but what a diversity of experience these highpoints provide! Lucky indeed is the climber who can spend a summer visiting highpoints throughout the West.

Humphreys Peak (Arizona), Wheeler Peak (New Mexico), Mauna Kea (Hawaii), Borah Peak (Idaho), and Mount Elbert (Colorado) are strenuous one-day hikes, although Borah has been known to show its mettle on inexperienced parties. Boundary Peak (Nevada) is just that—on the border with California and the only one of the West's highpoints that is a lower summit of a higher mountain in another state.

Mount Whitney (California) can certainly be climbed in one very long day, although one is apt to go crazy counting the switchbacks on the Mount Whitney Trail. Most parties backpack and make a two-day trip or climb one of the technical routes on the east face.

Gannett Peak (Wyoming) and Granite Peak (Montana) require multi-day backpacks to approach, followed by strenuous climbs for experienced mountaineers only. Gannett Peak is heavily glaciated and, along with Granite Peak, may be the most difficult of the highpoints to reach after Mount McKinley. Kings Peak (Utah) presents no technical difficulties, but its twelve-mile approach discourages beginners.

Mount Rainier ▲ Washington

Montana

Granite Peak ▲

Mount Hood ▲

Idaho

Oregon

Borah Peak ▲

Gannett Peak ▲

Wyoming

Nevada

Kings Peak ▲

Colorado

Boundary Peak ▲

Utah

Mount Elbert ▲

Mount Whitney ▲

California

Humphreys Peak ▲

Wheeler Peak ▲

New Mexico

Arizona

Alaska

Mount McKinley ▲

Hawaii

Mauna Kea ▲

West

Mount Rainier (Washington) and Mount Hood (Oregon) are both heavily glaciated volcanoes that require ropes, ice axes, crampons, and adequate knowledge of their use. Mount McKinley (Alaska) is, of course, in a class by itself, and an ascent of this highest point in North America is undertaken only by experienced mountaineers prepared for the rigors of expedition climbing at high altitudes.

Highpoints of the West

State	Highpoint	Elevation (Feet)	Class
Montana	Granite Peak	12,799	4
Idaho	Borah Peak	12,662	3
Wyoming	Gannett Peak	13,804	4
Washington	Mount Rainier	14,410	4
Oregon	Mount Hood	11,239	4
Colorado	Mount Elbert	14,433	1
Utah	Kings Peak	13,528	2
Nevada	Boundary Peak	13,140	2
California	Mount Whitney	14,494	1
New Mexico	Wheeler Peak	13,161	1
Arizona	Humphreys Peak	12,633	1
Alaska	Mount McKinley	20,320	4
Hawaii	Mauna Kea	13,796	1

Highpoints of the United States by Elevation

State	Highpoint	Elevation (Feet)	Class
Alaska	Mount McKinley	20,320	4
California	Mount Whitney	14,494	1
Colorado	Mount Elbert	14,433	1
Washington	Mount Rainier	14,410	4
Wyoming	Gannett Peak	13,804	4
Hawaii	Mauna Kea	13,796	1
Utah	Kings Peak	13,528	2
New Mexico	Wheeler Peak	13,161	1
Nevada	Boundary Peak	13,140	2
Montana	Granite Peak	12,799	4
Idaho	Borah Peak	12,662	3
Arizona	Humphreys Peak	12,633	1
Oregon	Mount Hood	11,239	4
Texas	Guadalupe Peak	8,749	1
South Dakota	Harney Peak	7,242	1
North Carolina	Mount Mitchell	6,684	Drive-up
Tennessee	Clingmans Dome	6,643	1
New Hampshire	Mount Washington	6,288	Drive-up
Virginia	Mount Rogers	5,729	1
Nebraska	Panorama Point (815398)	5,424	Drive-up
New York	Mount Marcy	5,344	1
Maine	Mount Katahdin	5,267	1
Oklahoma	Black Mesa	4,973	1
West Virginia	Spruce Knob	4,861	Drive-up
Georgia	Brasstown Bald	4,784	1
Vermont	Mount Mansfield (736344)	4,393	2
Kentucky	Black Mountain (312868)	4,139	Drive-up
Kansas	Mount Sunflower	4,039	Drive-up

South Carolina	Sassafras Mountain	3,560	Drive-up
North Dakota	White Butte	3,506	1
Massachusetts	Mount Greylock	3,487	Drive-up
Maryland	Backbone Mountain (309440)	3,360	1
Pennsylvania	Mount Davis	3,213	Drive-up
Arkansas	Magazine Mountain (413916)	2,753	1
Alabama	Cheaha Mountain	2,405	Drive-up
Connecticut	Mount Frissell - South Slope	2,380	1
Minnesota	Eagle Mountain	2,301	1
Michigan	Mount Arvon	1,979	1
Wisconsin	Timms Hill	1,951	1
New Jersey	High Point	1,803	Drive-up
Missouri	Taum Sauk Mountain (007605)	1,772	1
Iowa	Hawkeye Point (806153)	1,670	Drive-up
Ohio	Campbell Hill	1,549	Drive-up
Indiana	Hoosier High Point (835298)	1,257	1
Illinois	Charles Mound	1,235	1
Rhode Island	Jerimoth Hill	812	1
Mississippi	Woodall Mountain	806	Drive-up
Louisiana	Driskill Mountain (097873)	535	1
Delaware	Ebright Azimuth (555095)	448	Drive-up
Florida	Lakewood Park (686282)	345	Drive-up

Appendix D

Highpointers Club

The Highpointers Club was formed in 1987 by Jack Longacre, current club president, to provide a forum for the exchange of information regarding the highpoints of the United States. The organization is growing rapidly as more and more "Highpointers" become aware of the club. The Highpointers Club official website, www.highpointers.org, has considerable information regarding the club and state highpoints.

Purpose
The purpose of the club is to promote climbing to the highest point in each of the 50 states and to provide a vehicle through which persons with a common goal can meet and correspond with one another.

Membership
Membership is open to anyone interested in climbing or promoting climbing of the highpoints of the states. The membership fee is $10.00 per year per household. The whole family can be members for the one annual fee. To become a member, send $10.00 for a one-year subscription to the newsletter and membership to R. Craig Noland, Membership Chairman, Highpointers Club, P.O. Box 6364, Sevierville, TN 37864-6364.

Newsletter
Apex to Zenith, the club newsletter, is published quarterly and is sent to all members. The newsletter contains articles on the highpoints, trip reports, upcoming events, club news, and other items of interest.

Climbing Awards
In order to recognize Highpointer accomplishments and to encourage continued highpointing progress, the club has established a system of awards. Each of the awards contains a full-color representation of the Highpointers' logo. Awards are attained by (1) being a member of the Highpointers Club, (2) climbing the number of highpoints required to qualify for a particular award, and (3) sending appropriate payment to the awards chairman (address and prices given in the newsletter).

The following awards are available:

Embroidered patch: Ascend any 5 highpoints.

Emblem pin: Ascend 30 highpoints, with at least 5 from each of 4 geographical areas (see Appendix B).

Emblem pin with red border: Ascend 40 highpoints, with at least 5 from each of 4 geographical areas.

Highpointer plaque: Ascend all 48 contiguous state highpoints or all 50 highpoints (member's choice, but only one award to any one member). The plaque is inscribed with the member's name and completion date.

Annual Banquet and Highpoint Climb

The Highpointers Club holds an annual banquet that includes a climb of the nearby highpoint. The location of the banquet is moved around the country in order to afford all members an opportunity to attend.

Acknowledgments

The author wishes to thank the many members of the Highpointers Club for their support, encouragement, and help in the development of this guide. Its accuracy has certainly been enhanced by their contributions.

Highpoints of the United States
Personal Log

State	Highpoint	Elevation (Feet)	Date
Alabama	Cheaha Mountain	2,405	_____
Alaska	Mount McKinley	20,320	_____
Arizona	Humphreys Peak	12,633	_____
Arkansas	Magazine Mountain (413916)	2,753	_____
California	Mount Whitney	14,494	_____
Colorado	Mount Elbert	14,433	_____
Connecticut	Mount Frissell (South Slope)	2,380	_____
Delaware	Ebright Azimuth (555095)	448	_____
Florida	Lakewood Park (686282)	345	_____
Georgia	Brasstown Bald	4,784	_____
Hawaii	Mauna Kea	13,796	_____
Idaho	Borah Peak	12,662	_____
Illinois	Charles Mound	1,235	_____
Indiana	Hoosier High Point (835298)	1,257	_____
Iowa	Hawkeye Point (806153)	1,670	_____
Kansas	Mount Sunflower	4,039	_____
Kentucky	Black Mountain (312868)	4,139	_____
Louisiana	Driskill Mountain (097873)	535	_____
Maine	Mount Katahdin	5,267	_____
Maryland	Backbone Mountain (309440)	3,360	_____
Massachusetts	Mount Greylock	3,487	_____
Michigan	Mount Arvon	1,979	_____
Minnesota	Eagle Mountain	2,301	_____
Mississippi	Woodall Mountain	806	_____
Missouri	Taum Sauk Mountain (007605)	1,772	_____
Montana	Granite Peak	12,799	_____
Nebraska	Panorama Point (815398)	5,424	_____
Nevada	Boundary Peak	13,140	_____

New Hampshire	Mount Washington	6,288	_____
New Jersey	High Point	1,803	_____
New Mexico	Wheeler Peak	13,161	_____
New York	Mount Marcy	5,344	_____
North Carolina	Mount Mitchell	6,684	_____
North Dakota	White Butte	3,506	_____
Ohio	Campbell Hill	1,549	_____
Oklahoma	Black Mesa	4,973	_____
Oregon	Mount Hood	11,239	_____
Pennsylvania	Mount Davis	3,213	_____
Rhode Island	Jerimoth Hill	812	_____
South Carolina	Sassafras Mountain	3,560	_____
South Dakota	Harney Peak	7,242	_____
Tennessee	Clingmans Dome	6,643	_____
Texas	Guadalupe Peak	8,749	_____
Utah	Kings Peak	13,528	_____
Vermont	Mount Mansfield (736344)	4,393	_____
Virginia	Mount Rogers	5,729	_____
Washington	Mount Rainier	14,410	_____
West Virginia	Spruce Knob	4,861	_____
Wisconsin	Timms Hill	1,951	_____
Wyoming	Gannett Peak	13,804	_____

Useful Websites

General Websites

These websites provide general information relative to more than one state highpoint.

www.highpointers.org ▲ This is the official website of the Highpointers Club. It has information about the club, the highpoints, and other pertinent data. Updates relative to the highpoint descriptions in this book will also be found here.

www.americasroof.com ▲ This website is complimentary to the website listed above. It offers additional information regarding the highpoints.

www.nps.gov ▲ This is the National Park Service website. Information on all of the National Parks can be found here.

www.nps.gov/aptr/ ▲ This is the National Park Service website for the Appalachian Trail.

www.atconf.org ▲ The Appalachian Trail conference maintains this website.

www.fred.net/kathy/at.html ▲ This is a privately maintained website with useful information on the Appalachian Trail. It includes a list of state highpoints on or near the trail.

www.peakware.com ▲ This is the *Peakware World Mountain Encyclopedia* website. It lists virtually all of the significant mountains in the world. The link to the state highpoints is www.peakware.com/encyclopedia/ranges/fiftystates.htm.

www.fs.fed.us/links/forests.shtml ▲ This is the U.S. Forest Service website that links to all National Forests.

www.outdoorreview.com ▲ This is a website operated by *Outdoor Review*. It is a consumer review website that includes all manner items related to outdoor recreation. It has an extensive section of trail reviews.

info.er.usgs.gov ▲ This is the home page of the U.S. Geological Survey.

www.gorp.com ▲ This is the website for Great Outdoor Recreation Pages (GORP). There is an abundance of information on trails, wilderness areas, and many other outdoor recreation activities. The link to the wilderness areas is www.gorp.com/gorp/resource/us_wilderness_area/main.htm.

www.llbean.com ▲ This website is maintained by L. L. Bean of Freeport, Maine. It has a wealth of information on America's parks. Click on "Outdoors Online."

Books

www.chesslerbooks.com ▲ Books pertaining to mountaineering, hiking, climbing, polar exploration, adventure travel, trekking, and much more can be found at this website. In fact, nearly all the books referenced in this book may be found here.

Clubs

www.americanalpineclub.org ▲ This website is operated by the American Alpine Club.

www.mountaineers.org ▲ This is the Seattle Mountaineers website.

www.outdoors.org ▲ This website is operated by the Appalachian Mountain Club.

mcak.org ▲ The Mountaineering Club of Alaska website. Several links to other useful websites are provided in addition to information about the club.

www.coloradotrail.org ▲ This website is maintained by the Colorado Trail Foundation.

www.adk.org ▲ This website is operated by the Adirondack Mountain Club with a link to lodging and camping including Adirondak Loj.

State Specific Websites

These websites usually have information pertaining to one highpoint. However, some of them will have information useful for more than one.

Alabama

www.al.com/parks/parks.html ▲ A link to the Alabama State Parks website.

www.alapark.com/parks/cheaha_1a.html ▲ A direct link to Cheaha State Park.

www.talladega.com/tourism/odum.htm ▲ The Odum Scout Trail website.

Alaska

www.nps.gov/dena/mountaineering ▲ This is the National Park Service website for the Denali Mountaineering Ranger. Up-to-date information on climbing Mount McKinley may be obtained here.

www.nps.gov/dena/ ▲ This is the National Park Service website for Denali National Park.

homepage2.rconnect.com/kbayne/denali.html ▲ A private website with lots of useful information on climbing Mount McKinley.

mcak.org ▲ The Mountaineering Club of Alaska website. Several links to other useful websites are provided in addition to information about the club.

www.alaska.net/~adg/ ▲ The Alaska-Denali Guiding, Inc. website.

www.alaska.net/flyk2/ ▲ The K2 Aviation website.

Arizona

www.fs.fed.us/r3/ ▲ The Coconino National Forest may be contacted via this website. Search for "Humphreys Peak."

www.fs.fed.us/r3/coconino/rec_volcanic.html ▲ One can access information on the trail system in the San Francisco Peaks area directly. Information on the Humphreys Trail, the Kachina Trail, and Weatherford Trail may be obtained in addition to information on several other trails in the area.

www.arizonasnowbowl.com ▲ This is the Arizona Snowbowl website.

www.arizonasnowbowl.com/skyride.cfm ▲ This is the Arizona Snowbowl Skyride website.

Arkansas

www.arkansasstateparks.com ▲ This is the Arkansas State Parks website. Mount Magazine State Park may be accessed by clicking on "Park Finder" and navigating to Mount Magazine State Park.

California

www.r5.fs.fed.us/inyo/ ▲ This is the Inyo National Forest website. Up-to-date information on hiking Mount Whitney is available. Also see the next website.

www.nps.gov/seki/ ▲ This is the National Park Service website for Sequoia and Kings Canyon National Parks. This website and the one above offer a wealth of information about hiking Mount Whitney.

www.r5.fs.fed.us/inyo/vvc/index.htm ▲ This is the U.S. Forest Service website for the Eastern Sierra Inter-agency Visitor Center.

Colorado

www.fs.fed.us/r2/psicc/ ▲ This is the U.S. Forest Service website for the San Isabel National Forest.

www.fs.fed.us/r2/psicc/leadville/leadrd.htm ▲ This is the Leadville Ranger District website within the above website. Click on "Climbing Peaks" for up-to-date information on climbing Mount Elbert and other 14ers in the Leadville Ranger District.

www.coloradotrail.org ▲ This website is maintained by the Colorado Trail Foundation.

Connecticut

www.ctwoodlands.org/index.html ▲ The website of the Connecticut Forest and Park Association. The CFPA is the oldest private, nonprofit conservation organization in Connecticut.

www.ctwoodlands.org/pubs.html ▲ This is the CFPA's bookstore. The "Connecticut Walk Book" may be purchased here.

Georgia

georgiatrails.com ▲ This website has information on walking, hiking, and backpacking trails of northern Georgia. This includes the Brasstown Bald Trail, the Arkaquah Trail, the Wagon Train Trail, and the Jacks Knob trail.

www.fs.fed.us/conf/ ▲ The U.S. Forest Service website for the Chattahoochee National Forest.

Hawaii

www.ifa.hawaii.edu/info/bif ▲ The Onizuka Center for International Astronomy maintains this website. Information on the observatory complex and access to the Mauna Kea summit area is available here.

Idaho

www.fs.fed.us/r4/sc/ ▲ This is the U.S. Forest Service website for the Salmon-Challis National Forest. Not much information here, but there is a good picture of Borah Peak.

www.peakware.com/encyclopedia/peaks/borah.htm ▲ This is the direct address to the Borah Peak listing on the peakware.com website.

Maine

www.mainerec.com/baxter1.html ▲ An extensive website with detailed information regarding Baxter State Park. It includes hiking guides and rules and regulations.

www.mtkahdin.com ▲ This website is devoted largely to Mount Katahdin.

Minnesota

www.snf.toofarnorth.org/bwcaw/index.html ▲ The Superior National Forest website for the Boundary Waters Canoe Area Wilderness.

www.snf.toofarnorth.org ▲ This is the U.S. Forest Service general website for the Superior National Forest.

canoecountry.com ▲ This website has comprehensive information regarding the Boundary Waters Canoe Area Wilderness.

Missouri

www.mostateparks.com ▲ This is the website for the Missouri State Parks with a link to Taum Sauk Mountain State Park.

Montana

www.fs.fed.us/r1/custer/main.html ▲ This is the U.S. Forest Service website for Custer National Forest. It provides a link to some historical climb information.

www.gorp.com/gorp/resource/US_Wilderness_Area/MT_absar.htm ▲ This is the Great Outdoor Recreation Pages (GORP) listing for the Absaroka-Beartooth Wilderness.

Nevada
www.r5.fs.fed.us/inyo/ ▲ This is the U.S. Forest Service website for the Inyo National Forest.
www.r5.fs.fed.us/inyo/vvc/index.htm ▲ This is the U.S. Forest Service website for the Eastern Sierra Interagency Visitor Center.

New Hampshire
www.mountwashington.com ▲ An extensive website covering Mount Washington with links to the Mount Washington Cog Railway and Mount Washington Auto Road websites.

New Jersey
www.nj.com/outdoors/parks.html ▲ This is the New Jersey State Parks website with a link to High Point State Park.

New Mexico
www.fs.fed.us/r3/ ▲ This is the U.S. Forest Service website for the Carson National Forest. Click on "Wheeler Peak" for climbing information and maps.
www.taoswebb.com/skitaos/base.phtml ▲ This website has information on Taos Ski Valley.

New York
www.adk.org ▲ This website is operated by the Adirondack Mountain Club with a link to Lodging and Camping including Adirondak Loj.

North Carolina
ils.unc.edu/parkproject/ncparks.html ▲ This is the North Carolina Division of Parks and Recreation website with a link to Mount Mitchell State Park.
www.nps.gov/blri/ ▲ This is the National Park Service website for the Blue Ridge Parkway.

Oklahoma
www.shopoklahoma.com/blackmes.htm ▲ This is the website for Black Mesa State Park.

Oregon
www.fs.fed.us/r6/mthood ▲ This is the U.S. Forest Service website for Mount Hood.
www.timberlinelodge.com ▲ This is the Timberline Lodge website.

Pennsylvania

www.dcnr.state.pa.us/forestry/forbes.htm ▲ This is the Pennsylvania Department of Conservation and Natural Resources website for Forbes State Forest. It includes a link to the Mount Davis Natural Area.

www.parec.com/state_parks/lrlrstpk.htm ▲ This website is for the Laurel Ridge State Park and includes information on the Laurel Highlands Hiking Trail.

South Carolina

www.greenvilleonline.com/outdoors/foothill.html ▲ This is the Foothills Trail website.

www.southcarolinaparks.com/home.html ▲ This is the South Carolina State Parks website with a link to the Table Rock State Park.

South Dakota

www.fs.fed.us/r2/blackhills/ ▲ This is the U.S. Forest Service website for the Black Hills National Forest. A quick jump to trail information is via www.fs.fed.us/r2/blackhills/trails.htm.

www.state.sd.us/state/executive/tourism/sdparks/ ▲ This is the South Dakota State Parks website with a link to Custer State Park.

Tennessee

www.nps.gov/grsm/ ▲ The National Park Service website for Great Smoky Mountains National Park.

Texas

www.nps.gov/gumo/ ▲ The National Park Service website for Guadalupe Mountains National Park.

Vermont

www.longtrail.org ▲ This website is maintained by the Green Mountain Club.

Virginia

www.fs.fed.us/gwjnf/ ▲ This is the U.S. Forest Service website for the George Washington and Jefferson National Forests. The quick link to the hiking trails in the Mount Rogers National Recreation Area is provided via www.fs.fed.us/gwjnf/JNFhikingtrailsNRA.html.

www.llbean.com/parksearch/parks/html/194lln.htm ▲ Although this is a website maintained by L. L. Bean of Freeport, Maine, it has useful information on Grayson Highlands State Park.

www.gorp.com/gorp/resource/us_trail/va_virgi.htm ▲ This is the Great Outdoor Recreation Pages (GORP) website listing for the Virginia Creeper Trail.

Washington

www.nps.gov/mora/ ▲ This is the National Park Service website for Mount Rainier National Park.

West Virginia

www.wvparks.com ▲ This is the website for the West Virginia State Parks System. It has information on the Cass Scenic Railroad State Park, as well as other parks in the system.

www.wvonline.com/wvsta/ ▲ This website is maintained by the West Virginia Scenic Trails Association.

www.fs.fed.us/r9/mnf/ ▲ This is the U.S. Forest Service website for Monongahella National Forest.

Wisconsin

www.nps.gov/iatr/ ▲ This is the National Park Service website for the Ice Age Trail.

Wyoming

www.fs.fed.us/outernet/btnf/ ▲ This is the U.S. Forest Service website for Bridger-Teton National Forest.

www.fs.fed.us/r2/shoshone/ ▲ This is the U.S. Forest Service website for Shoshone National Forest.

Index

This index includes all highpoints, all route names to the highpoints, significant road names, place names, and individuals associated with a highpoint. Please see the individual highpoint chapters for U.S.G.S. and other map information, individual highpoint guidebooks, and other road names.